Origami Symphony No. 8

An Octet of Cats

Books by John Montroll
www.johnmontroll.com
Instagram: @montrollorigami

Origami Symphonies

Origami Symphony No. 1: The Elephant's Trumpet Call
Origami Symphony No. 2: Trio of Sharks & Playful Prehistoric Mammals
Origami Symphony No. 3: Duet of Majestic Dragons & Dinosaurs
Origami Symphony No. 4: Capturing Vibrant Coral Reef Fish
Origami Symphony No. 5: Woodwinds, Horns, and a Moose
Origami Symphony No. 6: Striped Snakes Changing Scales
Origami Symphony No. 7: Musical Monkeys
Origami Symphony No. 8: An Octet of Cats

General Origami

Origami Fold-by-Fold
DC Super Heroes Origami
Origami Worldwide
Teach Yourself Origami: Third Edition
Christmas Origami: Second Edition
Storytime Origami
Origami Inside-Out: Third Edition

Animal Origami

Arctic Animals in Origami
Origami Aquarium
Dogs in Origami
Perfect Pets Origami
Dragons and Other Fantastic Creatures in Origami
Bugs in Origami
Horses in Origami: Second Edition
Origami Birds: Second Edition
Origami Gone Wild
Dinosaur Origami
Origami Dinosaurs for Beginners
Prehistoric Origami: Dinosaurs and other Creatures: Third Edition
Mythological Creatures and the Chinese Zodiac Origami
Origami Sea Life: Third Edition
Bringing Origami to Life: Second Edition
Origami Sculptures: Fourth Edition
African Animals in Origami: Third Edition
North American Animals in Origami: Third Edition
Origami for the Enthusiast: Second Edition
Animal Origami for the Enthusiast: Second Edition

Geometric Origami

Origami Stars: Second Edition
Galaxy of Origami Stars: Second Edition
Origami and Math: Simple to Complex: Second Edition
Origami & Geometry
3D Origami Platonic Solids & More: Second Edition
3D Origami Diamonds
3D Origami Antidiamonds
3D Origami Pyramids
A Plethora of Polyhedra in Origami: Third Edition
Classic Polyhedra Origami
A Constellation of Origami Polyhedra
Origami Polyhedra Design

Dollar Bill Origami

Dollar Origami Treasures: Second Edition
Dollar Bill Animals in Origami: Second Revised Edition
Dollar Bill Origami
Easy Dollar Bill Origami

Simple Origami

Fun and Simple Origami: 101 Easy-to-Fold Projects: Second Edition
Origami Twelve Days of Christmas: And Santa, Too!
Super Simple Origami
Easy Dollar Bill Origami
Easy Origami
Easy Origami 2
Easy Origami 3
Easy Origami Coloring Book
Easy Origami Animals
Easy Origami Polar Animals
Easy Origami Ocean Animals
Easy Origami Woodland Animals
Easy Origami Jungle Animals
Meditative Origami

Origami Symphony No. 8

An Octet of Cats

Antroll Publishing Company

John Montroll

To Jim, Christine, and Evan

Origami Symphony No. 8: *An Octet of Cats*

Copyright © 2022 by John Montroll. All rights reserved.
No part of this publication may be copied or reproduced by any means without the express written permission of the author.

ISBN-10: 1-877656-60-7
ISBN-13: 978-1-877656-60-6

Antroll Publishing Company

Introduction

Welcome to the world premier of the Eighth Origami Symphony! Structured as a musical symphony in four movements, several themes and styles of origami are shown. Detailed cat breeds, a variety of fish and sea mammals, tall prisms and spherical shapes, and circus animals come alive in this symphony.

The 38 models are divided into four movements. Beginning with a theme and variation on cats, diagrams for eight distinct cats are provided. This includes an Exotic Shorthair, Munchkin, and Tomkinese. Sea creatures from the second movement include a Royal Blue Discus Fish with white eyes, Guppy, Stingray, and Blue Whale that also has white eyes. A series of tall prisms are shown in the minuet of the third movement. The trio contains three challenging spherical shapes. The symphony concludes with a display of circus animals, including a Seal, Lion, and Elephant with white tusks.

Each model can be folded from a single square using standard origami paper. Given the complexity of the subjects, the models are designed to be as simple and large as possible. Several of the cats can be folded in under 30 steps. The Dolphin, with all the fin detail, is a 12-step model. The detailed Elephant with white tusks is diagrammed in 42 steps. A higher level of origami design is required to allow for fewer steps for the complex subjects. The simplicity in complexity adds a life-force to the models and a more enjoyable folding experience.

The diagrams are drawn in the internationally approved Randlett-Yoshizawa style. You can use any kind of square paper for these models, but the best results will be achieved with standard origami paper, which is colored on one side and white on the other (in the diagrams in this book, the shading represents the colored side). Large sheets, such as nine inches squared, are easier to use than small ones.

Origami supplies can be found in arts and craft shops, or at Dover Publications online: www.doverpublications.com. You can also visit OrigamiUSA at www.origamiusa.org for origami supplies and other related information including an extensive list of local, national, and international origami groups.

Please follow me on Instagram @montrollorigami to see posts of my origami.

I thank the folders who proof-read the diagrams and the ones who encouraged me to present origami through an origami symphony.

I hope you enjoy the fun themes from Origami Symphony No. 8.

John Montroll
www.johnmontroll.com

Contents

Symbols 9
Origami Symphony 9
Origami Symphony No. 8 10
First Movement 11
Second Movement 41
Third Movement 71
Fourth Movement 99

★ Simple
★★ Intermediate
★★★ Complex
★★★★ Very Complex

First Movement
Allegro: Theme and Variation on Cats

11 Exotic Shorthair ★★★	 15 Javanese ★★★	 18 Munchkin ★★★
 21 Calico ★★★	 25 Pixie-bob ★★★	 29 LaPerm ★★★
 33 Tomkinese ★★★	 37 Birman ★★★	

Second Movement
Andante: Sound Waves in the Sea

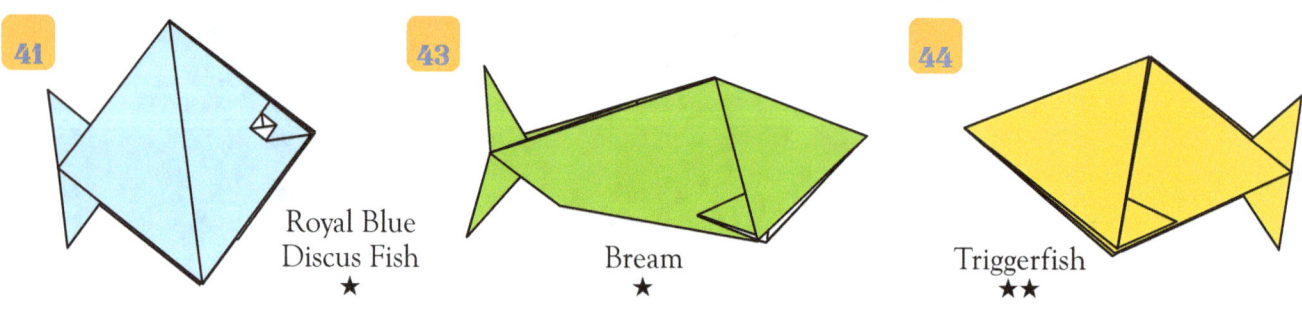

41 Royal Blue Discus Fish ★

43 Bream ★

44 Triggerfish ★★

6 *Origami Symphony No. 8*

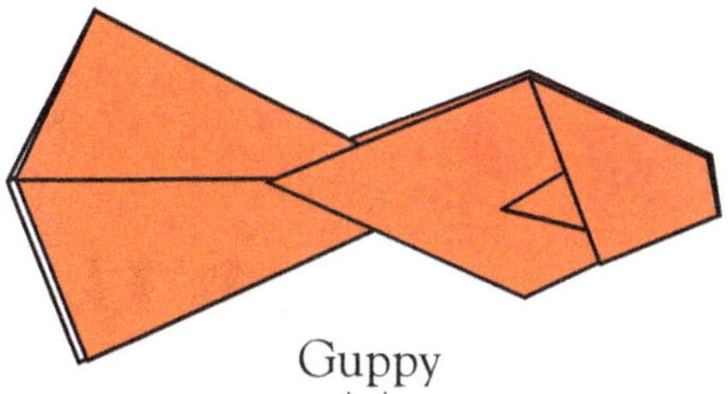

| 46 | 48 | 50 |

Guppy ★★ Angelfish ★★ Stingray ★★

| 52 | 55 | 58 |

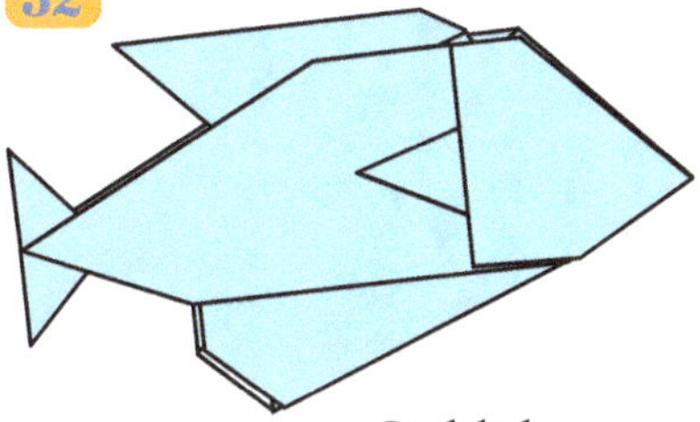

Cichlid ★★ Minnow ★★ Parrotfish ★★★

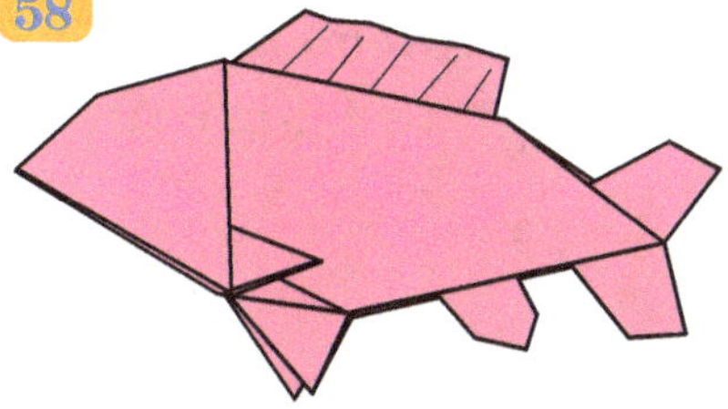

| 62 | 66 | 68 |

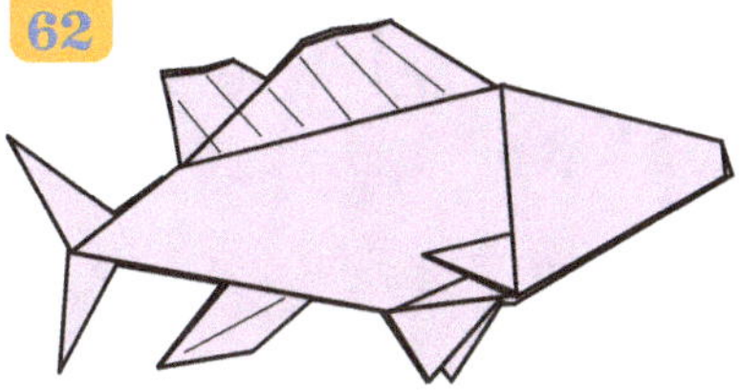

Perch ★★★ Dolphin ★★ Blue Whale ★★

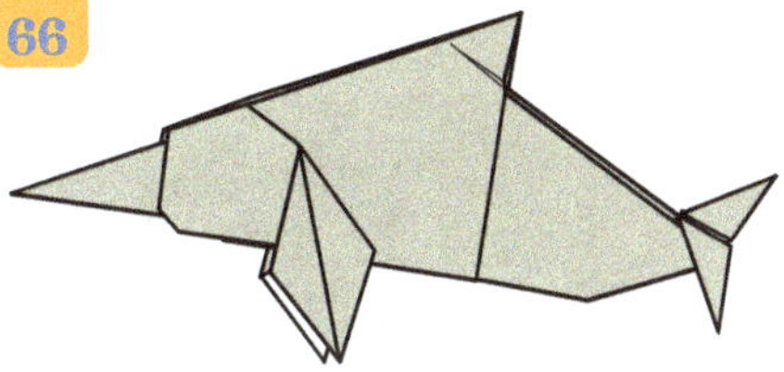

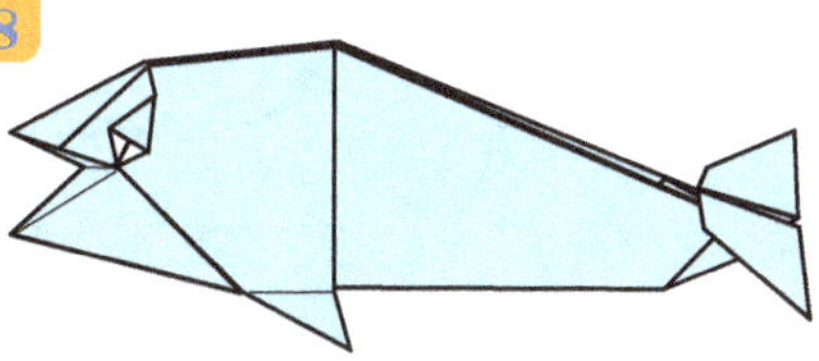

Third Movement
Minuet of Tall Prisms with a Trio of Spherical Shapes

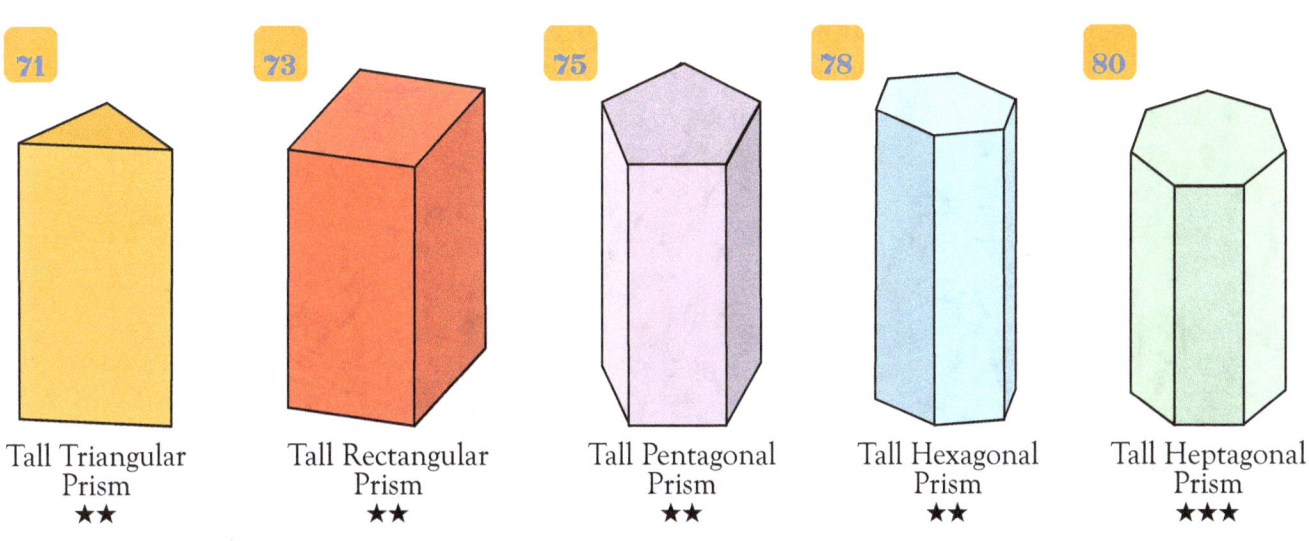

| 71 | 73 | 75 | 78 | 80 |

Tall Triangular Prism ★★
Tall Rectangular Prism ★★
Tall Pentagonal Prism ★★
Tall Hexagonal Prism ★★
Tall Heptagonal Prism ★★★

Contents 7

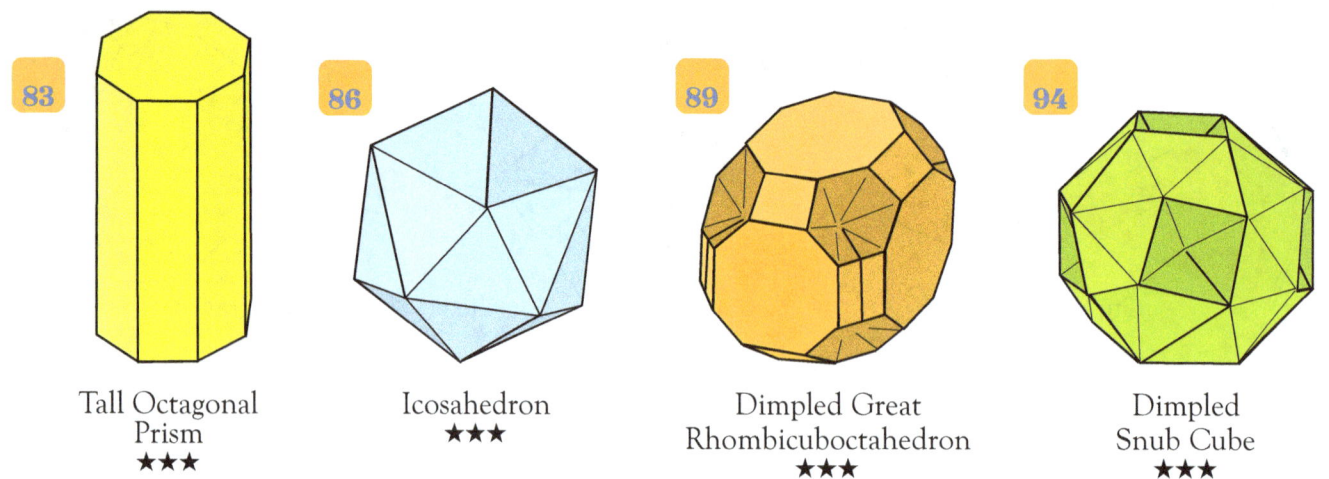

83 Tall Octagonal Prism ★★★

86 Icosahedron ★★★

89 Dimpled Great Rhombicuboctahedron ★★★

94 Dimpled Snub Cube ★★★

Fourth Movement
March of the Circus Animals

99 Seal ★★

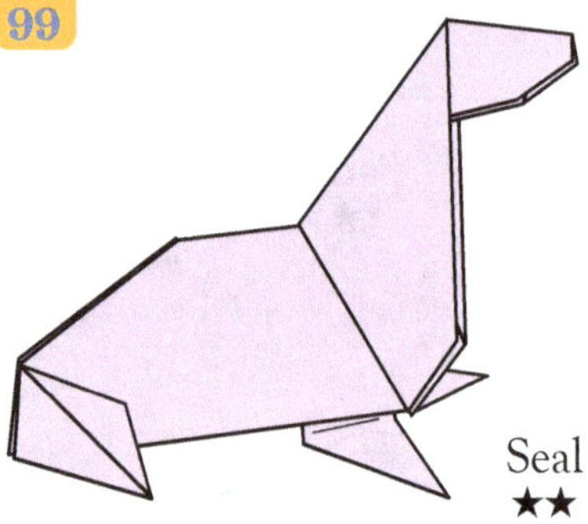

102 Parrot ★★

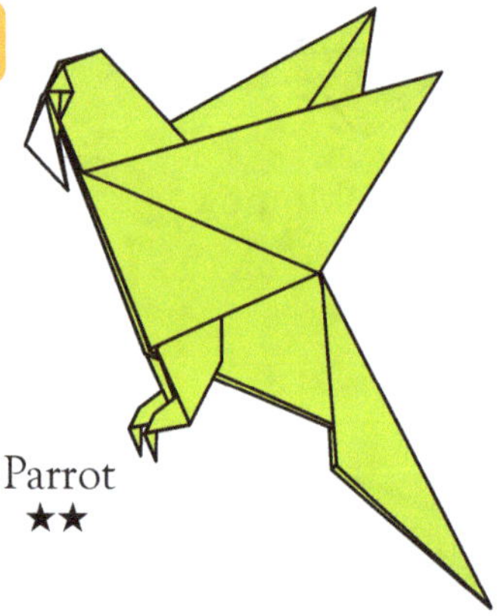

105 Bear ★★

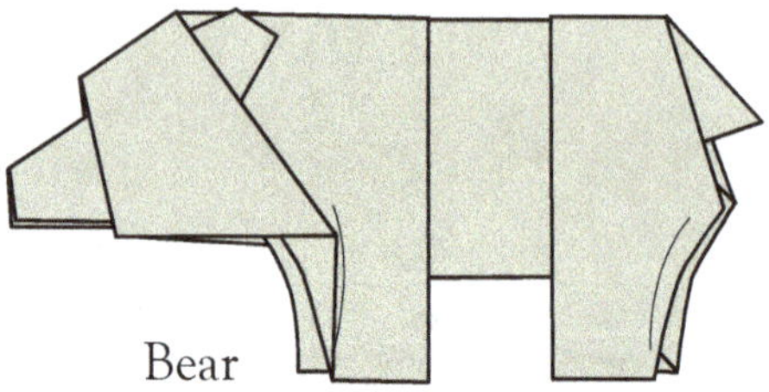

107 Lion ★★★

111 Panther ★★★

113 Dog ★★★

115 Horse ★★★

119 Giraffe ★★★

123 Elephant ★★★

8 Origami Symphony No. 8

Symbols

Lines

Valley fold, fold in front.

Mountain fold, fold behind.

Crease line.

X-ray or guide line.

Arrows

Fold in this direction.

Fold behind.

Unfold.

Fold and unfold.

Turn over.

Sink or three dimensional folding.

Place your finger between these layers.

Progression of Bases for this Symphony

One of the fascinations of origami design is that I am alway striving to create bases that allow for flexibility and make good use of the paper so the models will be as large as possible with as little thickness as possible, and hopefully as simple as possible with the given detail. From my previous work, *Origami Symphony No. 7*, I developed structures for some of the monkeys which were further explored in this work.

The cats from the first movement use a similar structure, I would call a family of bases. The base for the Exotic Shorthair is shown in step 16 (page 13). There is plenty of paper for the head, tail, and four legs. The beauty is that the top of the base is the length of the diagonal of the square, making it as large as possible.

As I contemplate the significance of this structure, I recall designs from an earlier generation. At that time, many mammals were folded from two bird bases, the ears were cut, and the two parts taped together. I would guess the designer did not think "what does it take to design a mammal" but rather "how could I fashion two bird bases with cuts to make a variety of mammals".

As we move to the circus animals in the fourth movement, the cat structure is used for the lion and a few more models. Then the base is modified to provide for a shorter tail, leading to the horse and giraffe. With my hope for simplicity, I am pleased that the structure allows the giraffe to be folded in (only) 29 steps. Applying the blintz fold to this structure provided a fun way to design an elephant with white tusks.

Exploring new structures keeps origami interesting. I hope you enjoy the variety in this symphony.

Origami Symphony No. 8

Small and large cats, friendly and ferocious, weave through Origami Symphony No. 8. Peaceful sea creatures, an array of tall prisms and fancy spherical shapes, along with circus animals add to the variety.

An octet of cats, presented as theme and variation, opens the symphony. The first movement begins with an Exotic Shorthair cat. It sits on stage, meows its melody, and waits for the Javanese to enter. More cats play their part, from the Munchkin, the Calico, and ending with the color-change depiction of the Birman cat. The cats use a unified family of bases that make them as large as possible.

The sea takes us to the second movement. Cats like fish but not water, so the fish are safe. Small aquarium fish swim around. A Royal Blue Discus Fish, Guppy, and Angelfish create sound waves in the sea. A Cichlid and Triggerfish from the coral reef swim in harmony. A Parrotfish and Perch add detail to design. The second movement closes as a Dolphin and Blue Whale sing their long songs and swim away.

The geometric side of origami is highlighted in the minuet and trio of the third movement. The minuet of tall prisms, from triangular to octagonal, makes for perfect stands for the cats and circus animals of the fourth movement. The challenging spherical shapes from the trio give the circus animals elaborate objects for their performances.

The symphony closes with the fanfare of a parade of circus animals. A Seal spins one of the spherical objects from the third movement while a Parrot does its antics. A trained Bear, roaring Lion, and stealthy Panther appear. Dogs dance, Horses trot around, and a Giraffe and Elephant add a majestic touch as the circus closes. All the origami animals enjoyed performing and none were harmed.

Cats from the first movement and the large cats from the fourth use similar folding structures, unifying symphonic themes. With wildly different folding styles for the fish and geometric shapes, the symphony offers a wide range of ideas. The symphony closes with one of my favorite subjects: a detailed Elephant with white tusks.

First Movement

Allegro: Theme and Variation on Cats

 Cats are one of our favorite pets. Historically, they were considered to be magical. It was through agriculture that cats enjoyed hunting mice and farmers were grateful for the pest control. Cats and humans began living together, new breeds were introduced and now friendly cats are everywhere. For this theme and variation on cats, I am showing a family of bases that make the origami cats as large as possible from a given size of paper.

Exotic Shorthair

The Exotic Shorthair cats have thick bodies and short legs from their dense bones. Their fur is short and plush. Bred from Persian cats, they are mellow with sweet personalities. These playful and kid-friendly cats have beautiful round heads.

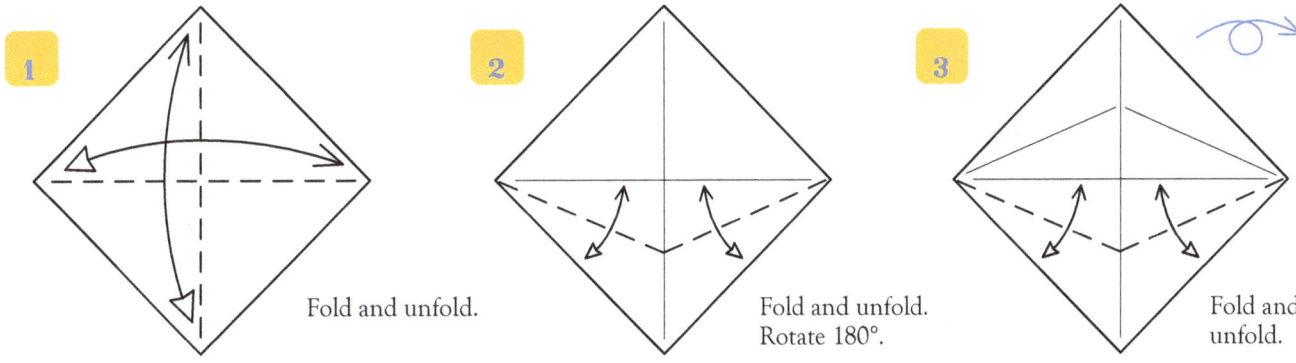

1 Fold and unfold.

2 Fold and unfold. Rotate 180°.

3 Fold and unfold.

Exotic Shorthair

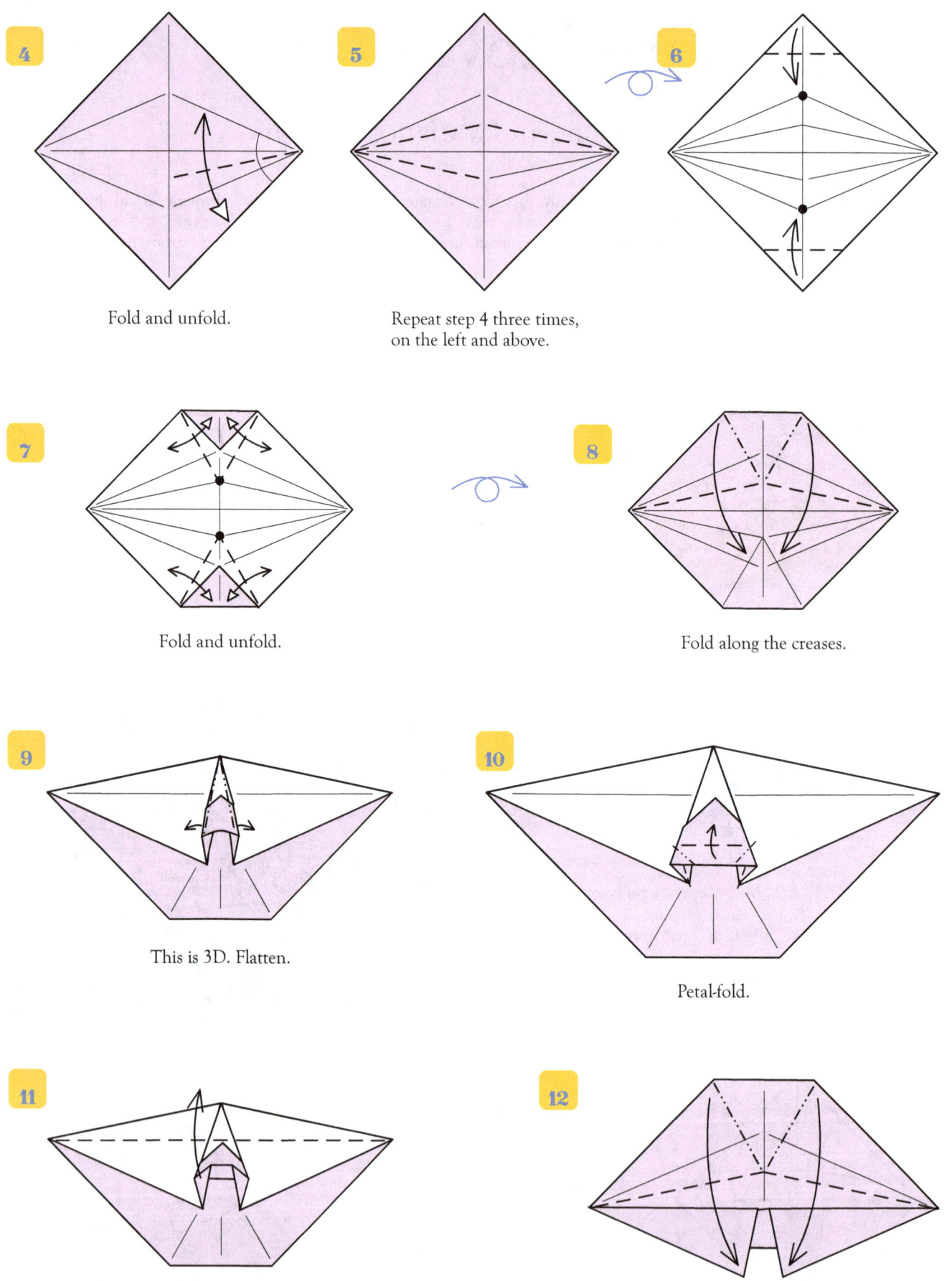

12 Origami Symphony No. 8

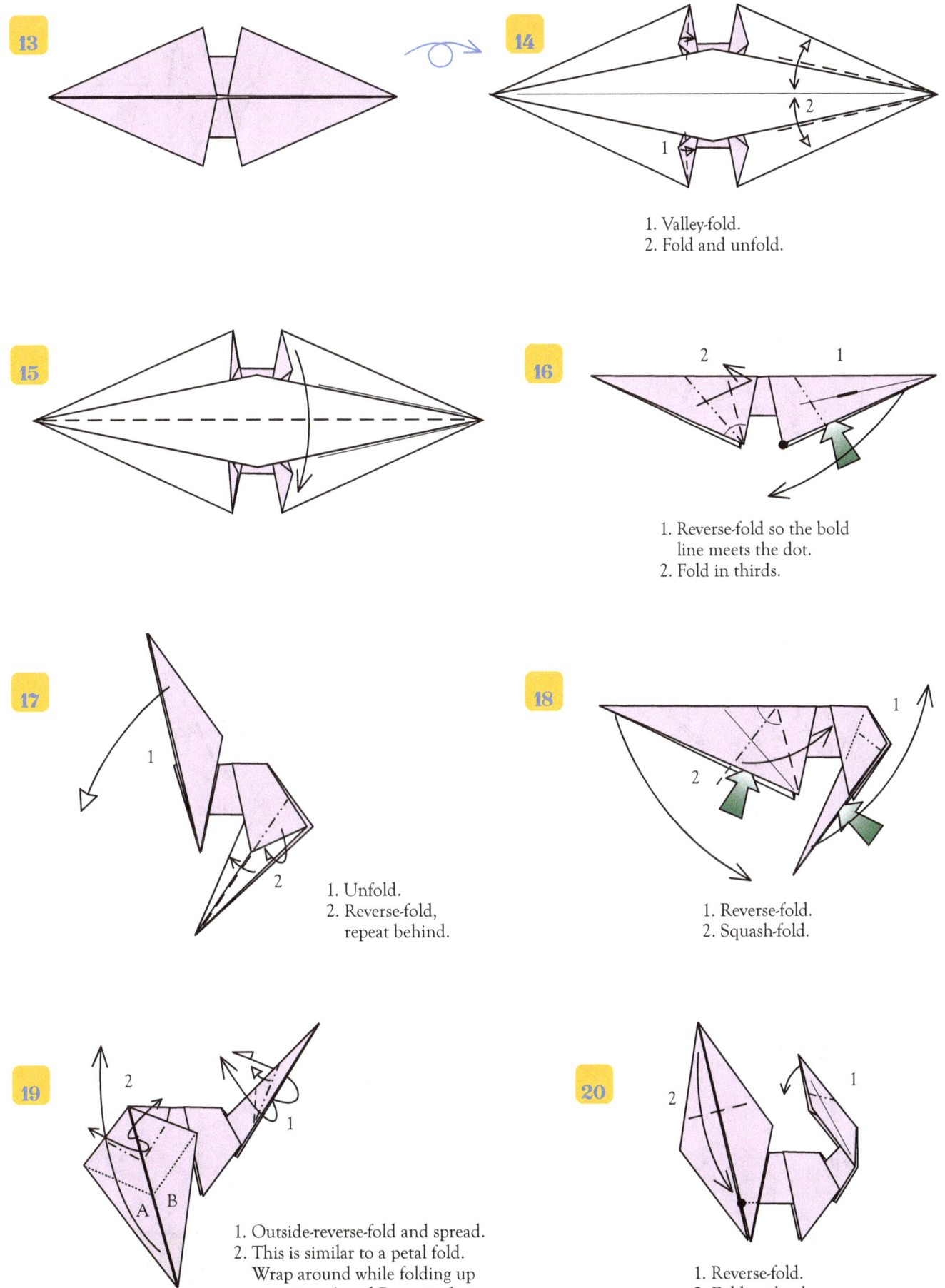

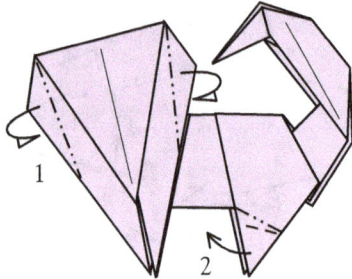

1. Make mountain folds.
2. Pleat-fold, repeat behind.

 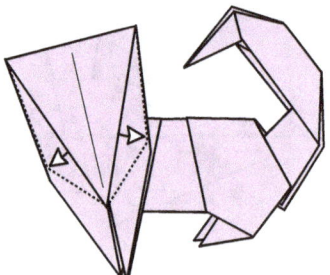

Spread from inside.

 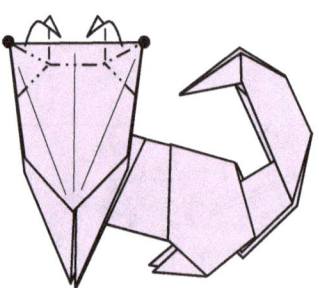

Fold behind so the dots meet.

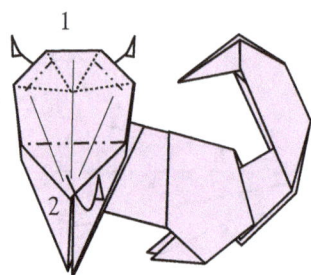

1. Fold the ears from behind.
2. Fold inside.

 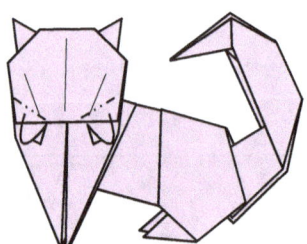

Fold inside.

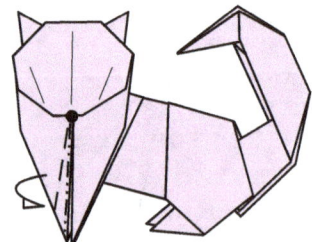

Puff out at the dot.

 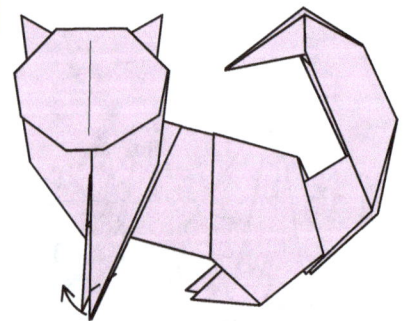

Outside-reverse-fold, repeat behind.

Exotic Shorthair

14 *Origami Symphony No. 8*

Javanese

The Javanese is a slender cat that is a skillful jumper. As an oriental breed, they are active and vocal. They like to sit in cat trees and high perches. The Javanese is smart, friendly, strong and active. They will be happy for plenty of attention from its owner, play-time with children, and get along well with other cats and dogs.

1. Fold and unfold.

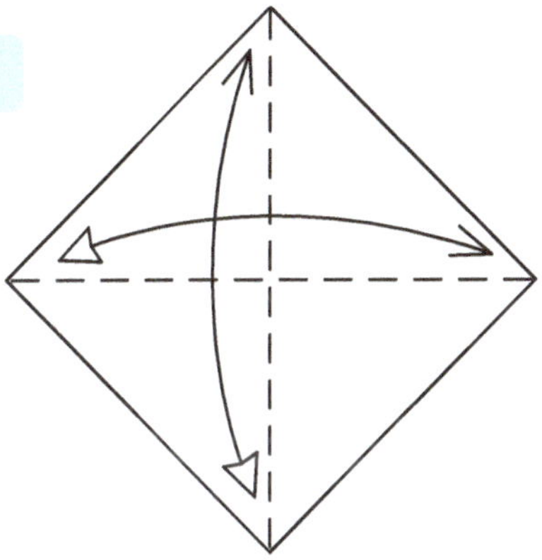

2. Fold and unfold. Rotate 180°.

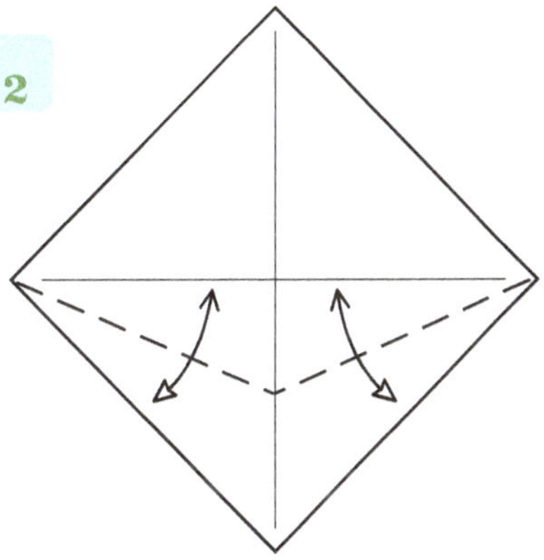

3. Fold and unfold.

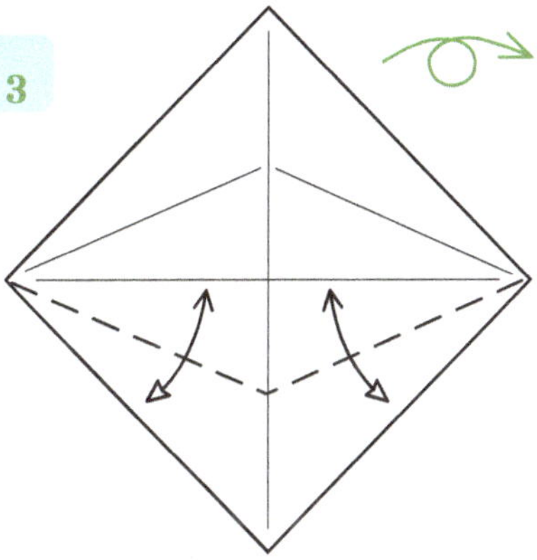

4. Fold and unfold.

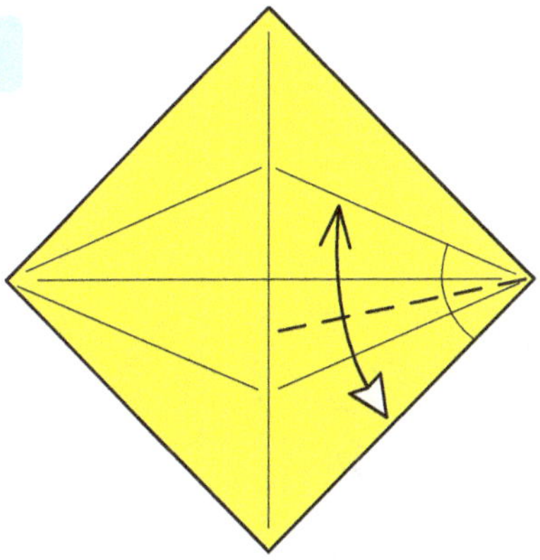

5. Repeat step 4 three times, on the left and above.

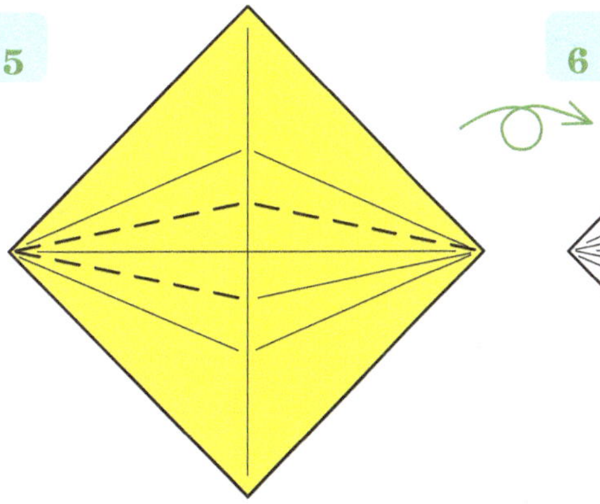

6.

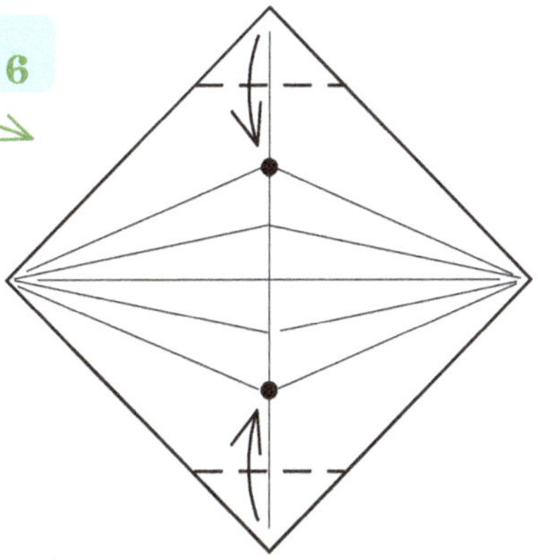

Javanese **15**

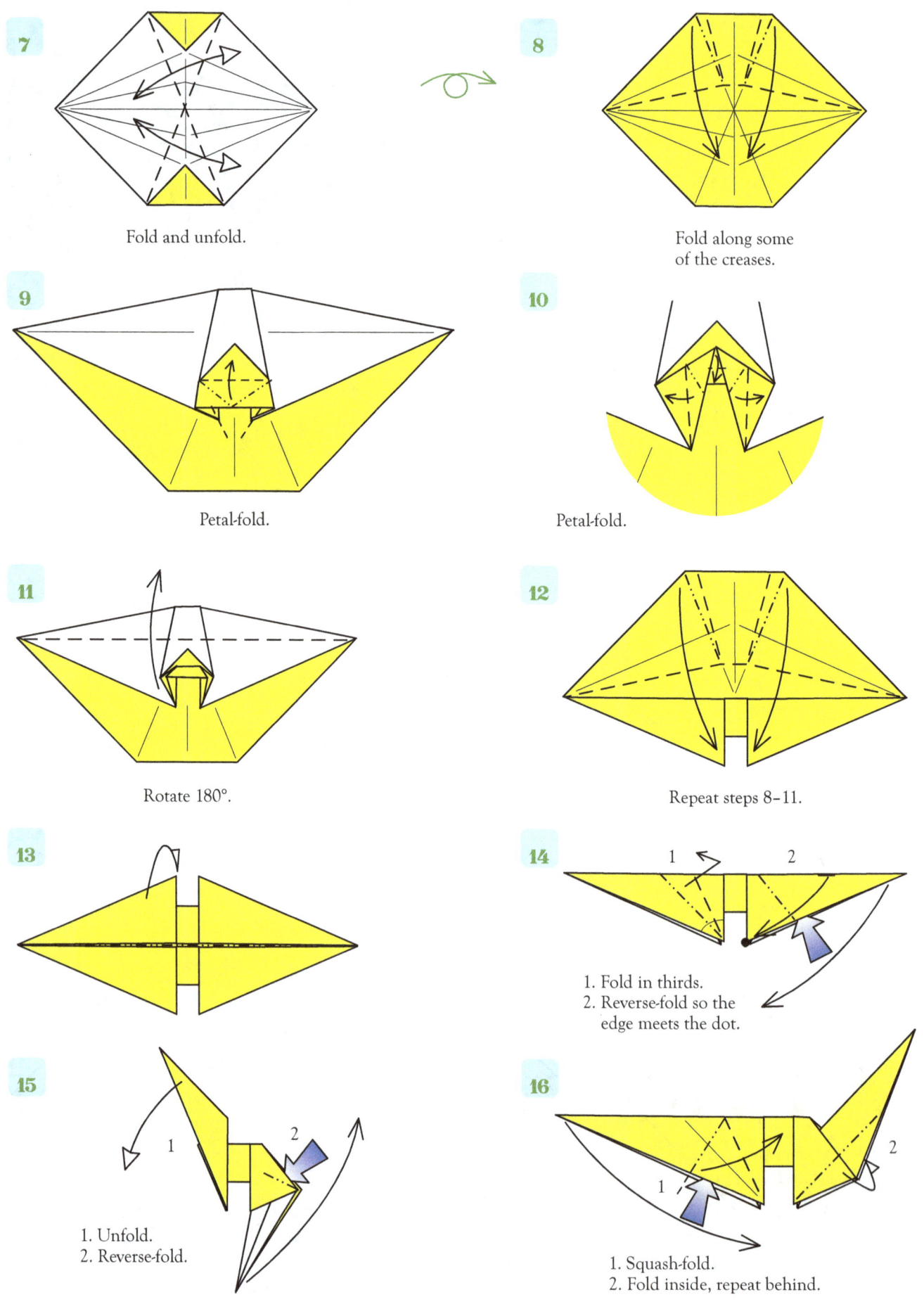

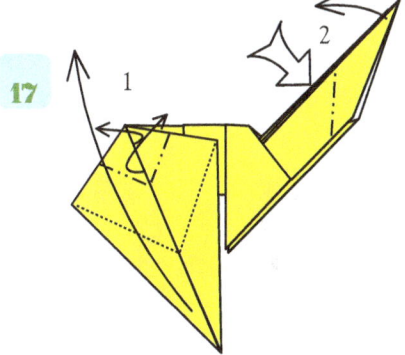

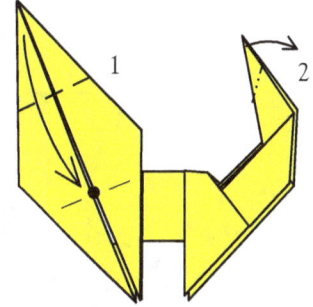

1. Wrap around and petal-fold.
2. Push in for this reverse fold.

1. Fold down.
2. Reverse-fold.

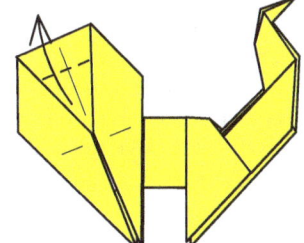

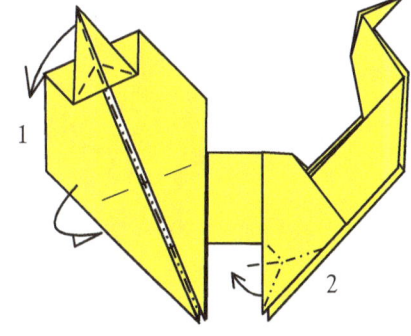

1. Rabbit-ear and fold behind.
2. Rabbit-ear, repeat behind.

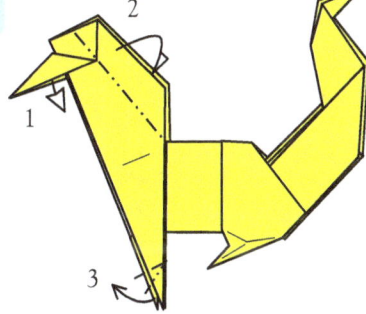

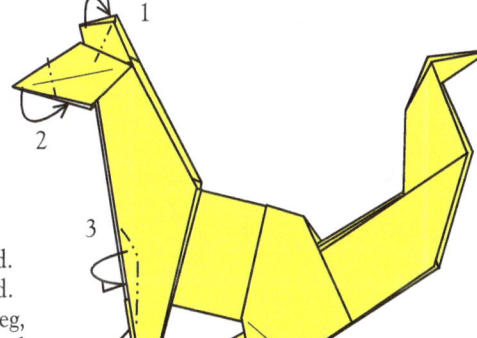

1. Pull out from inside.
2. Fold inside.
3. Squash-fold.
Repeat behind.

1. Reverse-fold.
2. Reverse-fold.
3. Shape the leg, repeat behind.

Javanese

Munchkin

Munchkin cats have uniquely short legs. Their hind legs are slightly larger allowing them to perch on two legs. They are friendly, curious, and easy to train. Because of their confidence and intelligence, they can follow commands as a dog would do. These small energetic cats enjoy running around and will look like kittens all their lives.

1. Fold and unfold.

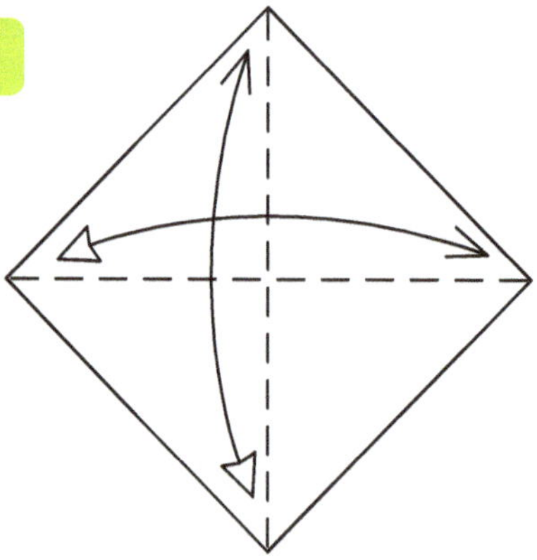

2. Fold and unfold. Rotate 180°.

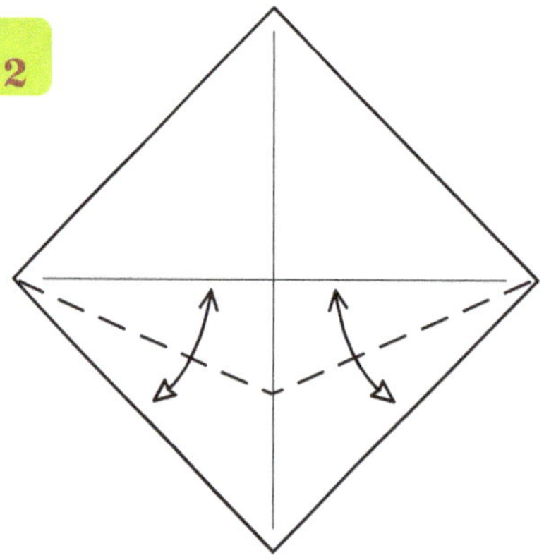

3. Fold and unfold.

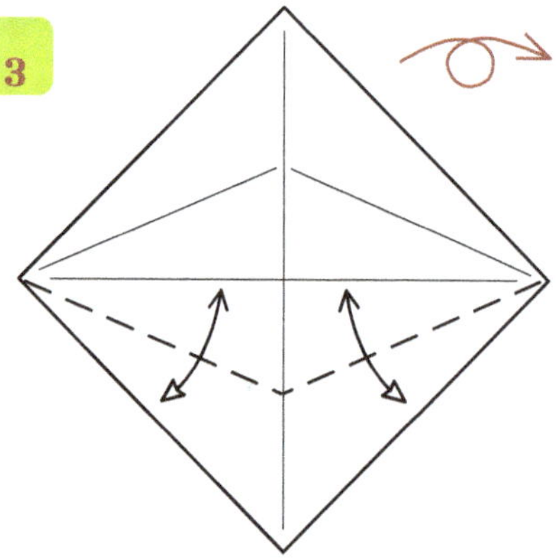

4. Fold and unfold.

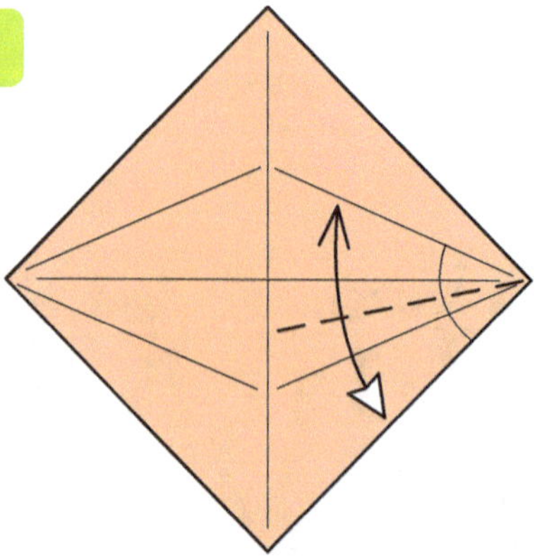

5. Repeat step 4 three times, on the left and above.

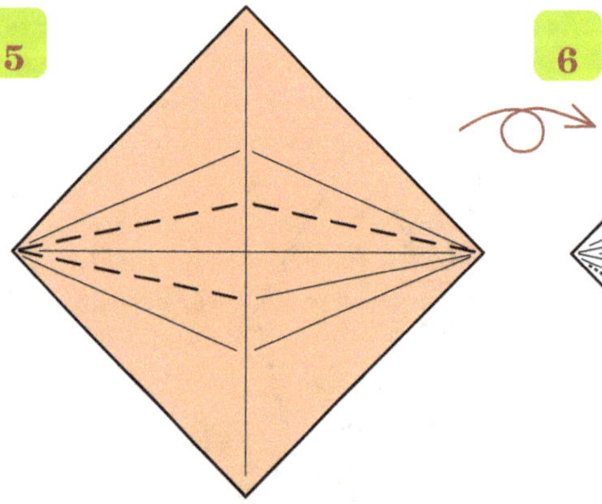

6. Bisect the angle and fold on the right.

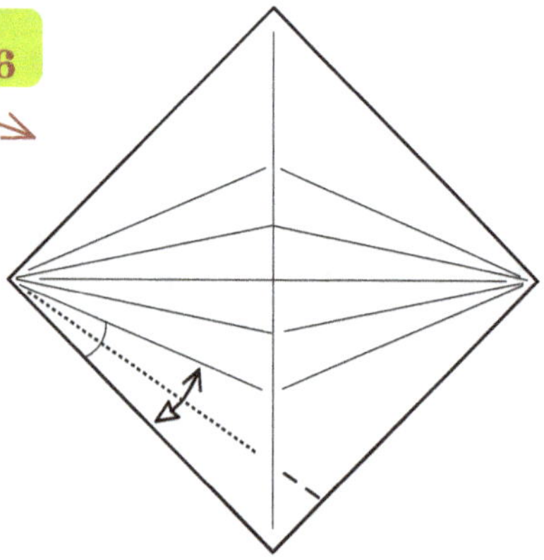

18   Origami Symphony No. 8

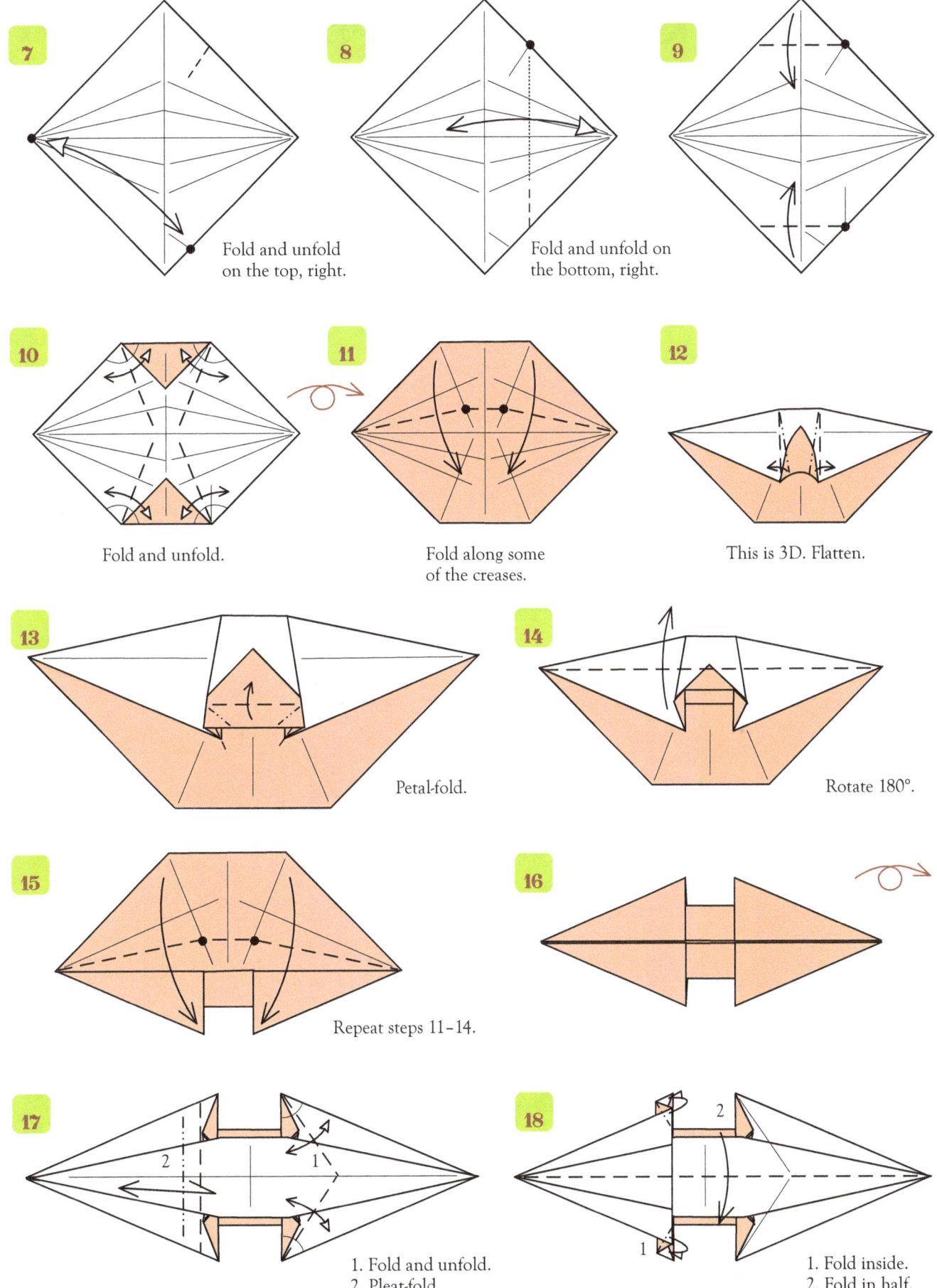

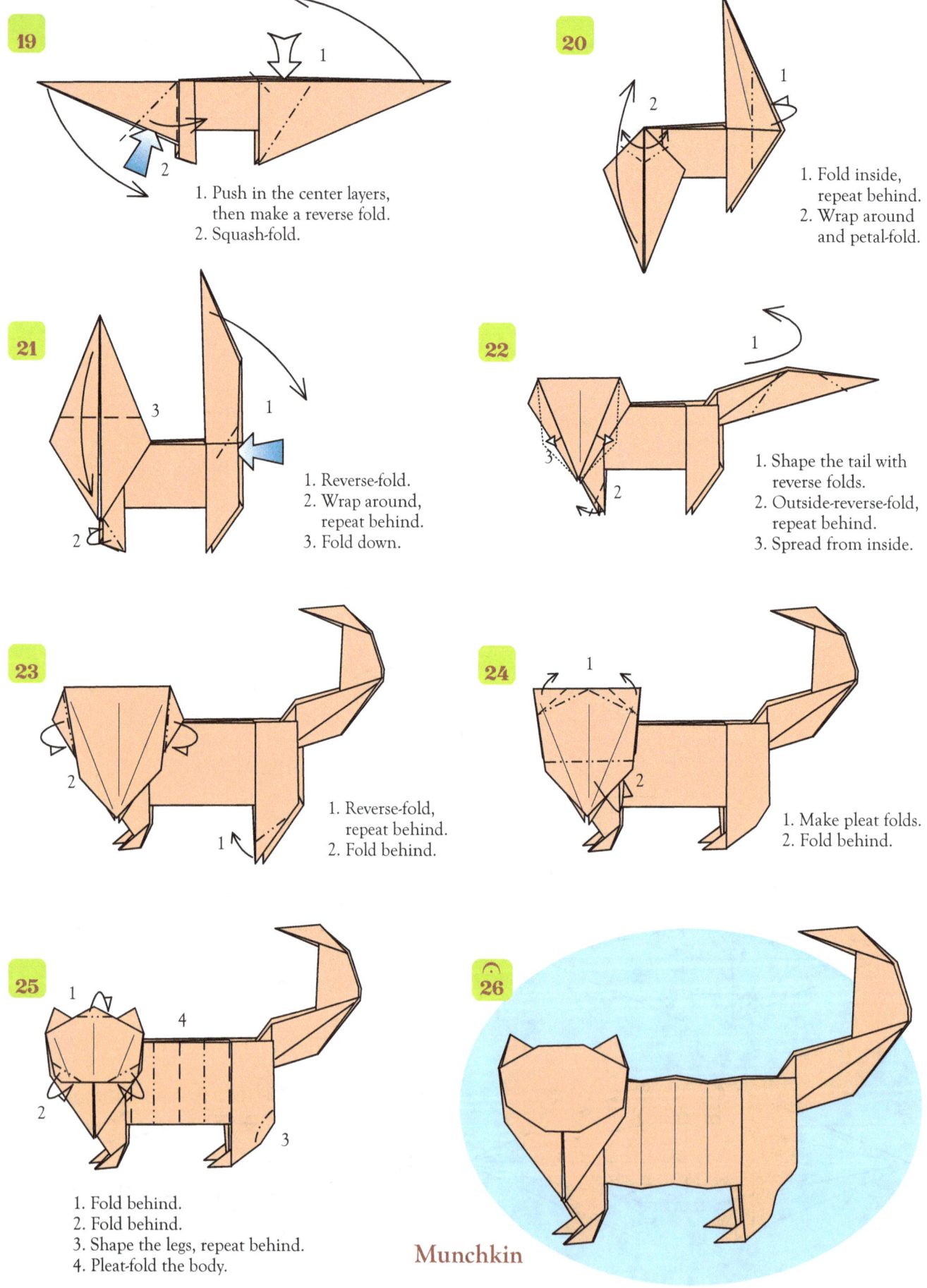

19
1. Push in the center layers, then make a reverse fold.
2. Squash-fold.

20
1. Fold inside, repeat behind.
2. Wrap around and petal-fold.

21
1. Reverse-fold.
2. Wrap around, repeat behind.
3. Fold down.

22
1. Shape the tail with reverse folds.
2. Outside-reverse-fold, repeat behind.
3. Spread from inside.

23
1. Reverse-fold, repeat behind.
2. Fold behind.

24
1. Make pleat folds.
2. Fold behind.

25
1. Fold behind.
2. Fold behind.
3. Shape the legs, repeat behind.
4. Pleat-fold the body.

26

Munchkin

Calico

Calico cats are usually orange, black, and white. The calico cat is not a breed but known for their tri-colored coat. Almost all are females and cannot be bred. Many cultures believe the calico cat brings good luck.

1. 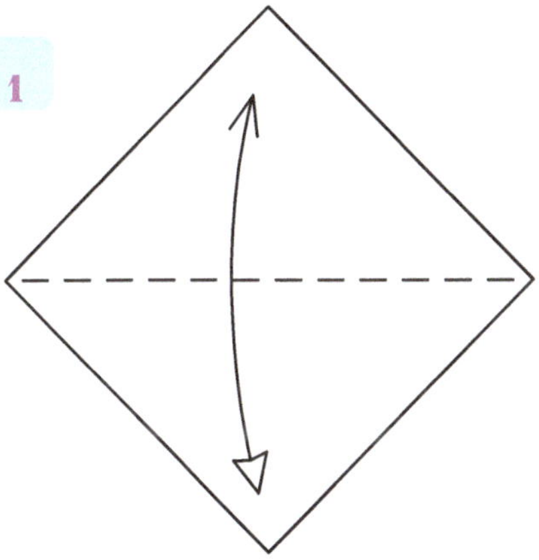 Fold and unfold.

2. Fold to the center.

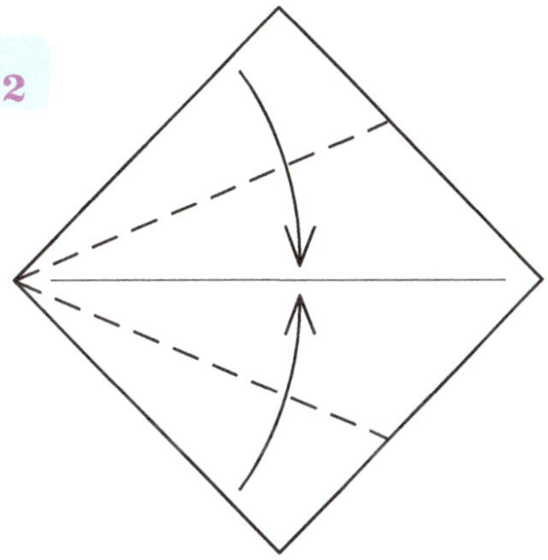

3. Fold to the center and swing out.

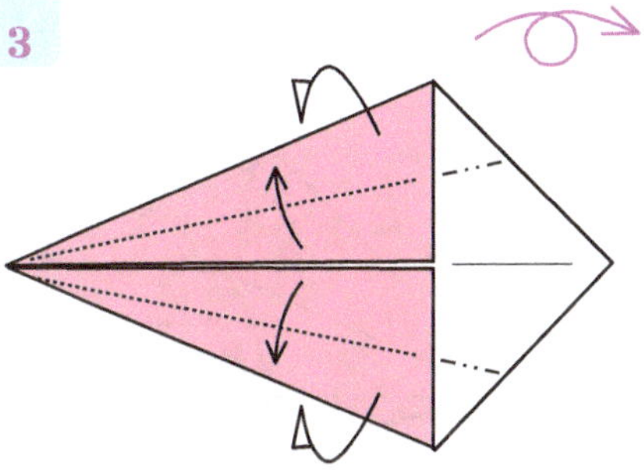

4.

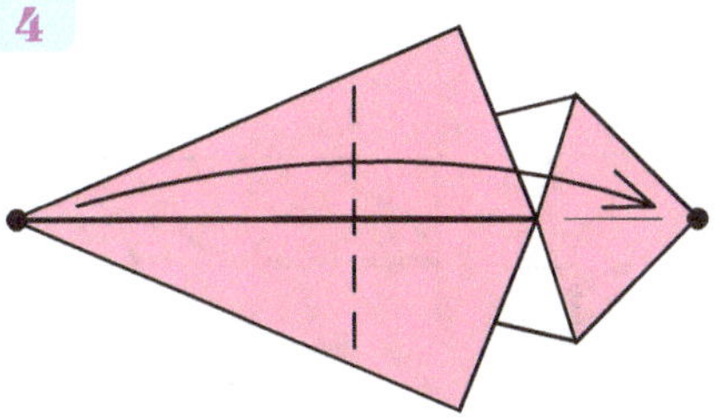

5. 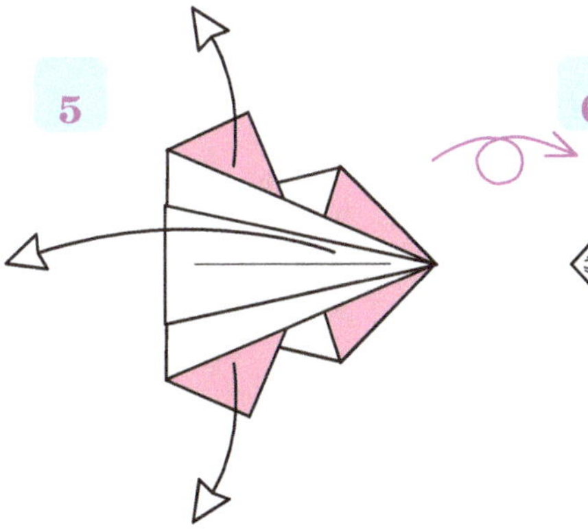 Unfold.

6. Fold and unfold.

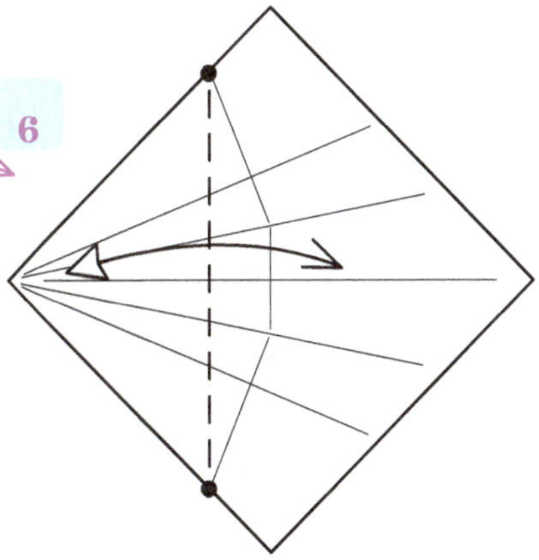

Calico **21**

7

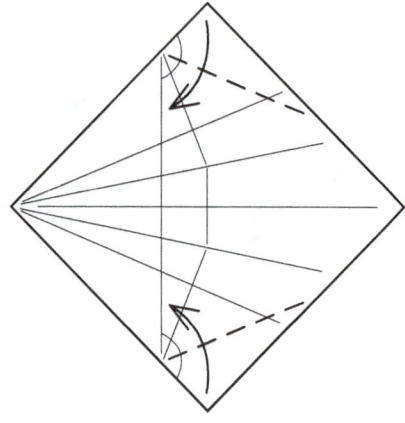

8

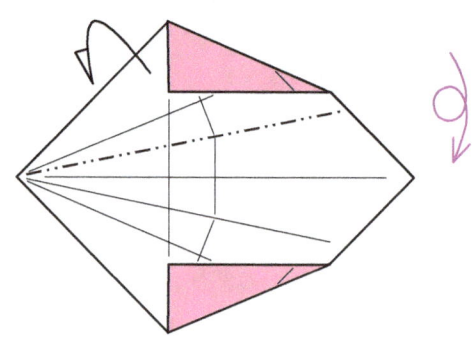

Fold along the crease.

9

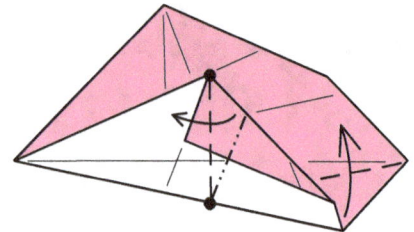

Valley-fold along the crease for this squash fold.

10

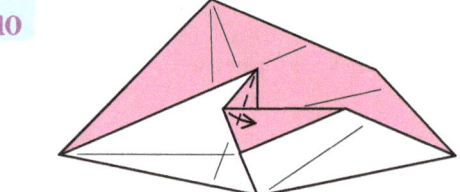

11

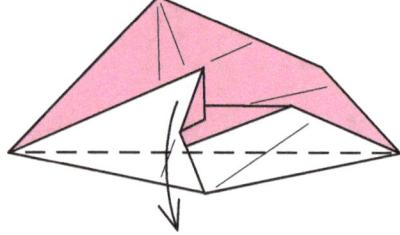

12

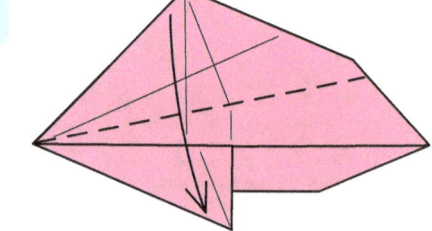

Repeat steps 8–11 on the top. This step is the same as step 8 except the paper is already on the other side.

13

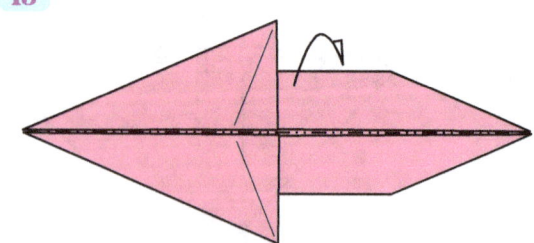

Fold in half.

14

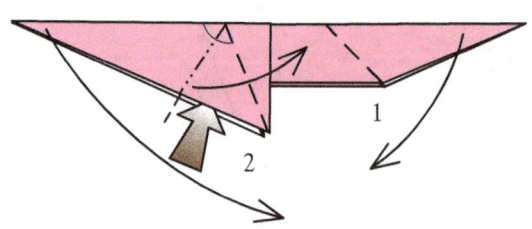

1. Valley-fold.
2. Squash-fold.

22 *Origami Symphony No. 8*

15
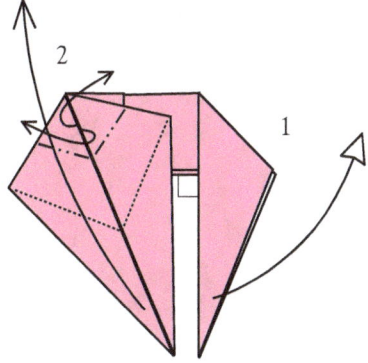

1. Note the right angle. Unfold.
2. Wrap around and petal fold.

16
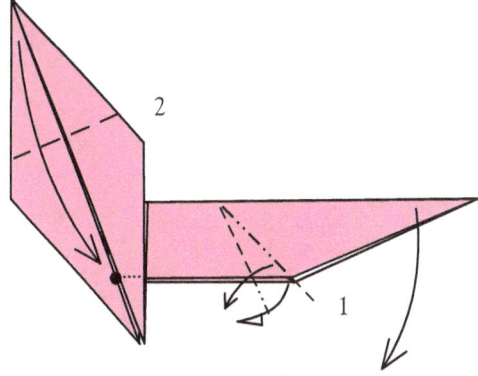

1. Crimp-fold.
2. Fold to the dot.

17
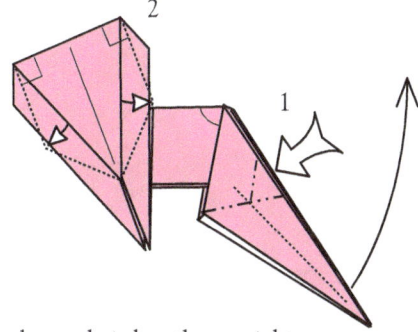

1. Note the angle is less than a right angle. Push in the center layers, then make a reverse fold.
2. Spread to form right angles.

18
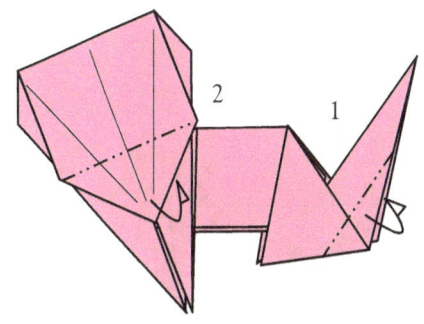

1. Fold inside, repeat behind.
2. Fold inside.

19
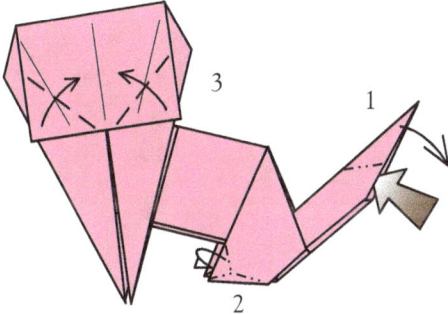

1. Reverse-fold.
2. Shape the feet, repeat behind.
3. Make valley folds.

20
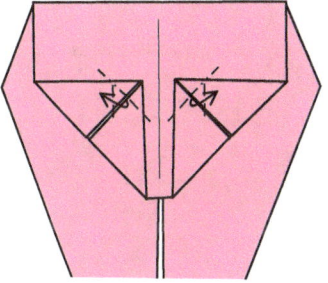

Head.

Make small squash folds.

21
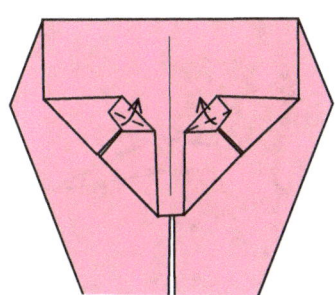

22
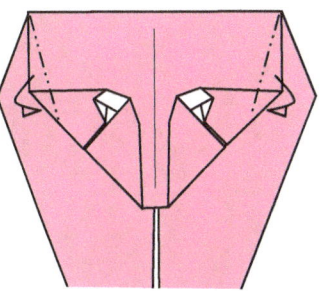

The small folds for the eyes show the white side of the paper. The results can vary.

Calico **23**

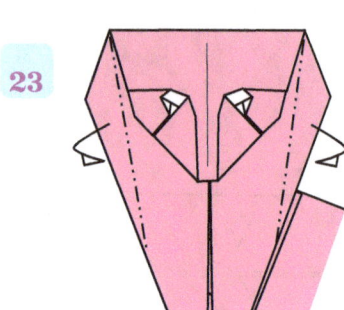

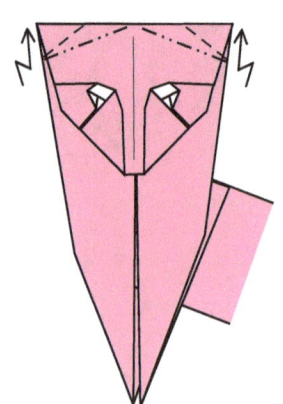

Make pleat folds.

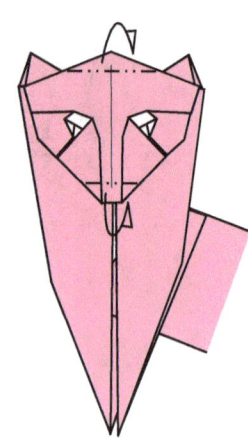

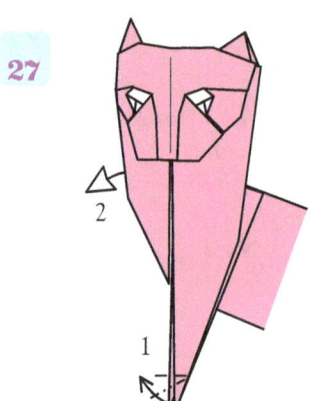

Do not flatten at the head.

1. Squash-fold, repeat behind.
2. Show the face.

Calico

24 Origami Symphony No. 8

Pixie-bob

The Pixie-bob is a very intelligent and muscular cat with a bobbed tail. It is one of the most dog-like of cat breeds and likes to go on walks, hikes, learn tricks, and will respond to simple commands. This easy-going cat will rarely meow. The Pixie-bob is loyal to its owner, plays well with children, and is friendly to other cats and dogs. Unlike most cats, they enjoy splashing in the water.

1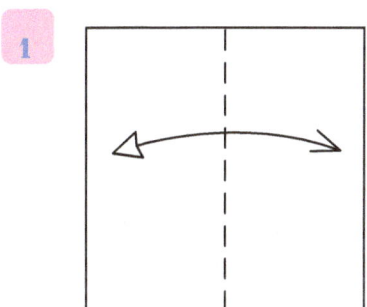

Fold and unfold.

2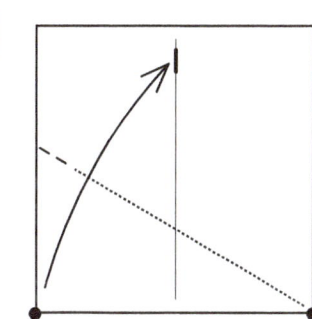

Bring the left dot to the line. Crease on the left.

3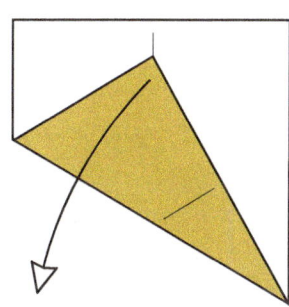

Unfold and rotate 180°.

4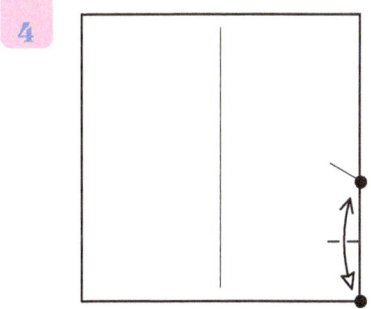

Fold and unfold.

5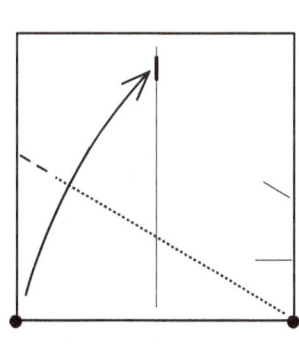

Repeat steps 2–4.

6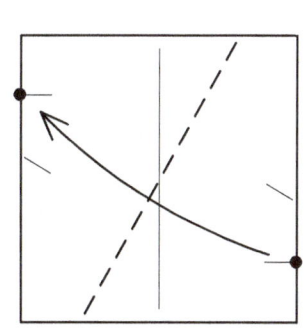

The dots will meet.

Pixie-bob

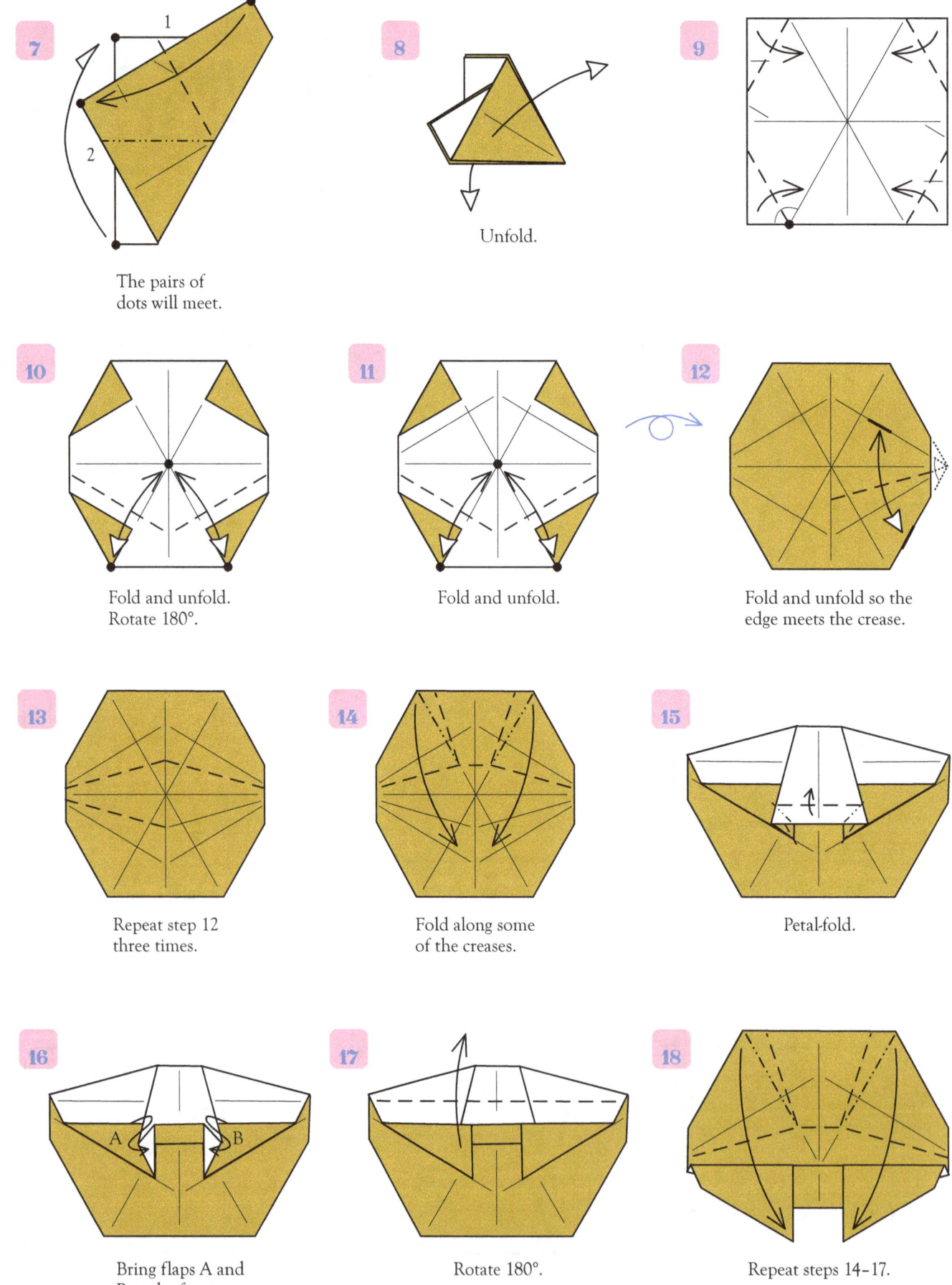

26 Origami Symphony No. 8

19

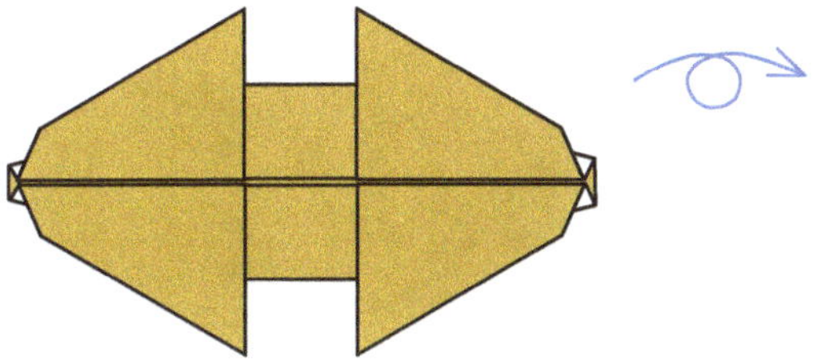

Rotate 90°.

20

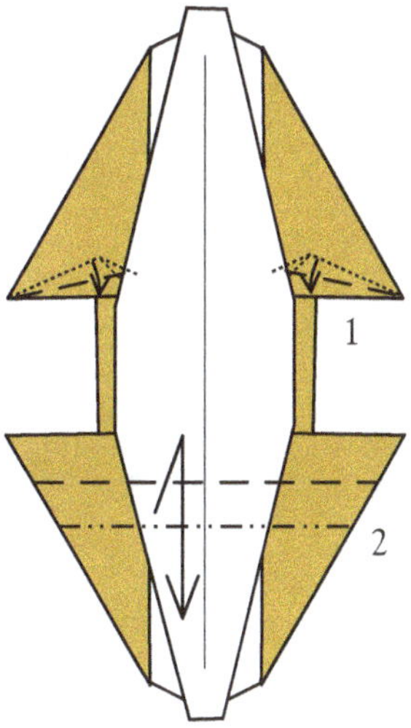

1. Fold the hidden flaps in half.
2. Pleat-fold.

21

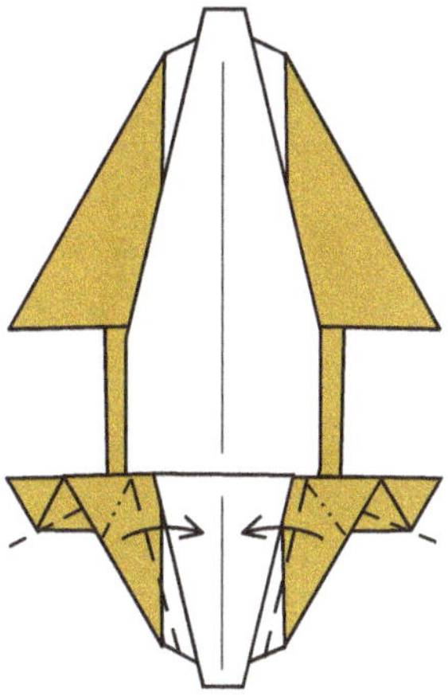

Make squash folds.

22

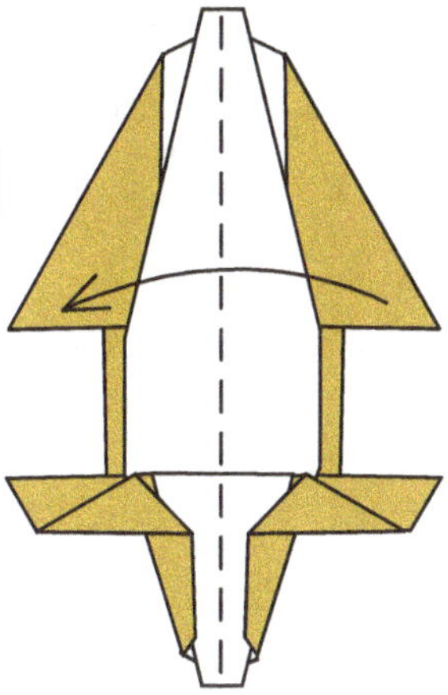

Fold in half and rotate 90°.

23

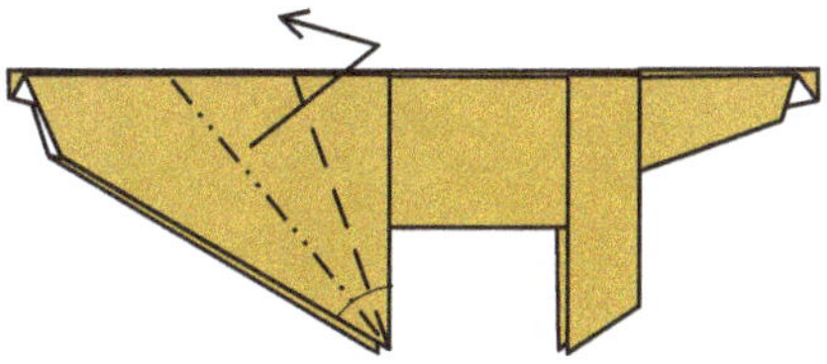

Fold in thirds.

24

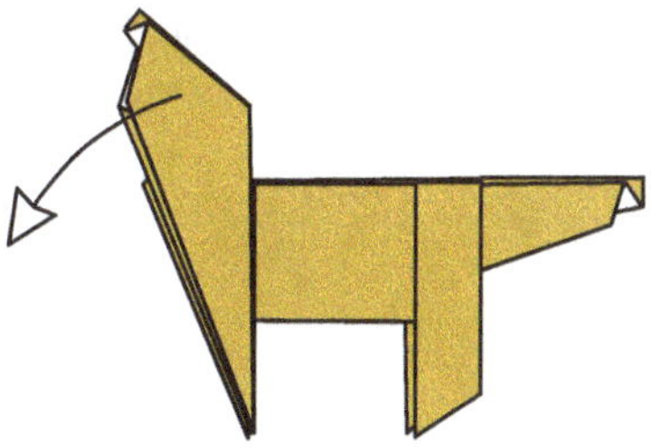

Unfold.

25

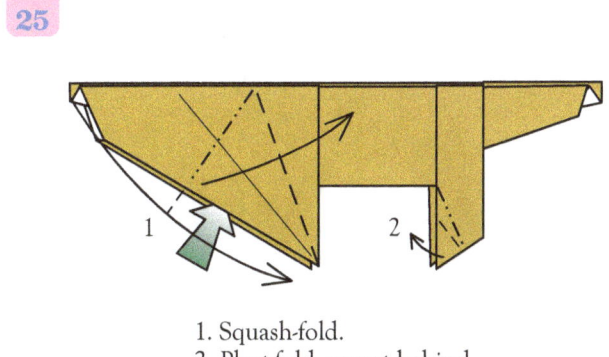

1. Squash-fold.
2. Pleat-fold, repeat behind.

26

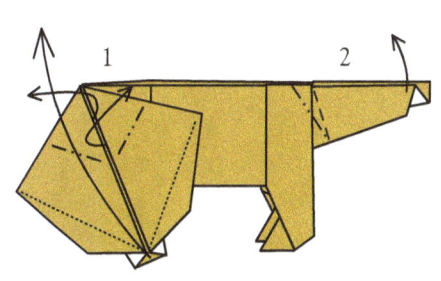

1. Wrap around and petal-fold.
2. Crimp-fold.

Pixie-bob **27**

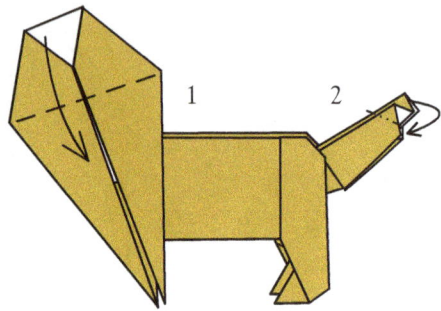

1. Fold down.
2. Reverse-fold.

Make pleat folds.

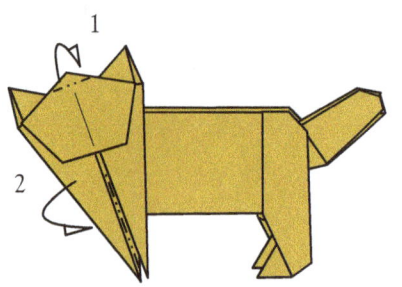

1. Fold behind.
2. Fold behind, but not the head.

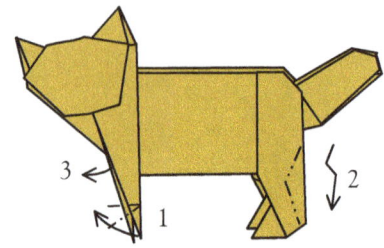

1. Squash-fold, repeat behind.
2. Shape the leg, repeat behind.
3. Spread.

Pixie-bob

LaPerm

Most LaPerms have soft, curly fur. Gentle and affectionate, LaPerms enjoy human company. They are easy-going, enjoy staying indoor while playing with toys, and sitting on a tall cat tree. They get along well with children and other pets. Originally bred from barn cats, they are very intelligent, active, and like to learn new tricks.

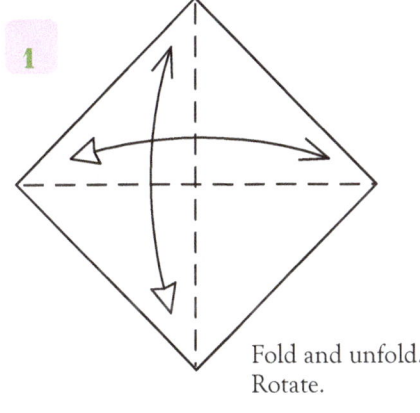

1. Fold and unfold. Rotate.

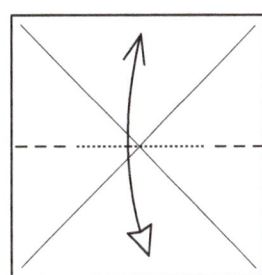

2. Fold and unfold on the edges.

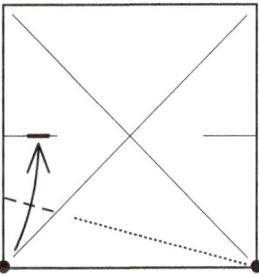

3. Bring the corner to the crease.

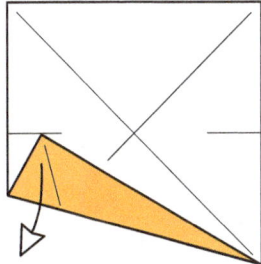

4. Unfold and rotate 180°.

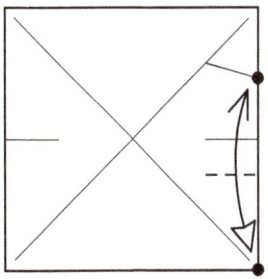

5. Fold and unfold.

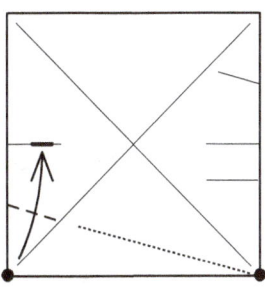

6. Repeat steps 3–5. Rotate 45°.

LaPerm 29

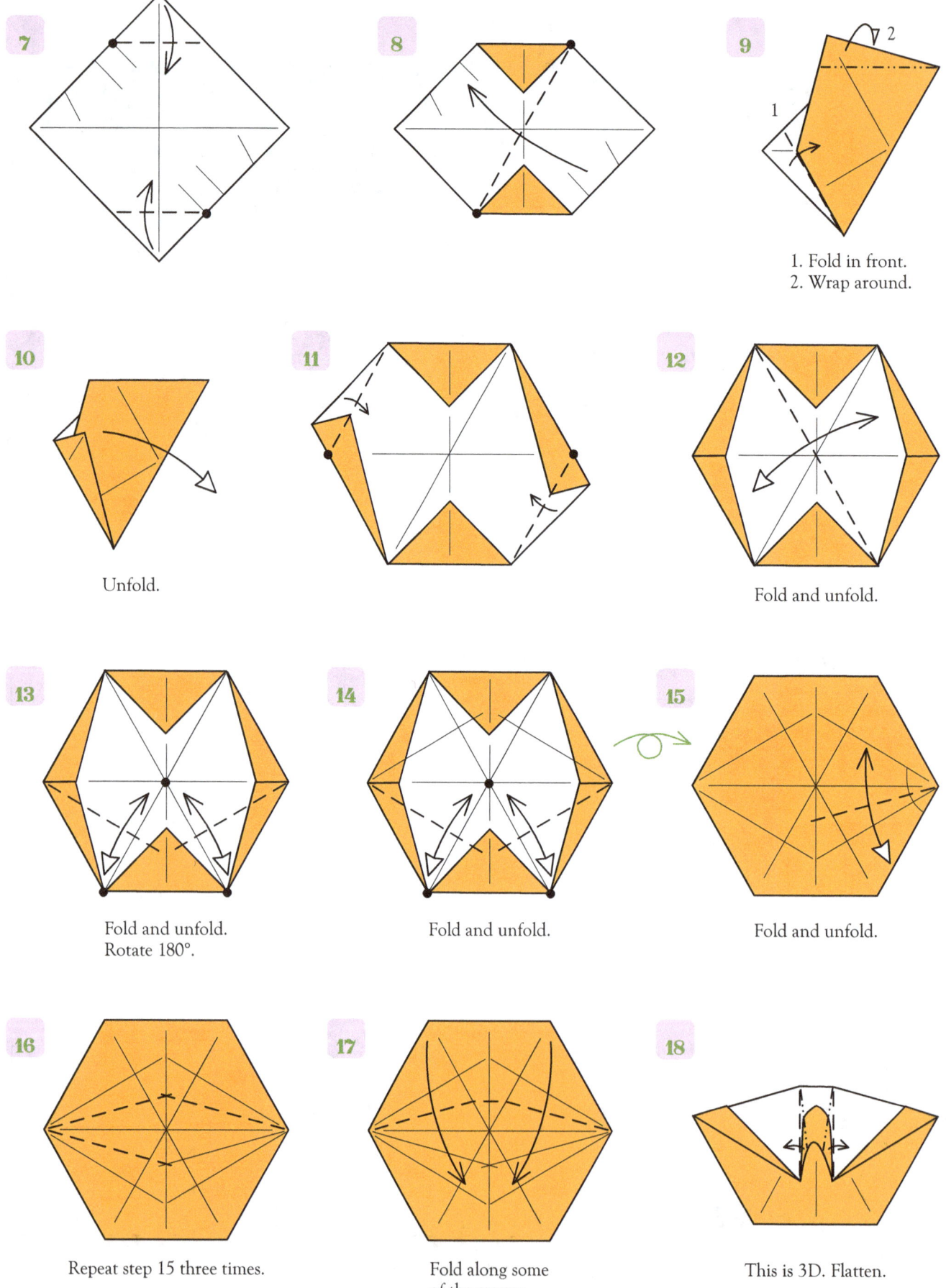

30 Origami Symphony No. 8

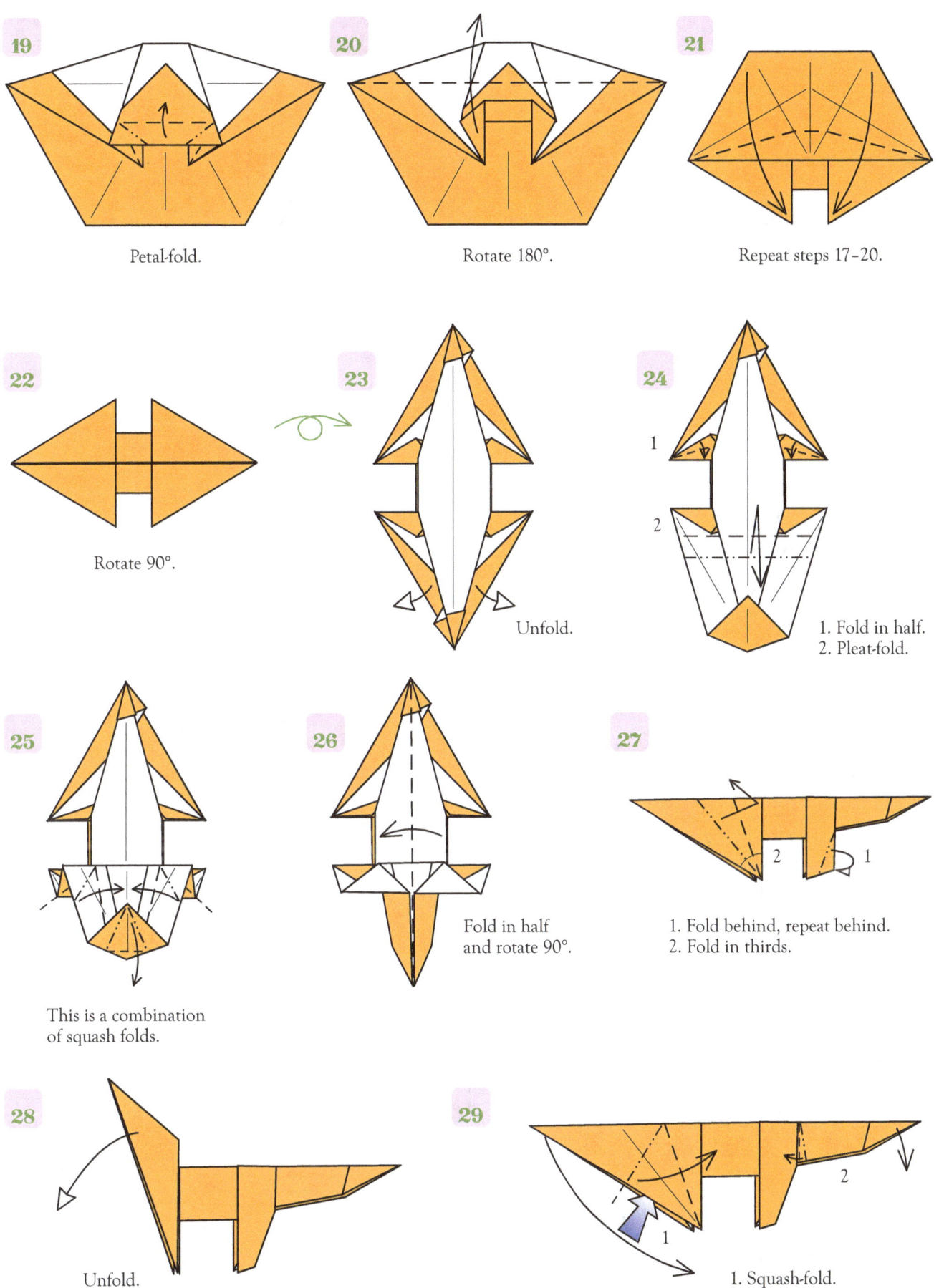

30

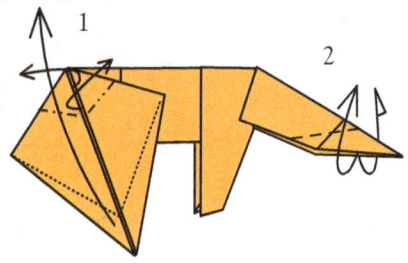

1. Wrap around and petal-fold.
2. Outside-reverse-fold.

31

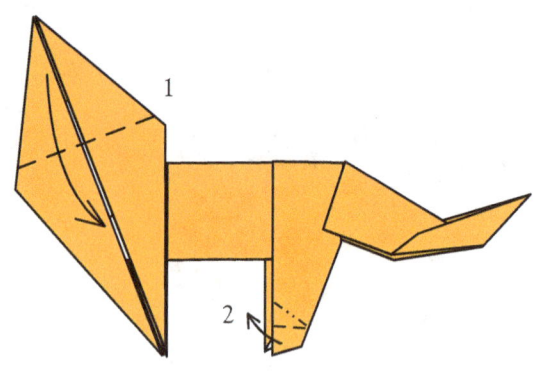

1. Fold down.
2. Pleat-fold, repeat behind.

32

Spread from inside.

33

34

Make pleat folds.

35

1. Fold behind.
2. Fold behind, but not the head.

36

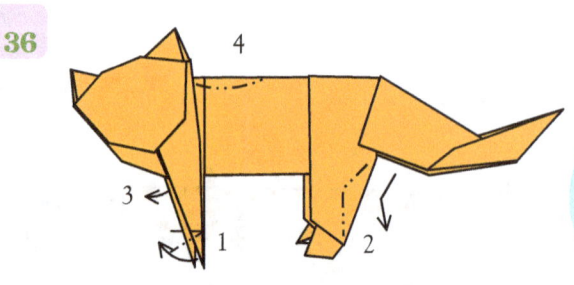

1. Squash-fold, repeat behind.
2. Shape the leg, repeat behind.
3. Spread.
4. Shape the back.

37

LaPerm

Tonkinese

The Tonkinese is a muscular indoor cat. This social cat enjoys enjoys human company and likes to "talk" a lot. They are perfect for children and get along with other cats and dogs. As a mix of Siamese and Burmese cat breeds, the Tonkinese is affectionate and playful. They are intelligent, active and like to jump and climb. Along with human interactions, a tall cat tree would keep them happy.

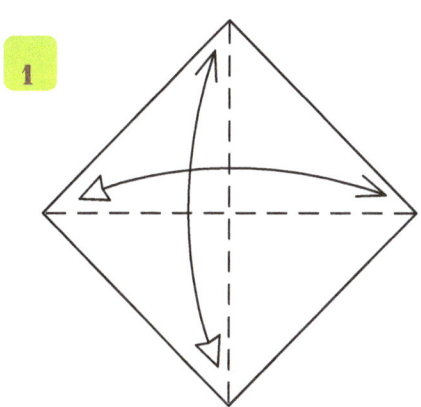

Fold and unfold.

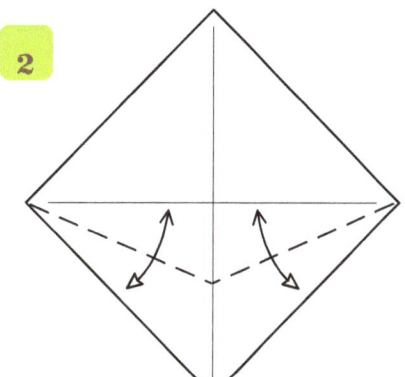

Fold and unfold.
Rotate 180°.

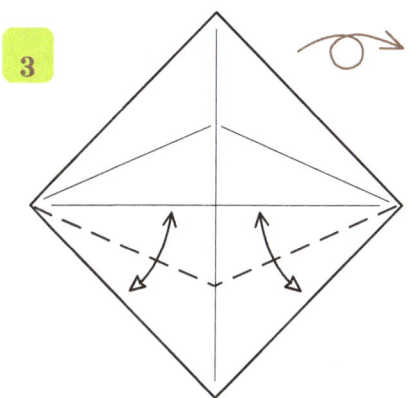

Fold and unfold.

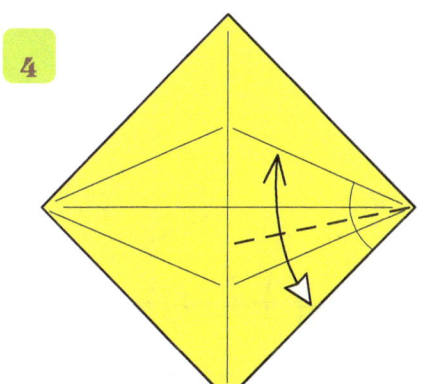

Fold and unfold.

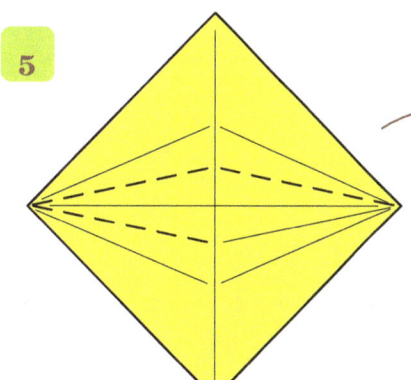

Repeat step 4 three times,
on the left and above.

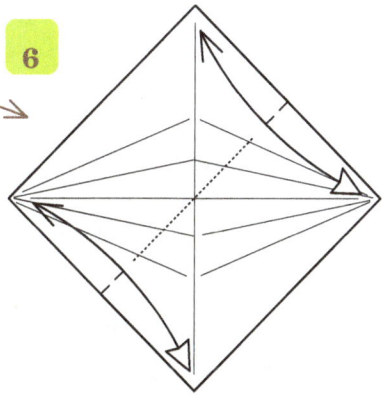

Fold and unfold
on the edges.

Tonkinese 33

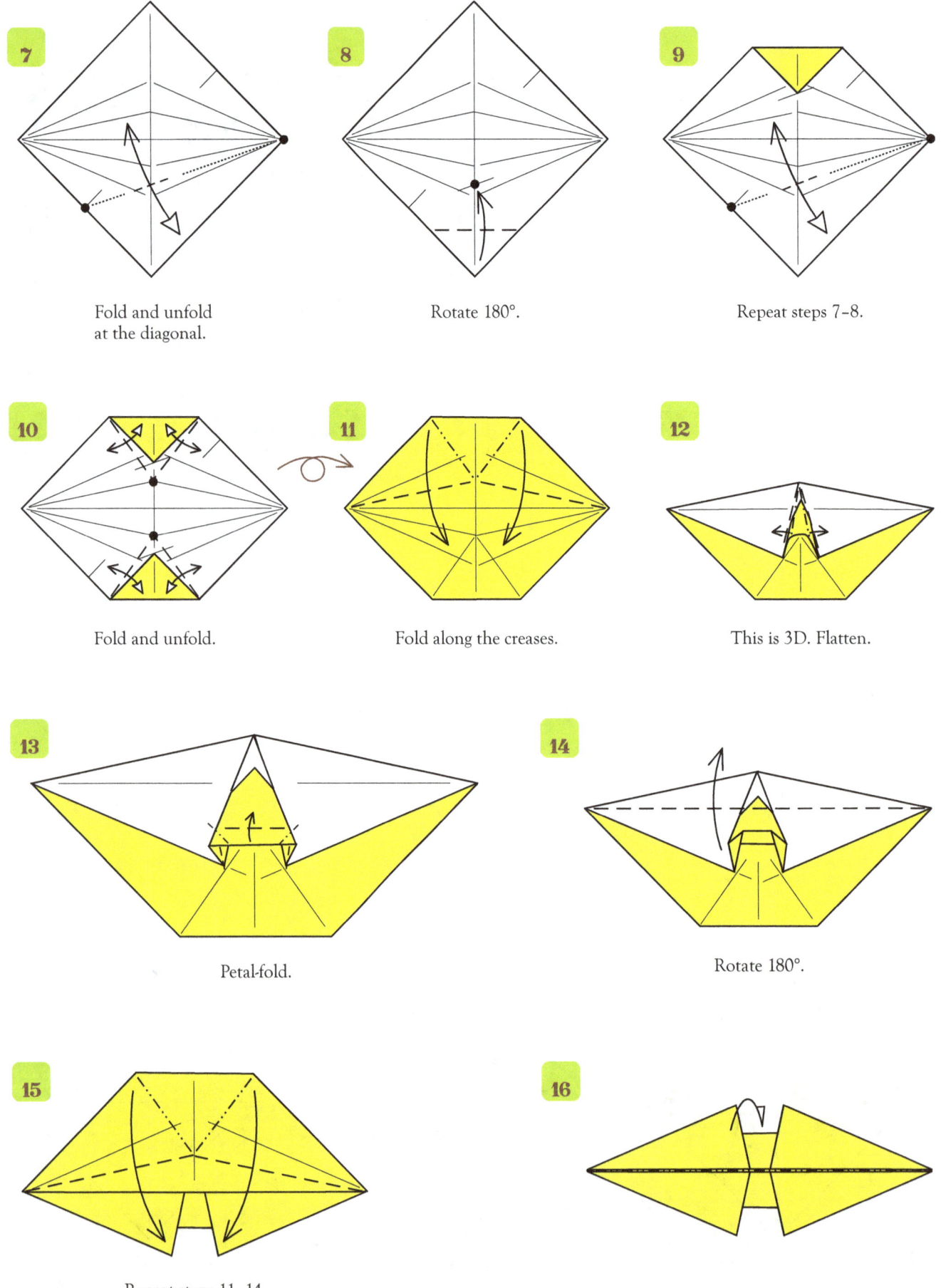

34 Origami Symphony No. 8

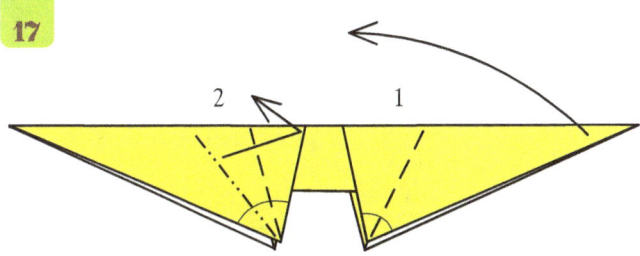

Fold all the layers.
1. Fold in half.
2. Fold in thirds.

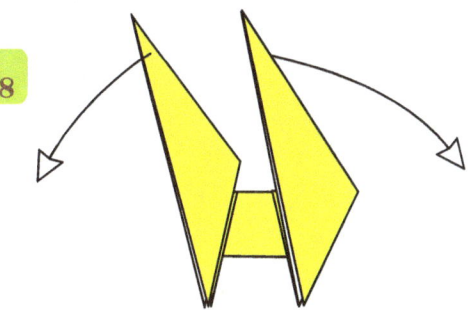

Unfold.

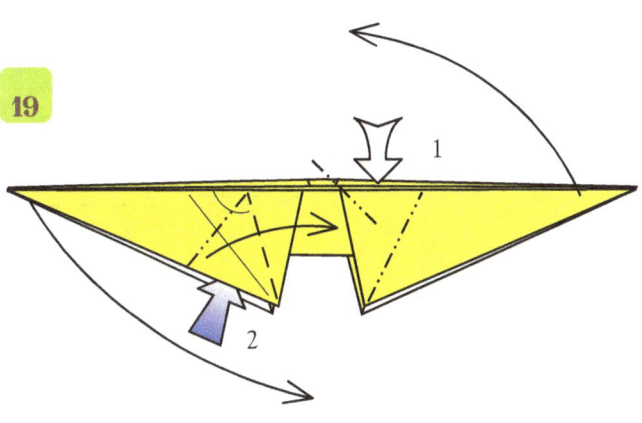

1. Push in the center layers, then make a reverse fold.
2. Squash-fold.

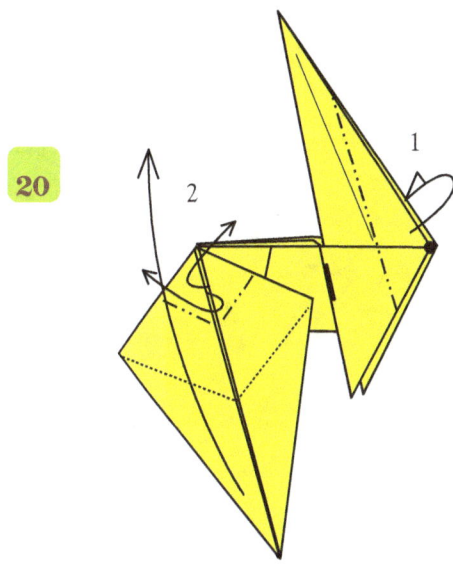

1. Fold inside so the dot meets the line, repeat behind.
2. Wrap around and petal-fold.

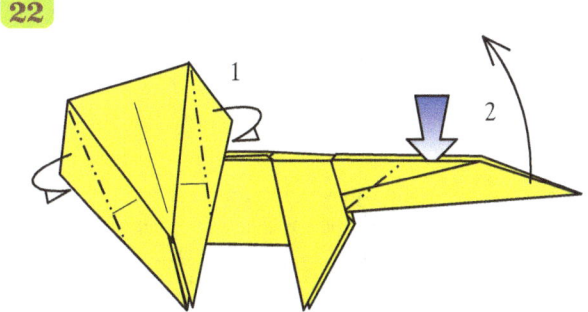

1. Reverse-fold.
2. Fold to the dot.

1. Make mountain folds.
2. Reverse-fold.

Tonkinese **35**

23

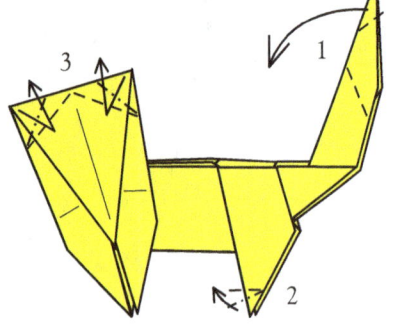

1. Make reverse folds including an outside reverse fold.
2. Squash-fold, repeat behind.
3. Make pleat folds.

24

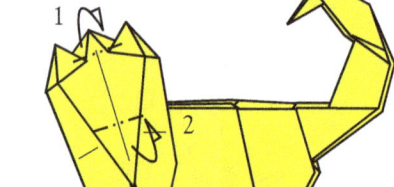

Fold behind at 1 and 2.

25

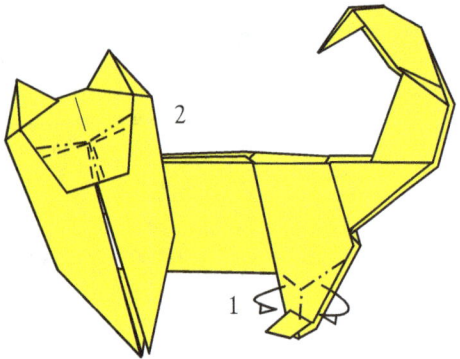

1. Shape the hind legs, repeat behind.
2. Shape the face with soft folds.

26

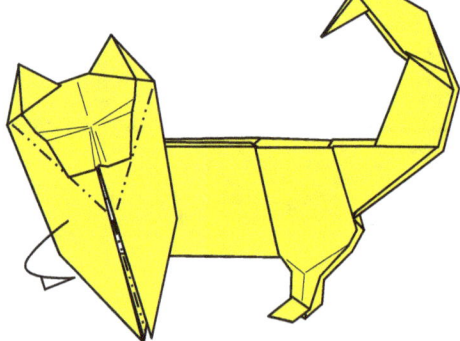

27

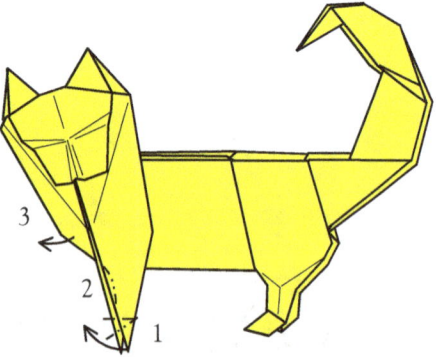

1. Squash-fold, repeat behind.
2. Shape the leg, repeat behind.
3. Show more of the face.

28

Tonkinese

36   Origami Symphony No. 8

Birman

The Birman is an affectionate, sweet, and playful cat. Birman kittens are all white. As they grow, their coat becomes darker on the head, tail, and legs. Unlike most cats, they like to hang out at ground level rather climb high. Gentle and very intelligent, they will greet visitors with curiosity. With distinctive blue eyes, Birmans are good with children and other pets.

1. 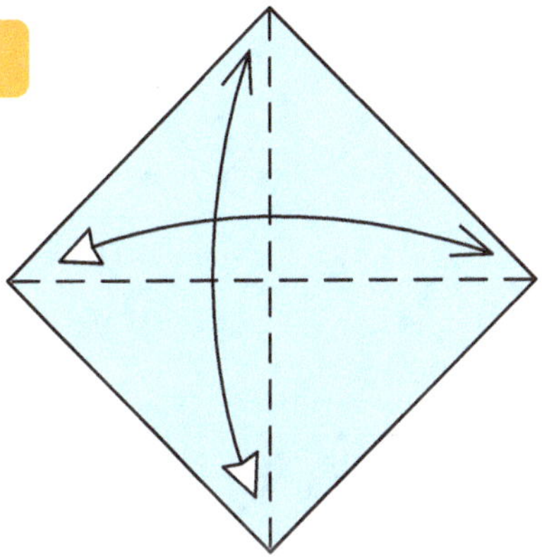 Fold and unfold.

2. Fold and unfold. Rotate 180°.

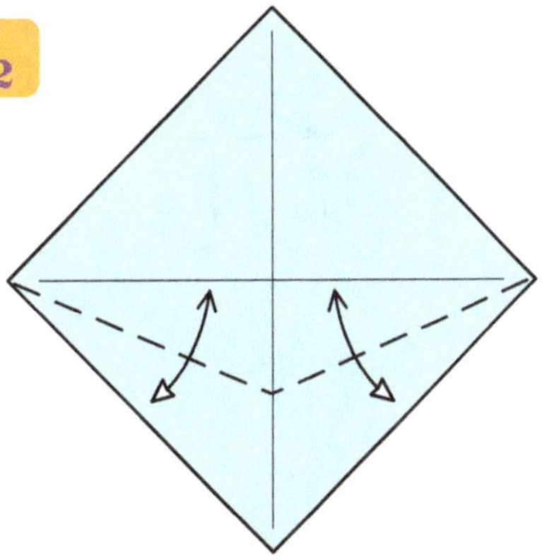

3. Fold and unfold.

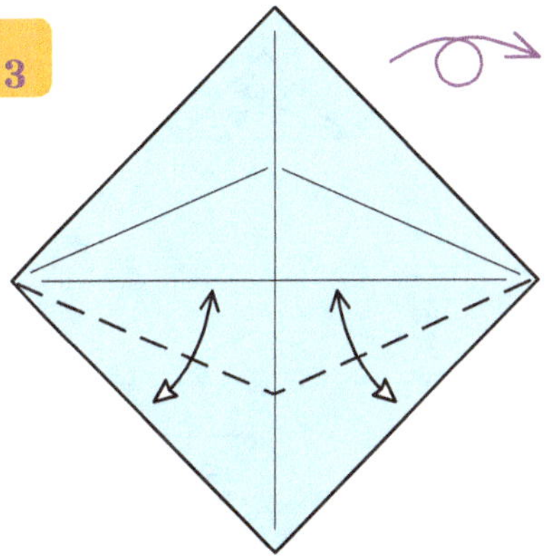

4. Fold and unfold.

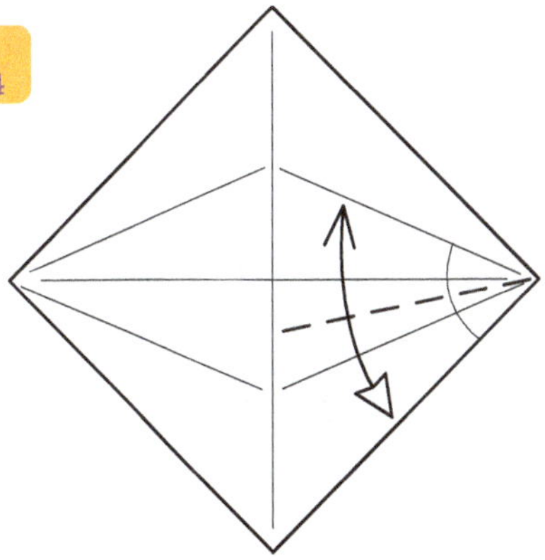

5. Repeat step 4 three times, on the left and above.

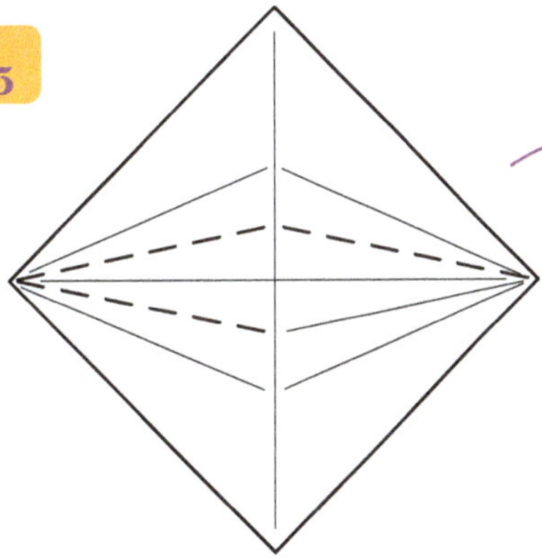

6. Fold and unfold on the edges.

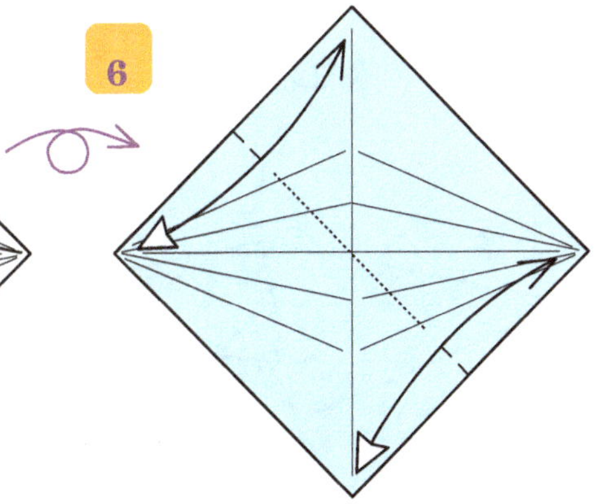

Birman **37**

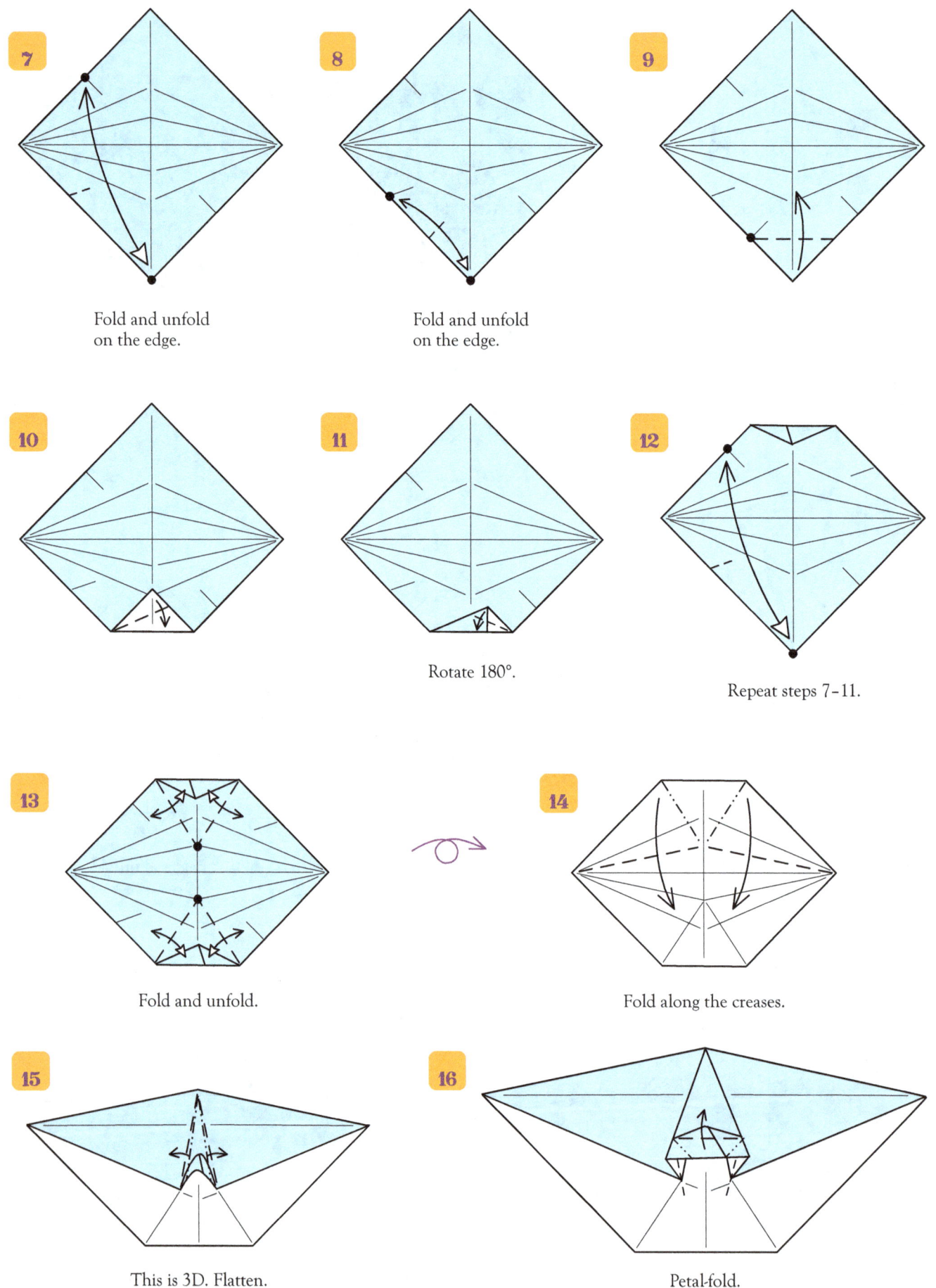

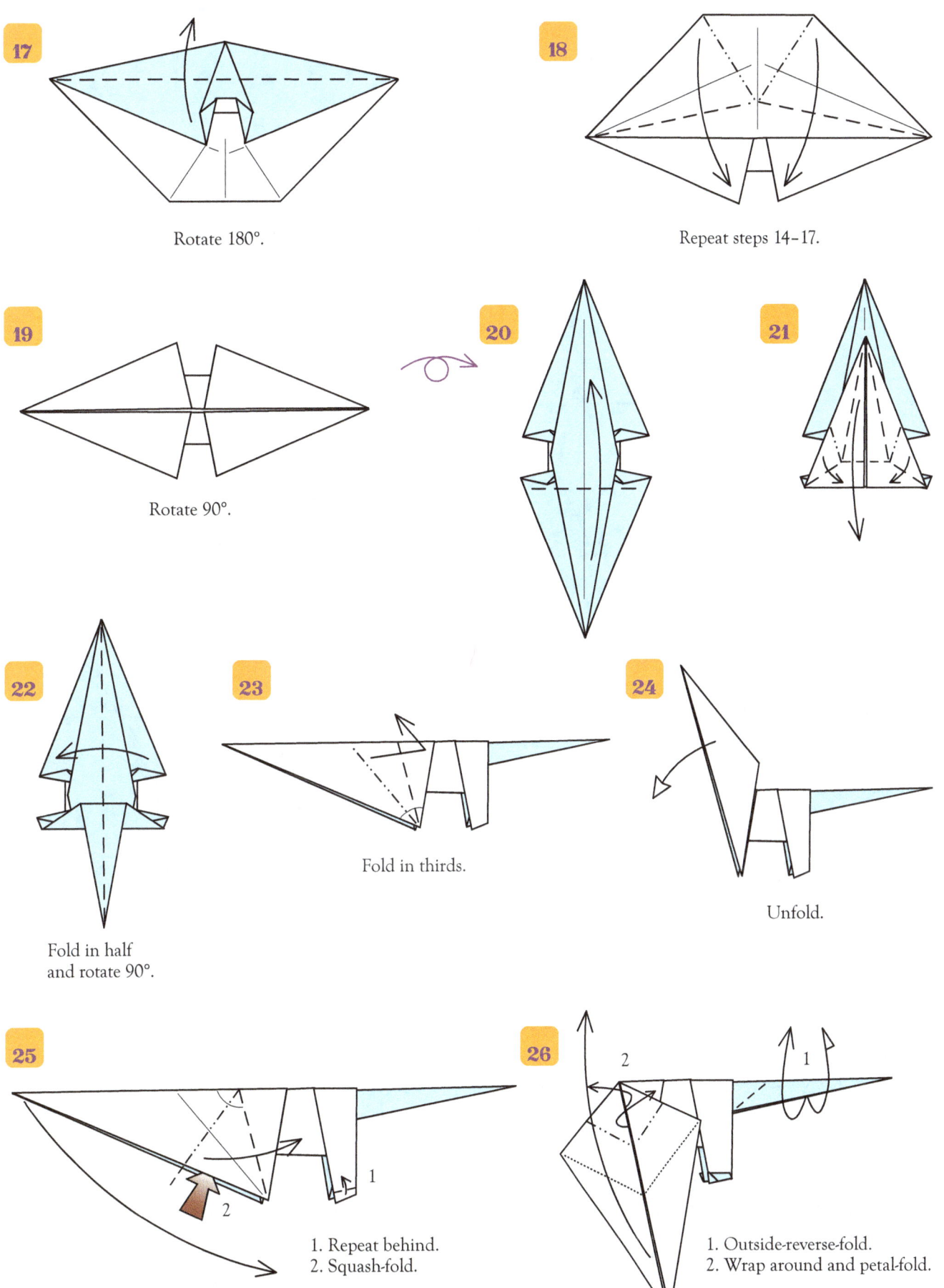

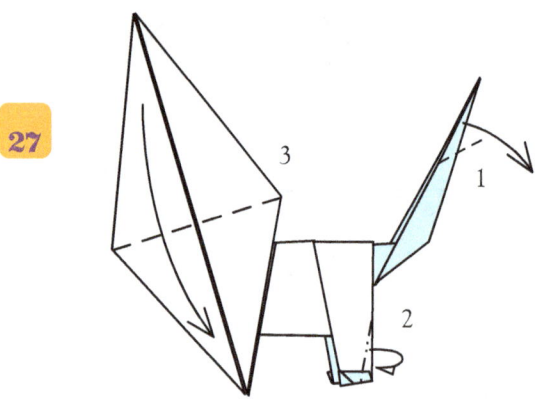

1. Outside-reverse-fold.
2. Repeat behind.
3. Fold down.

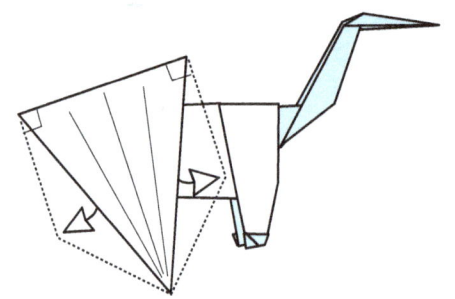

Spread to form 90° angles.

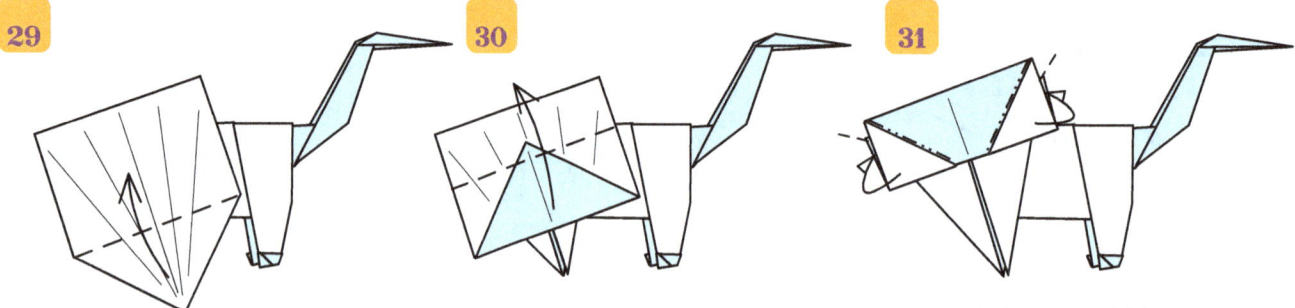

Make reverse folds.

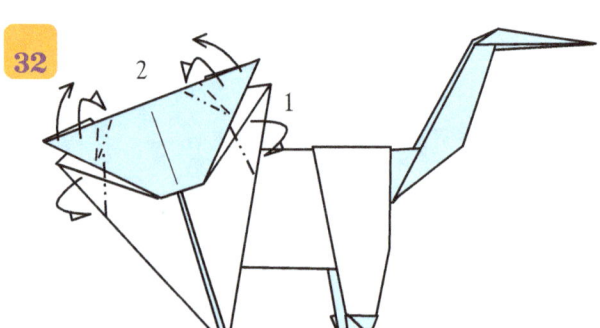

1. Fold behind.
2. Make pleat folds.

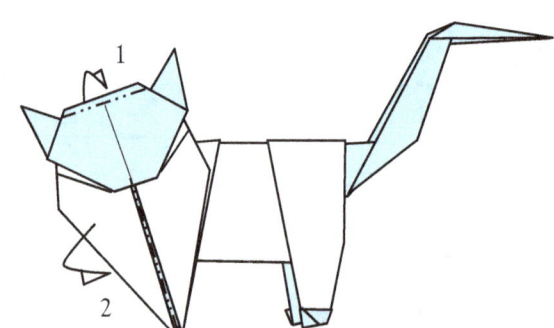

1. Fold behind.
2. Fold behind, but not the head.

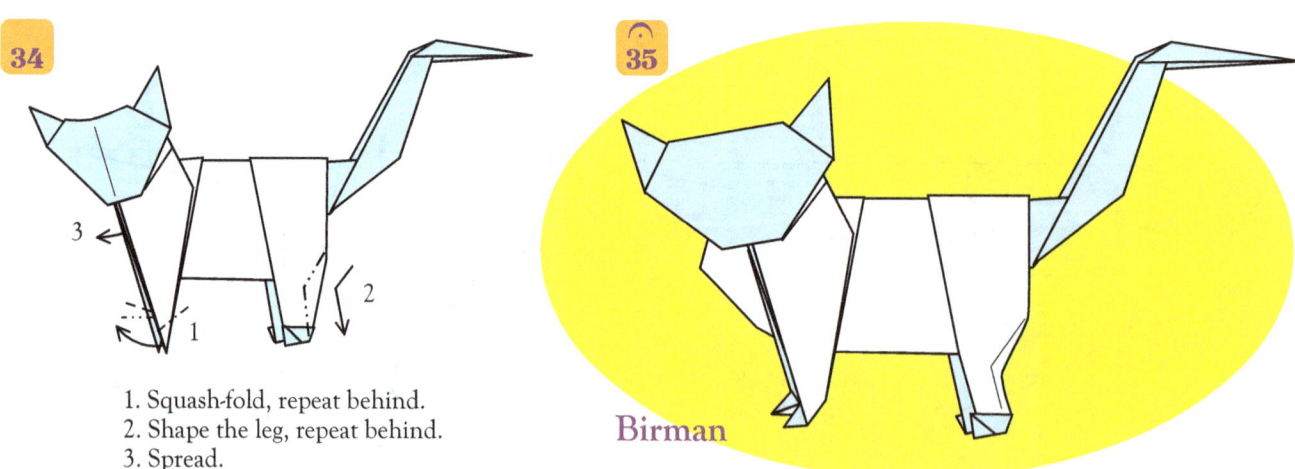

1. Squash-fold, repeat behind.
2. Shape the leg, repeat behind.
3. Spread.

Birman

Second Movement

Andante: Sound Waves in the Sea

The sea is filled with peaceful fish and other creatures. With a variety of shapes and fin displays, fish show the zany side of origami. The guppy, cichlid, and other small fish are perfect for aquariums. The intelligent dolphin and blue whale adds variety to origami design. Enjoy the sound waves as you fold these.

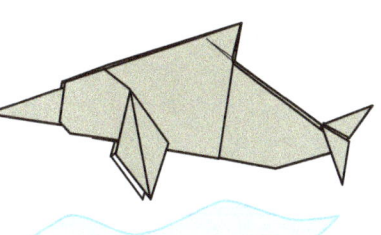

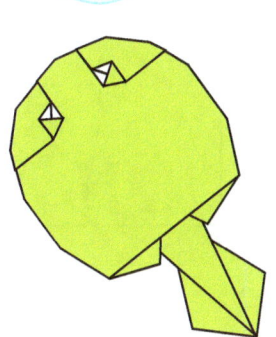

Royal Blue Discus Fish

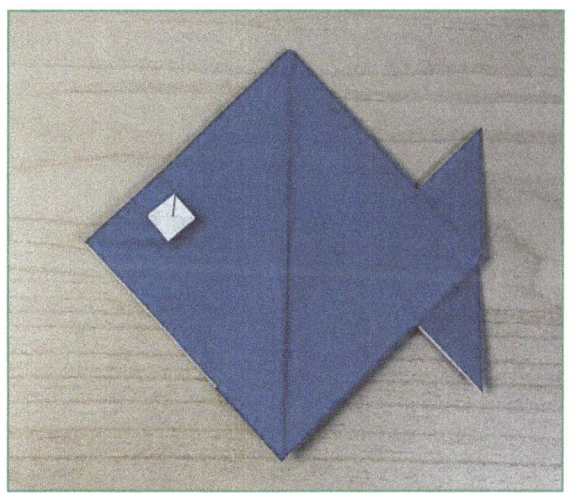

The royal blue discus fish is a member of the cichlid family. They swim in the Amazon River Basin in South America. At six to ten inches long, they feed on worms and small crustaceans. These beautiful and peaceful fish are called the "king of aquarium fish". Other discus fish sport a wide range of brilliant colors and patterns.

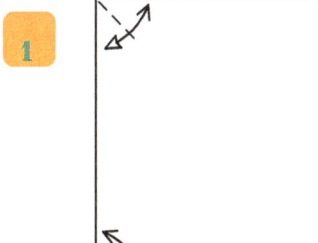
Fold and unfold on the corners.

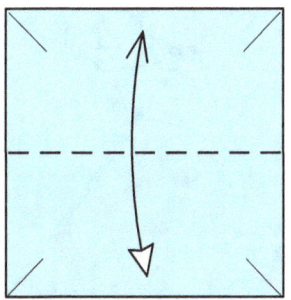
Fold and unfold.

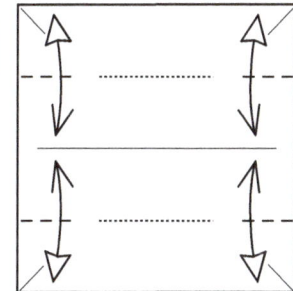
Fold and unfold.

Royal Blue Discus Fish **41**

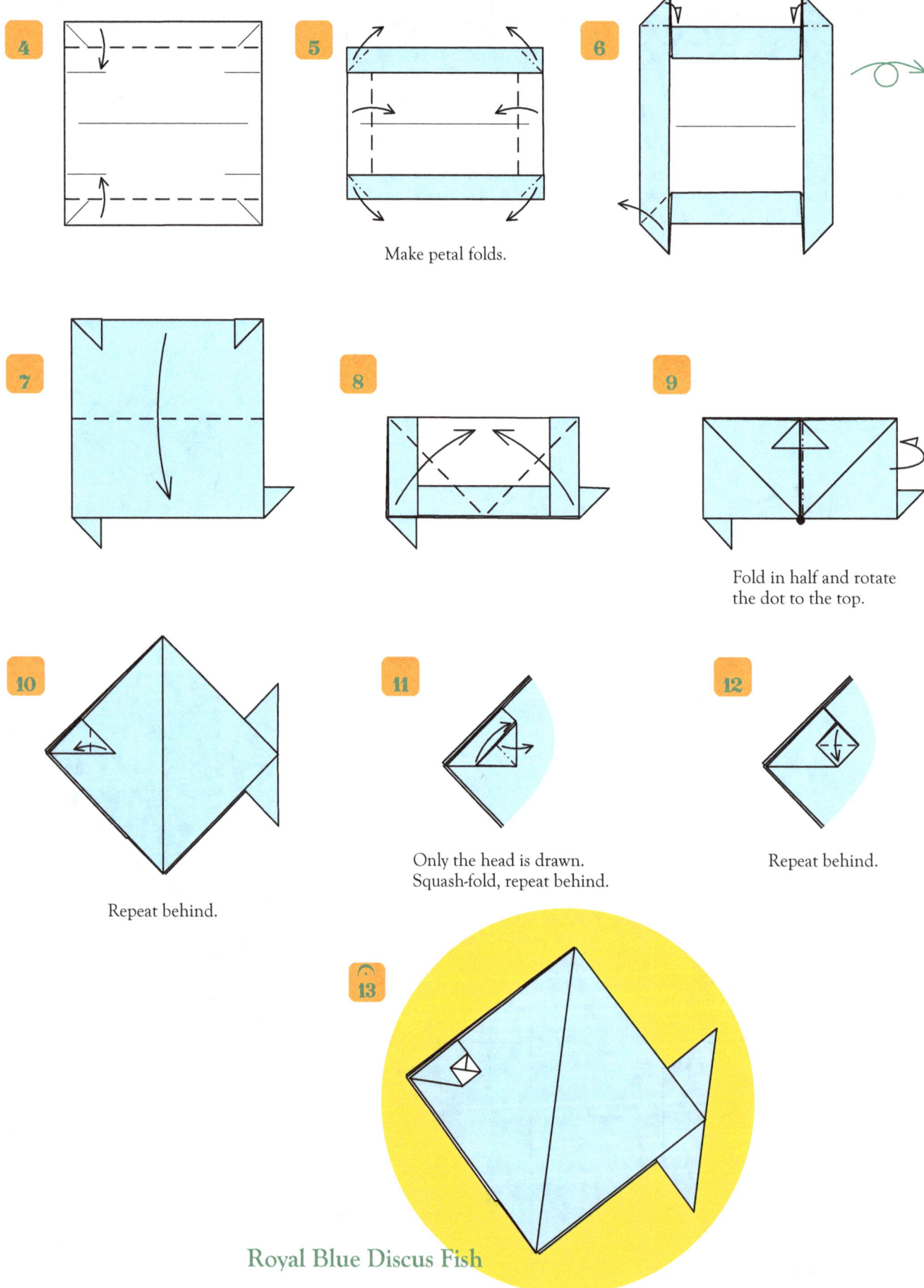

Royal Blue Discus Fish

Bream

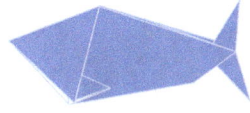

Breams have silver scales that become bronze as they age. At one to two feet long, breams are coastal and freshwater fish found in Europe and Australia. They swim in schools at the bottom of waters near the coast.

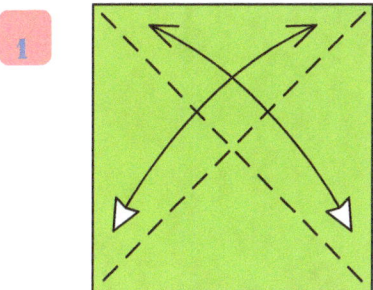

Fold and unfold.

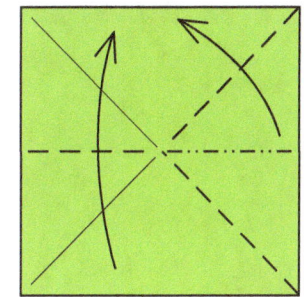

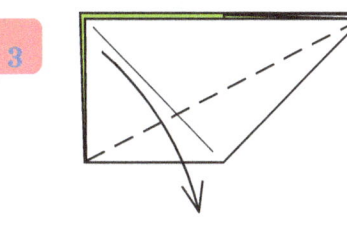

Repeat behind.

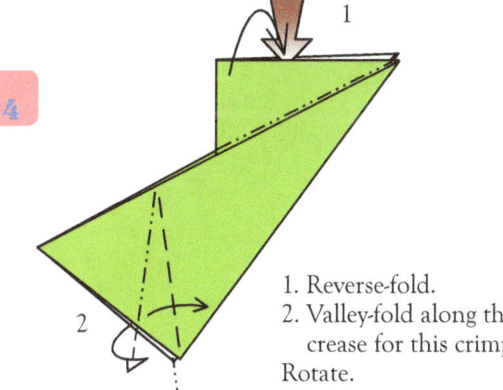

1. Reverse-fold.
2. Valley-fold along the crease for this crimp fold.
Rotate.

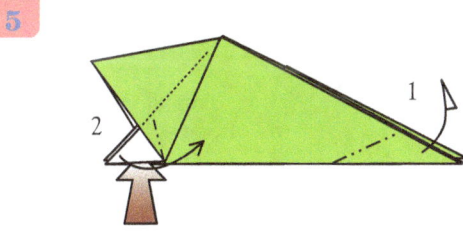

1. Mountain-fold.
2. Reverse-fold.
Repeat behind

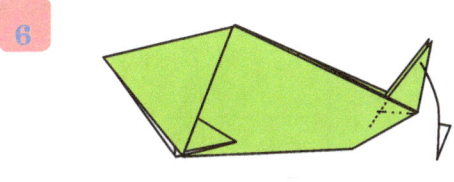

Mountain-fold one flap.

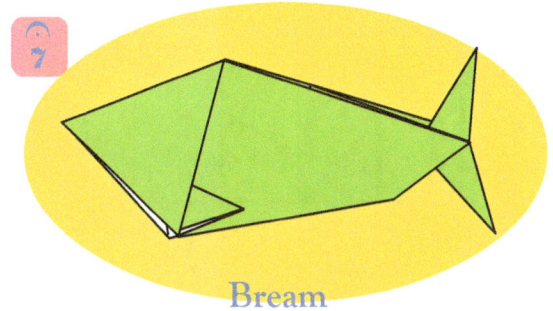

Bream

Bream **43**

Triggerfish

There are about 40 species of triggerfish, known for their stunning colorful patterns and oval shape. Most of the species are found in the coral reefs of Indonesia. For defense, a triggerfish can hide in crevices and use the fin on its back to lock in place, keeping the fish safe.

1. Fold and unfold. Rotate.

2. 1. Fold and unfold. 2. Fold up.

3. Fold and unfold.

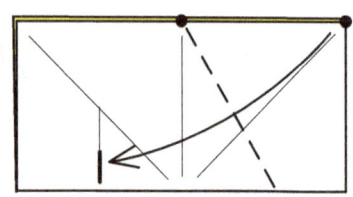

4. Bring the upper right corner to the line.

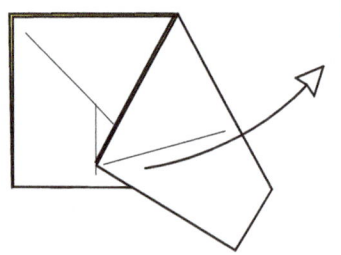

5. Unfold.

6. Fold the top layer down, repeat behind.

44   Origami Symphony No. 8

7

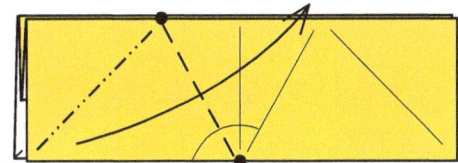

Spread the paper for this squash fold.

8

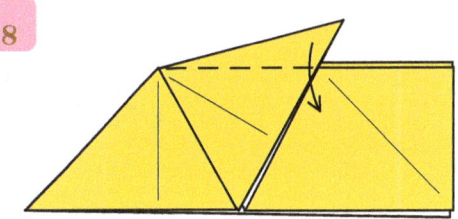

Fold along the hidden edge.

9

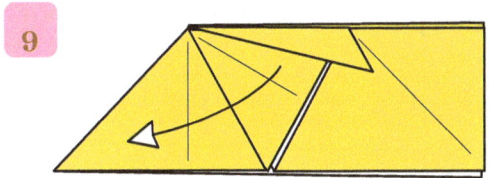

Unfold.

10

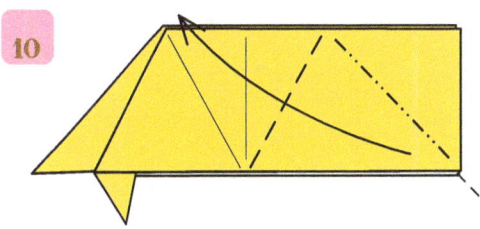

Spread the paper for this squash fold.

11

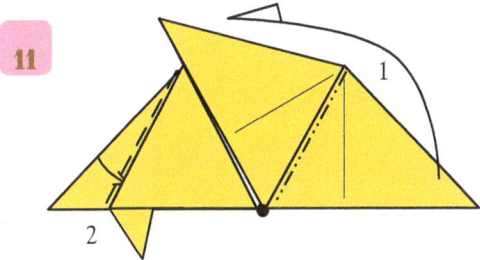

1. Mountain-fold.
2. Fold into the center. Rotate so the dot goes to the top.

12

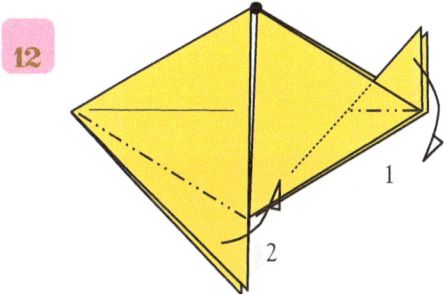

1. Mountain-fold one flap.
2. Mountain-fold along the hidden edge, repeat behind.

13

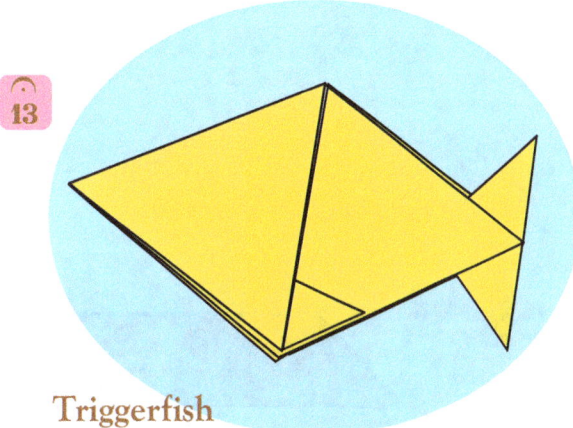

Triggerfish

Guppy

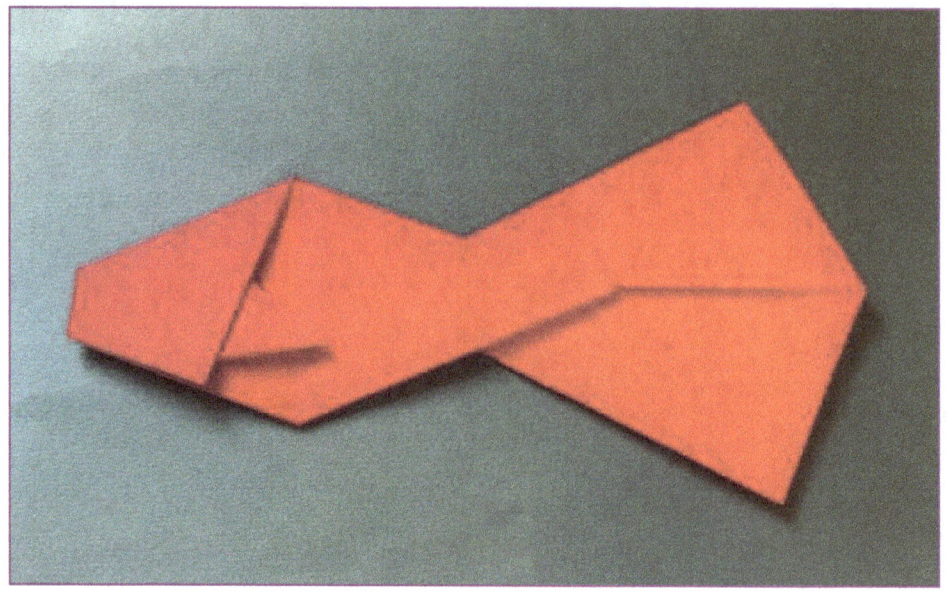

Guppies have large, flowing colorful tails. Averaging two inches long, the males are slightly shorter than the females, and sport vibrant colors. First found in the tropics of South America, they were known to control mosquitos. Guppies like to be surrounded by lush vegetation. These small, colorful fish with lively personalities and ease in care have made them very popular aquarium pets.

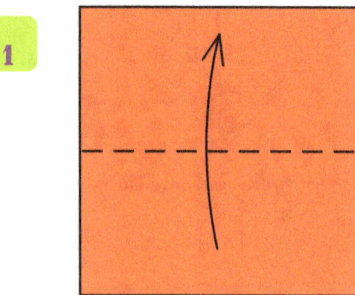

Fold in half.

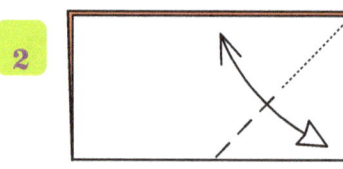

Fold and unfold.

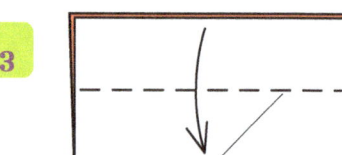

Repeat behind.

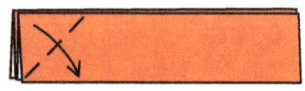

Repeat behind.

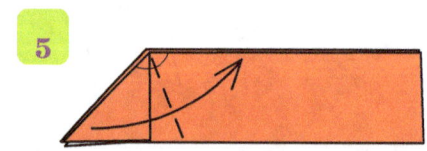

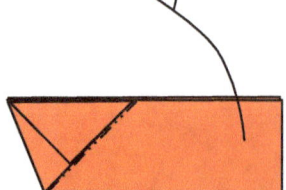

46   *Origami Symphony No. 8*

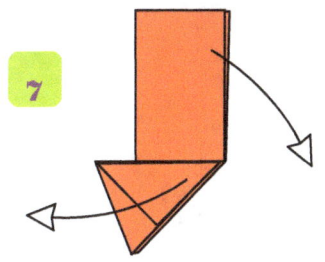

Unfold back to step 4.

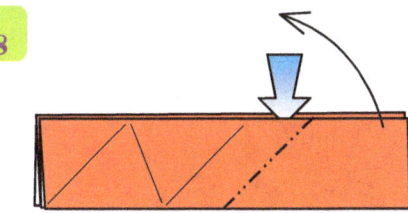

Reverse-fold along the hidden creases from step 2.

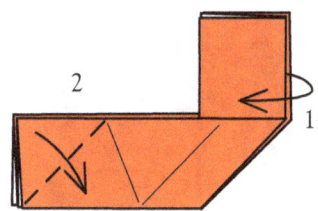

1. Wrap around.
2. Fold along the crease. Repeat behind.

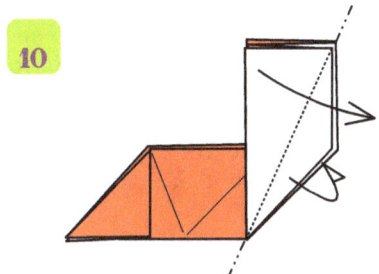

Fold inside along the dotted crease. Repeat behind.

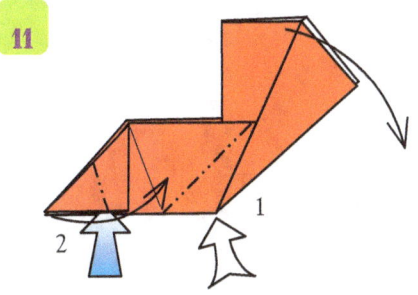

1. Push in at the bottom. This is a combination of a sink and reverse fold.
2. Reverse-fold, repeat behind.

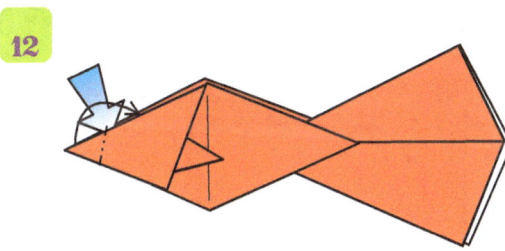

Reverse-fold.

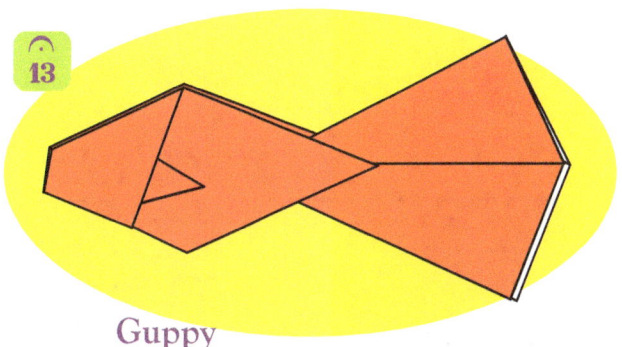

Guppy

Guppy **47**

Angelfish

Angelfish are graceful swimmers and native to the tropics of South America. They live among lush plants and tree branches that fall into the river. Angelfish are members of the cichlid family and can grow to six inches or more.

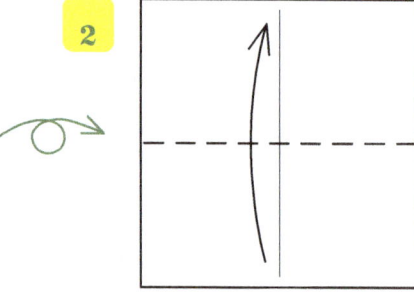

Fold and unfold. Fold in half.

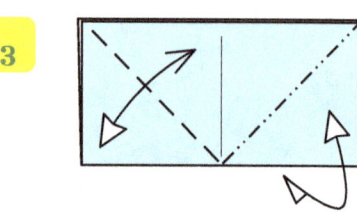

Fold and unfold.

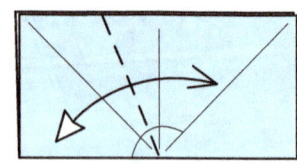

Fold and unfold.

Fold and unfold.

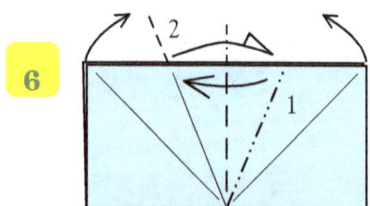

1. Only fold the top layer.
2. Turn over and repeat.
This is similar to a crimp fold.

48 *Origami Symphony No. 8*

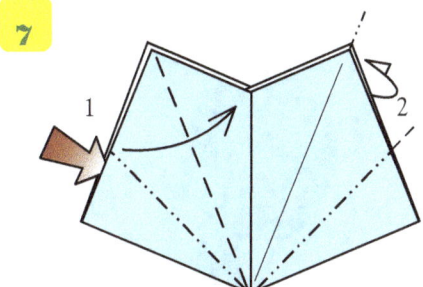

1. Squash-fold.
2. Turn over and repeat.

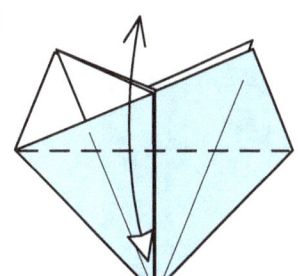

Fold and unfold all the layers. Rotate 90°.

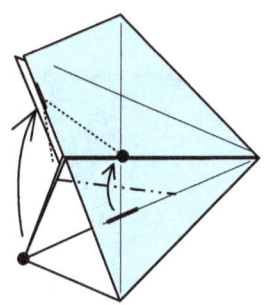

Reverse-fold so the lower dot meets the bold edge and the bold edge in the middle meets the center dot. The dotted lines show the result. Turn over and repeat.

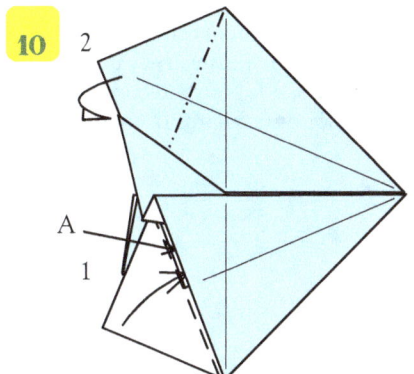

1. Fold inside and cover the hidden flap A.
2. Turn over and repeat.

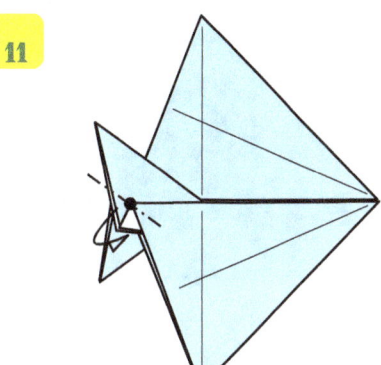

Mountain-fold two layers together. Turn over and repeat.

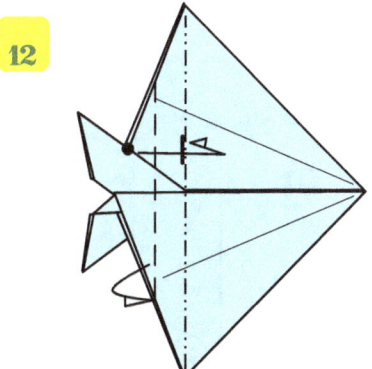

Pleat-fold so the dot meets the mountain fold line. Turn over and repeat.

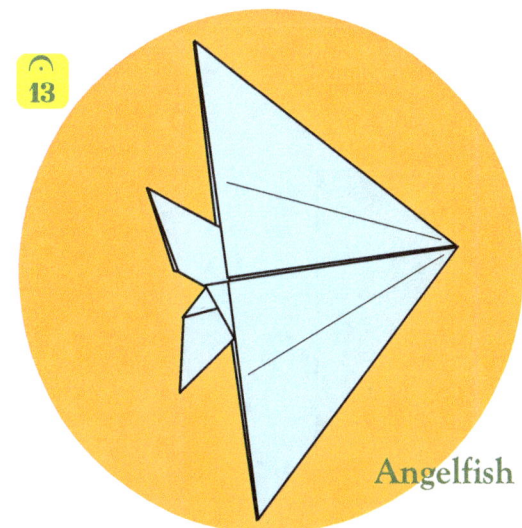

Angelfish

Angelfish **49**

Stingray

Stingrays are flattened fish with no bones and are closely related to sharks. They can detect electrical signals from other fish as they search for food. While resting, they bury themselves in the sand. For protection, stingrays have poisonous barbs in their tails.

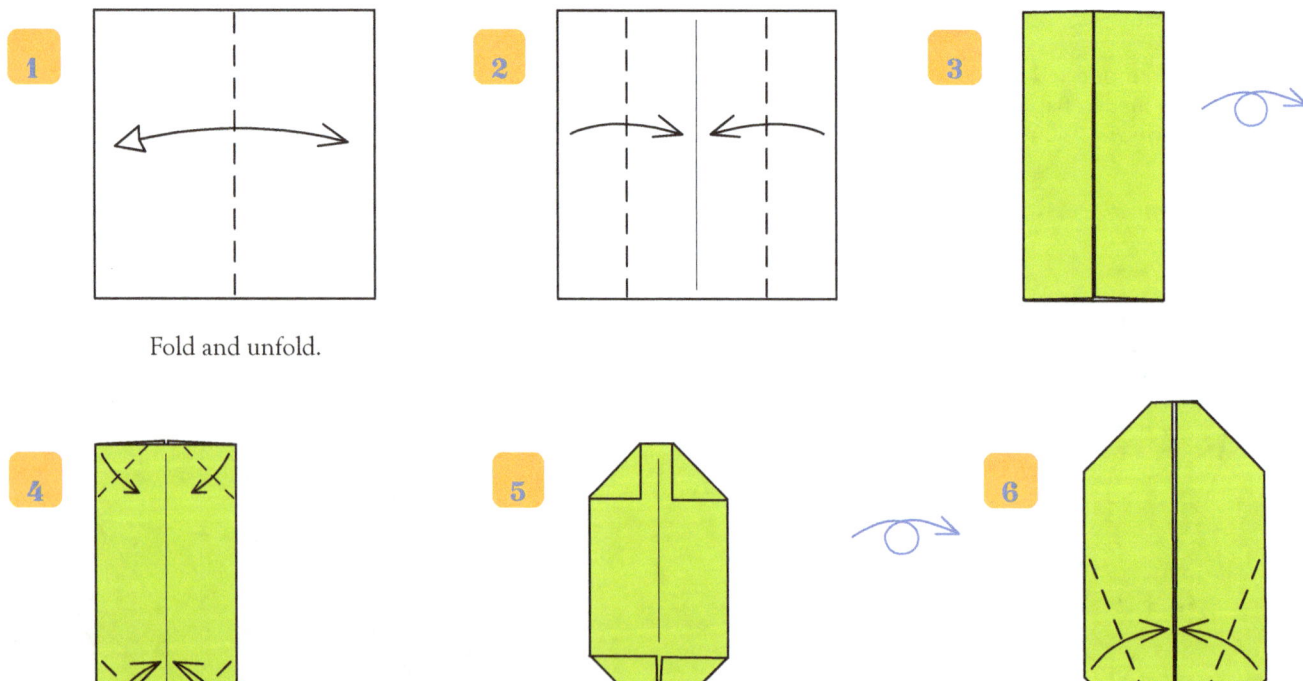

1. Fold and unfold.

6. Fold to the center and swing out from behind.

50   *Origami Symphony No. 8*

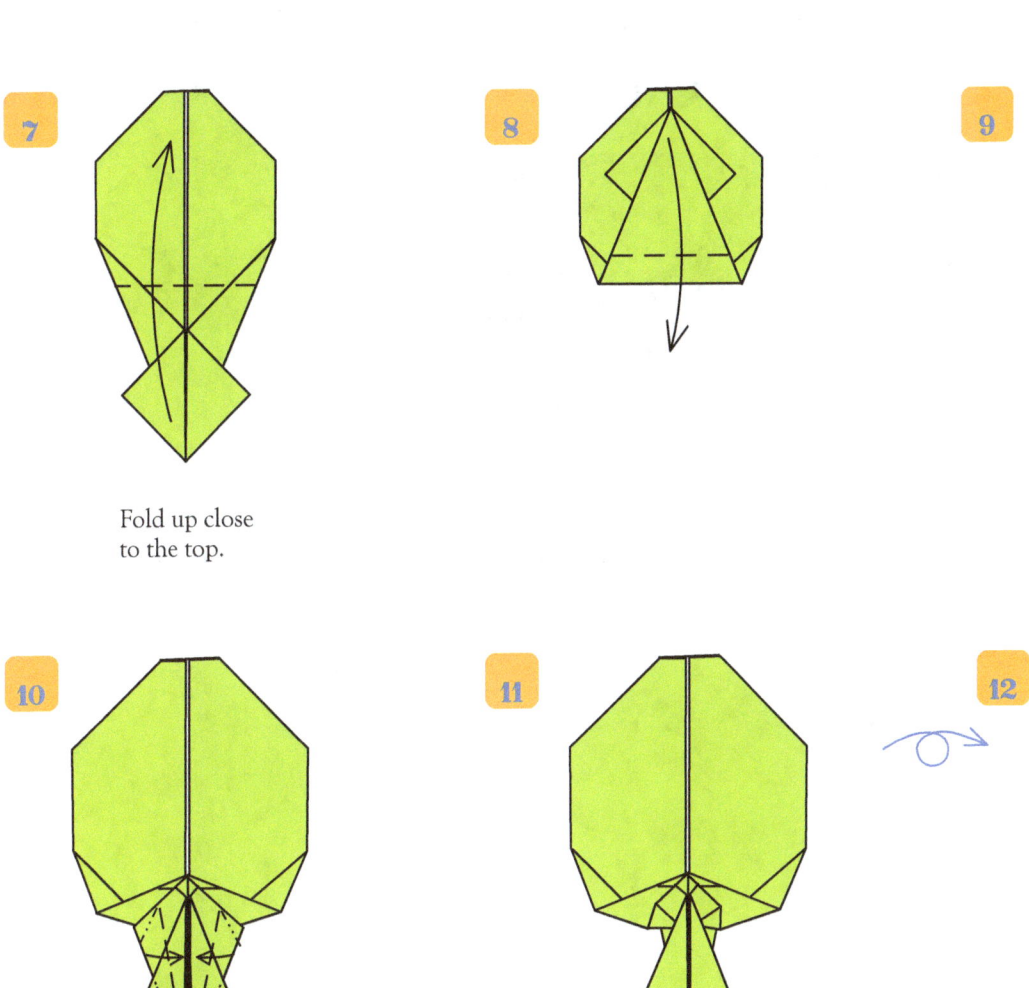

7. Fold up close to the top.

9.
1. Fold to the center.
2. Push in.

10. Make squash folds. Much of the folds are hidden.

12. Make squash folds.

13.
1. Rabbit-ear.
2. Fold behind.

Stingray

Stingray **51**

Cichlid

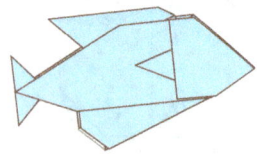

Cichlids are small fish that are seen in all the colors of the rainbow. Most are found in the lakes and rivers of Africa and South America. They are intelligent and will protect their territory. These colorful fish are favorites in aquariums.

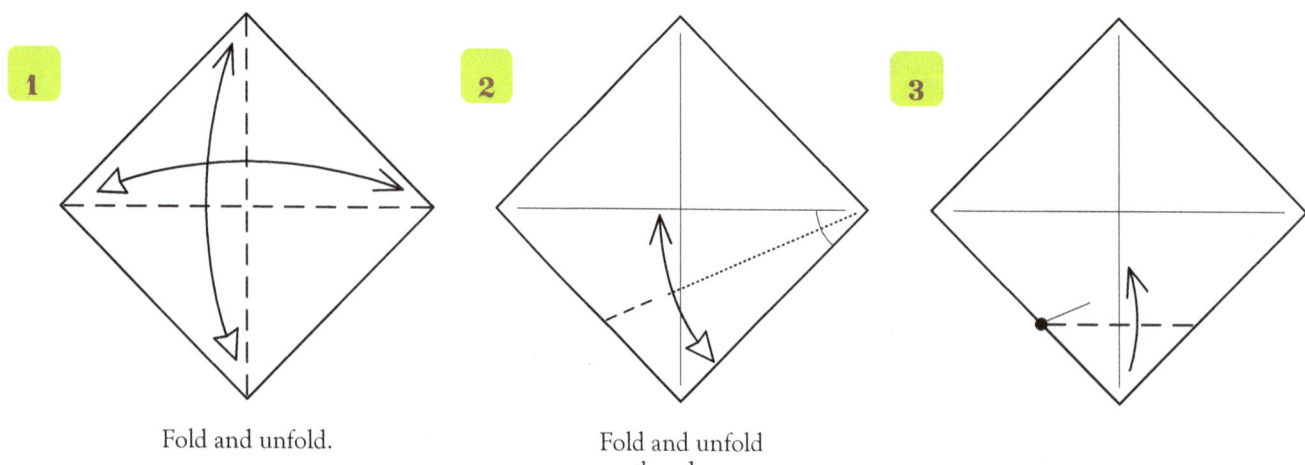

1. Fold and unfold.

2. Fold and unfold on the edge.

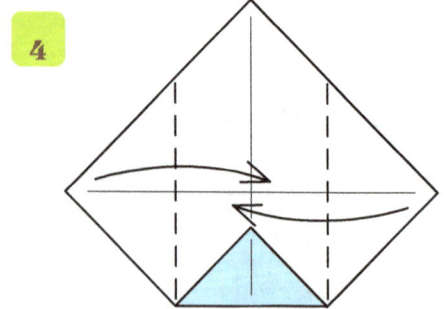

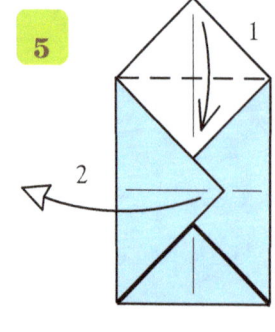

1. Fold down.
2. Unfold.

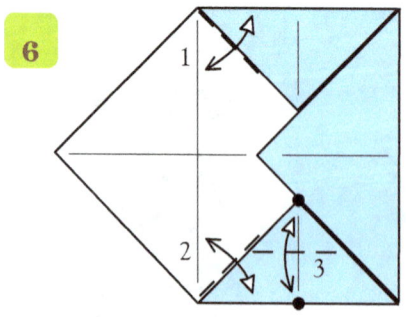

Fold and unfold at 1, 2, and 3.

52 *Origami Symphony No. 8*

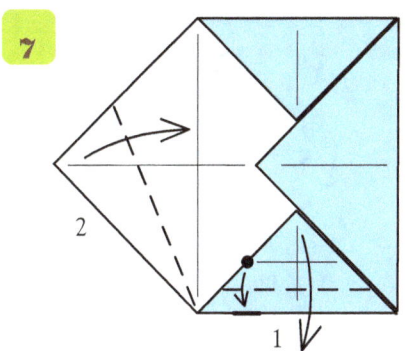

Make valley folds at 1 and 2.

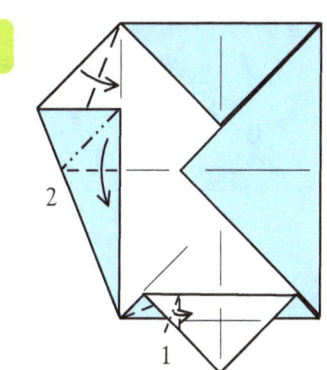

Make valley folds at 1 and 2.

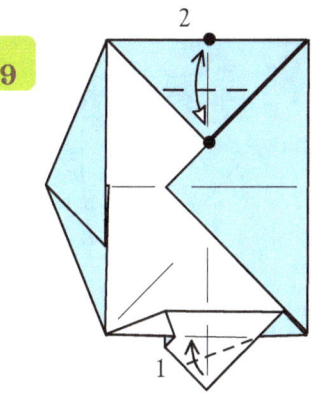

1. Valley-fold.
2. Repeat steps 6–9 on the upper fin.

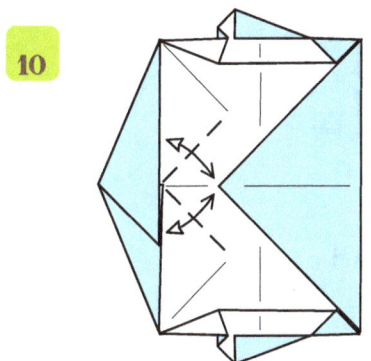

Fold and unfold.

Fold to the center.

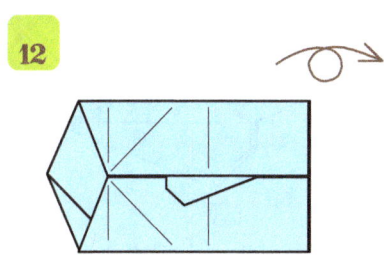

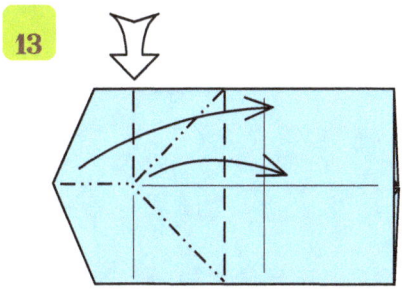

This is a conbination of squash folds.

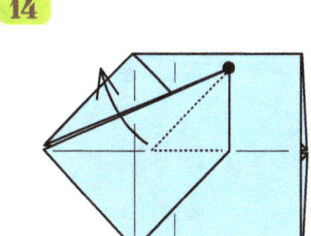

Pivot at the dot and slide out the hidden flap.

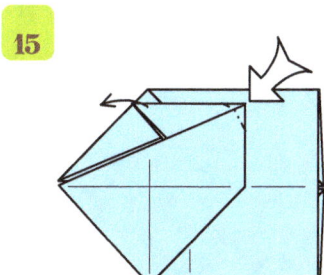

Pull the flap to the left.

Cichlid 53

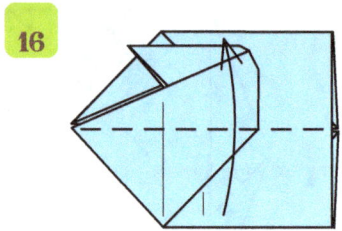

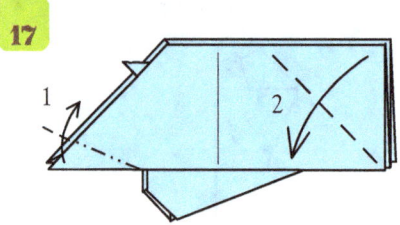

1. Reverse-fold.
2. Repeat behind.

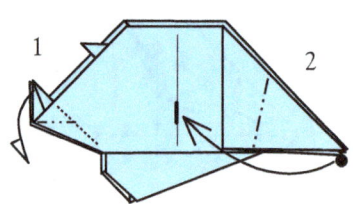

1. Fold one flap down.
2. Reverse-fold, repeat behind.

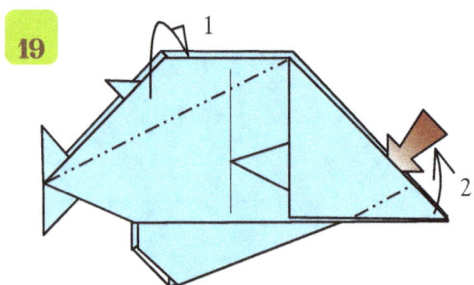

1. Repeat behind.
2. Reverse-fold.

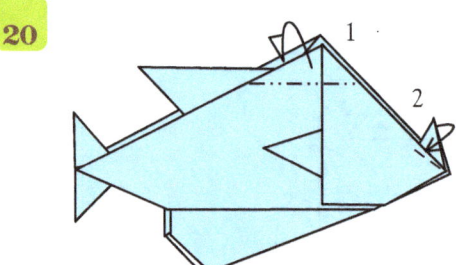

1. Repeat behind.
2. Tuck inside.

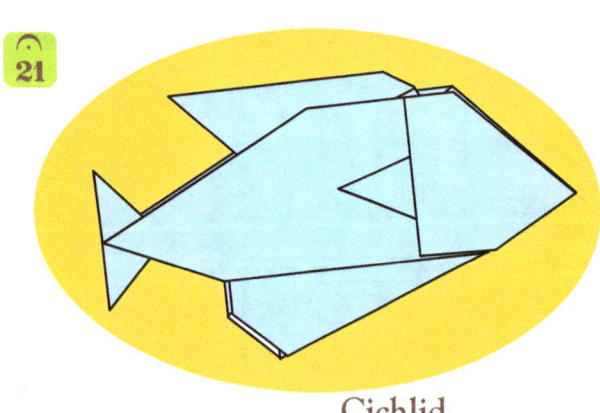

Cichlid

54 *Origami Symphony No. 8*

Minnow

Minnows refers to a large group of small fish including goldfish, carp, and chubs. Some minnows are used as fish bait. One of the more beautiful minnows is the striped zebrafish. Minnows are found in swamps, rivers, and lakes.

1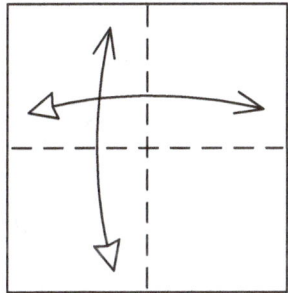

Fold and unfold.

2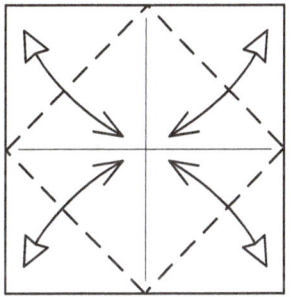

Fold to the center and unfold.

3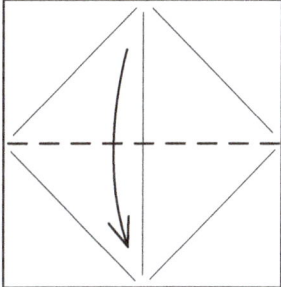

4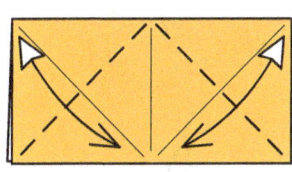

Fold and unfold.

5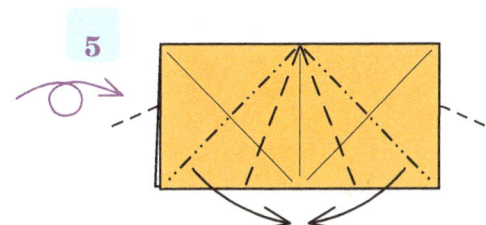

Make squash folds.

6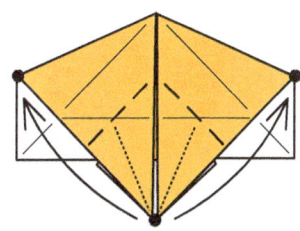

This is similar to a petal fold.

Minnow 55

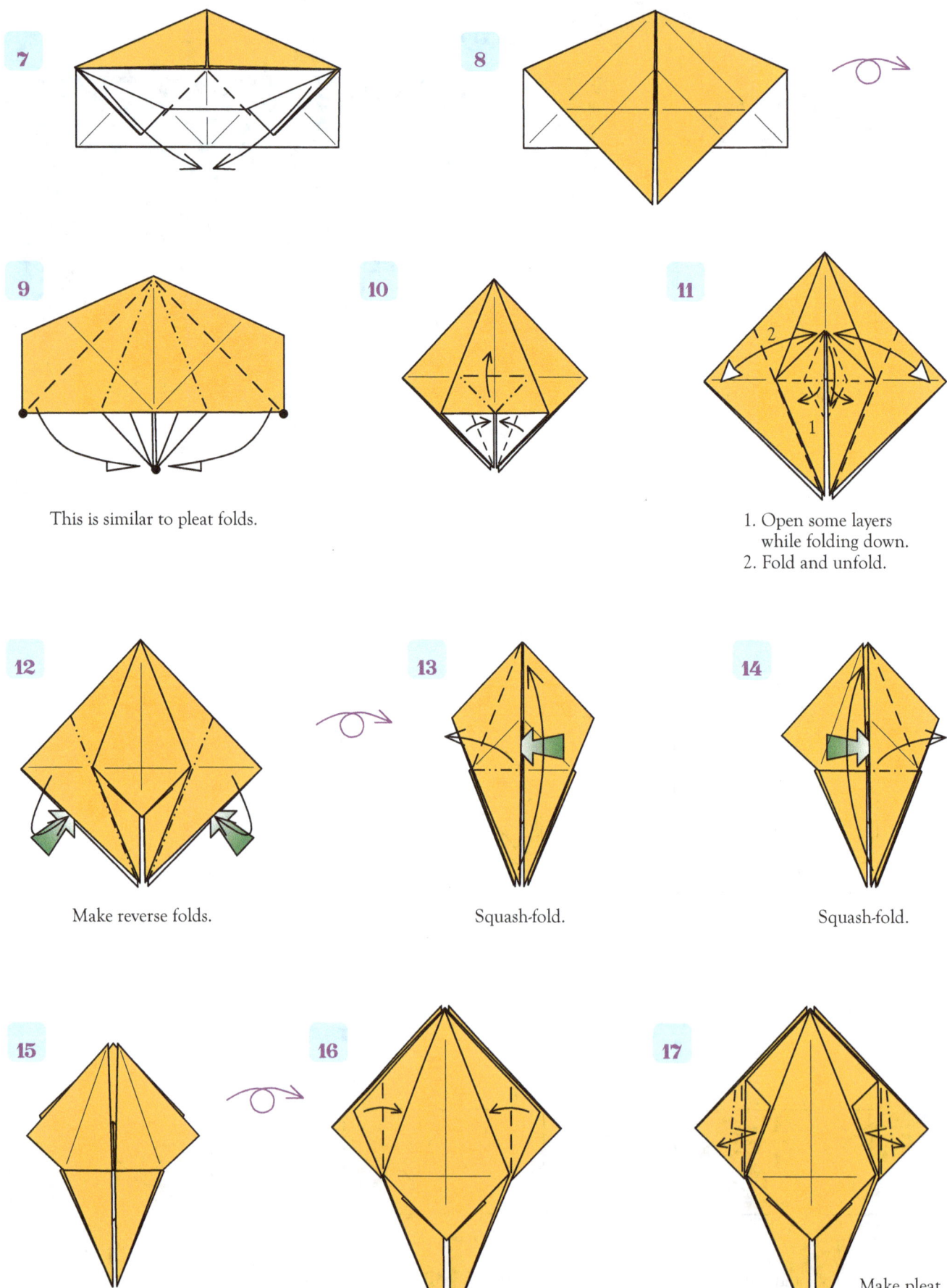

9. This is similar to pleat folds.

11.
1. Open some layers while folding down.
2. Fold and unfold.

12. Make reverse folds.

13. Squash-fold.

14. Squash-fold.

17. Make pleat folds.

56 *Origami Symphony No. 8*

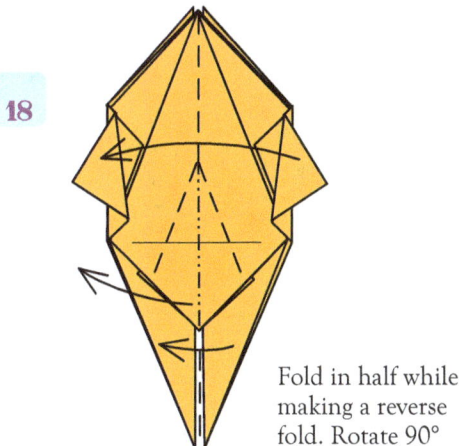

18

Fold in half while making a reverse fold. Rotate 90°.

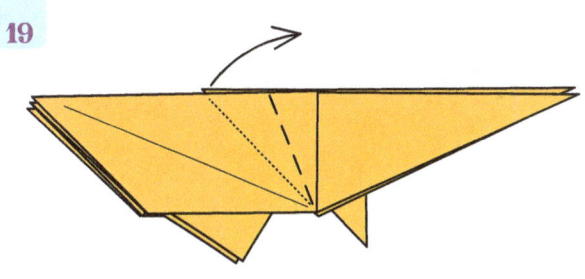

19

Outside-reverse-fold the hidden flap.

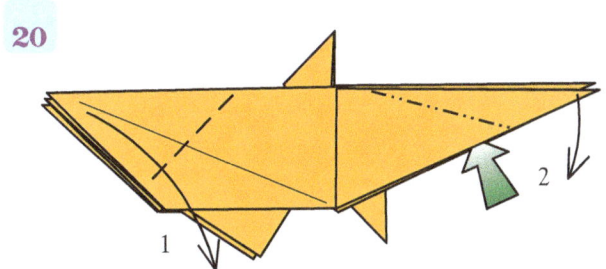

20

1. Fold down.
2. Reverse-fold.
Repeat behind.

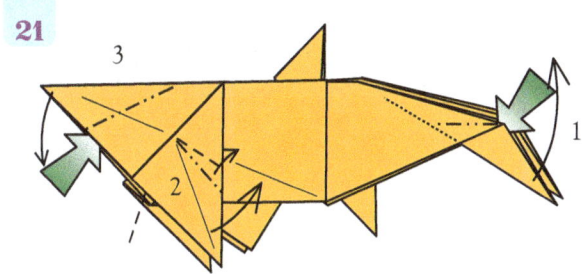

21

1. Reverse-fold one flap.
2. Squash-fold, repeat behind.
3. Reverse-fold.

22

Tuck inside.

23

Minnow

Parrotfish

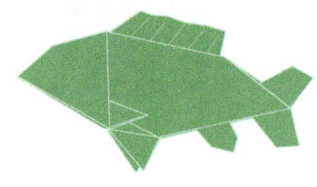

Parrotfishes are found around the world, often in shallow tropical waters, coral reefs, and seagrass beds. Their teeth resemble a parrot's beak. They feed on algae which they extract from coral. They are about 12 to 20 inches long. They are brightly colored and their coloring changes throughout their lives.

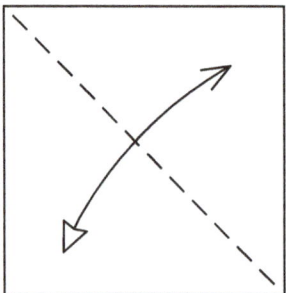

1. Fold and unfold.

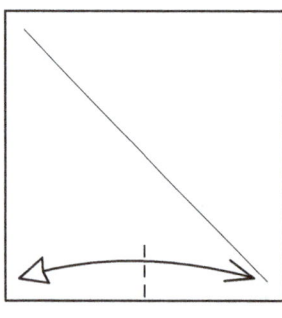

2. Fold and unfold at the bottom.

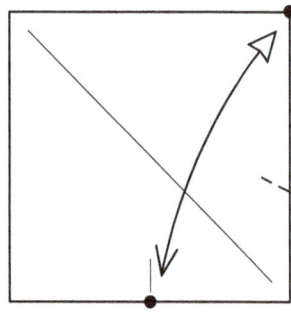

3. Fold and unfold on the right.

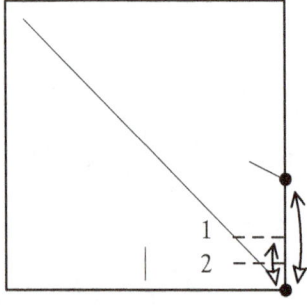

4. Fold and unfold on the right.

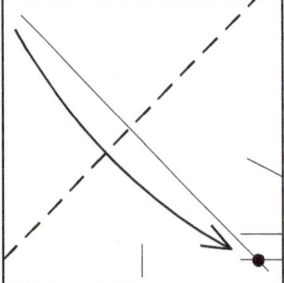

5.

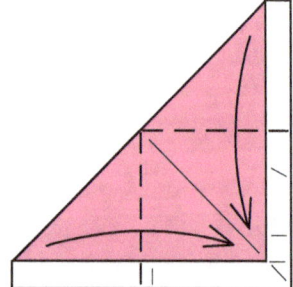

6.

58 *Origami Symphony No. 8*

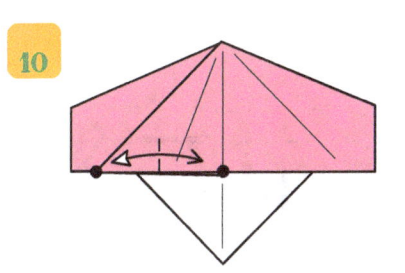

Unfold and rotate.

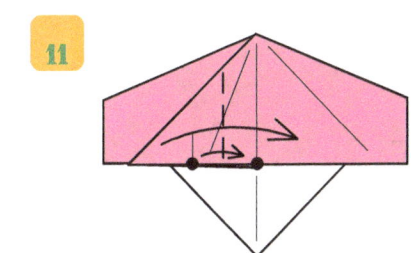

Squash-fold.

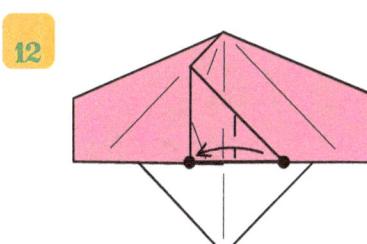

Squash-fold.

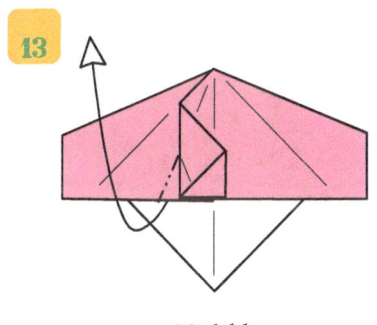

Fold and unfold.

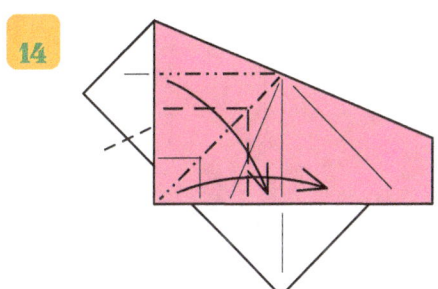

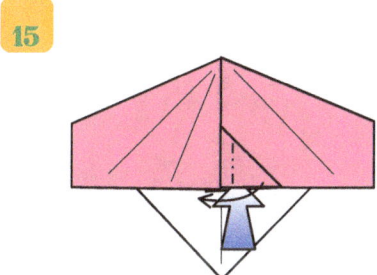

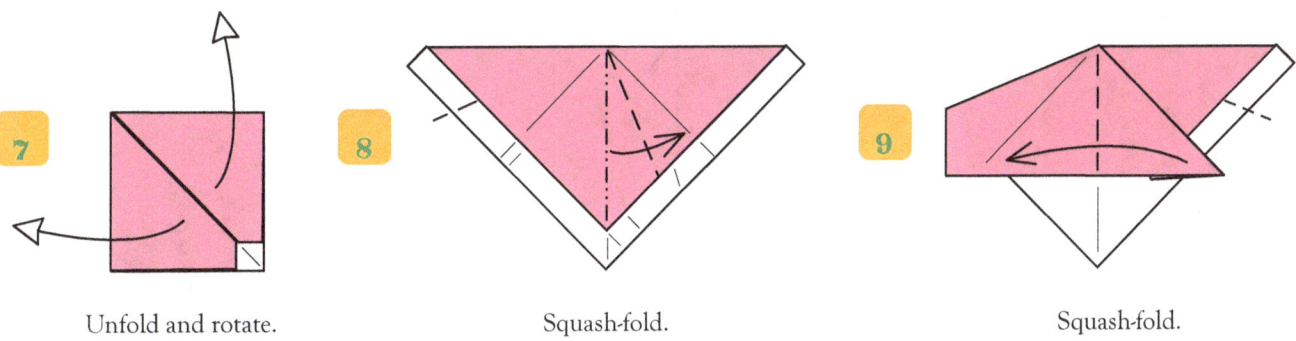

Unfold.

Fold along the creases.

Reverse-fold along the crease.

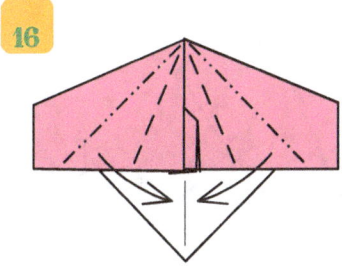

Squash-fold along the creases.
Fold behind the fin on the right.

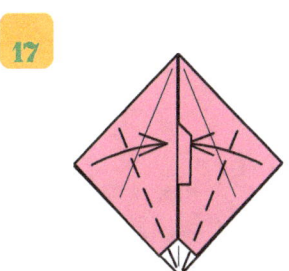

Fold to the center.

Unfold.

Parrotfish **59**

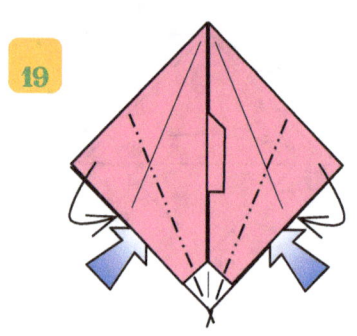

Make reverse folds.

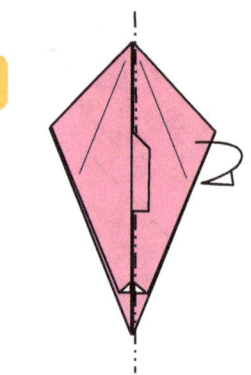

Fold in half and rotate.

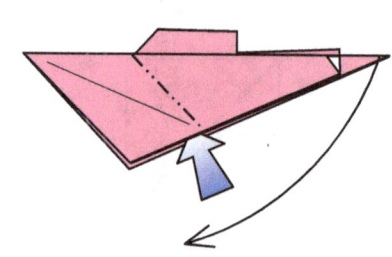

Reverse-fold.

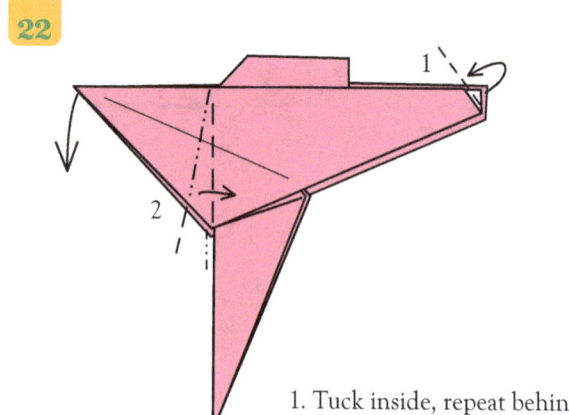

1. Tuck inside, repeat behind.
2. Crimp-fold.

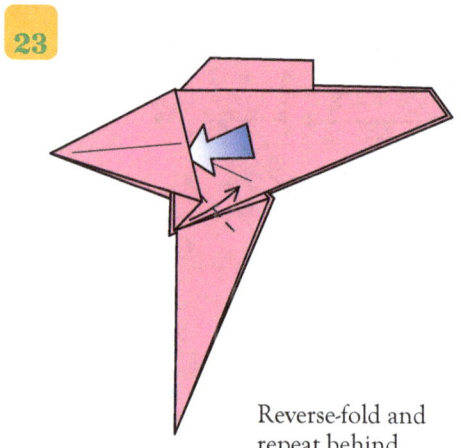

Reverse-fold and repeat behind.

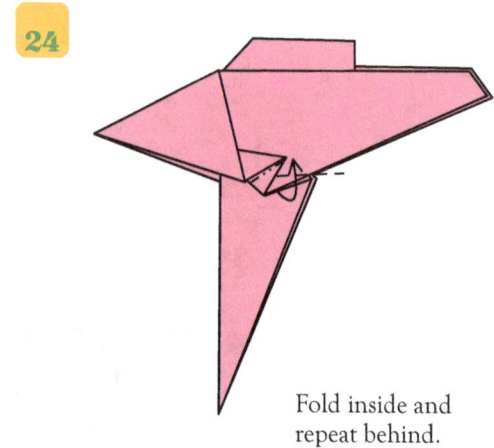

Fold inside and repeat behind.

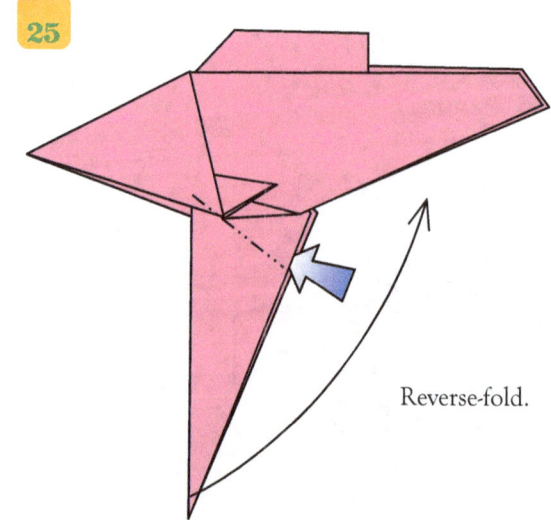

Reverse-fold.

60 *Origami Symphony No. 8*

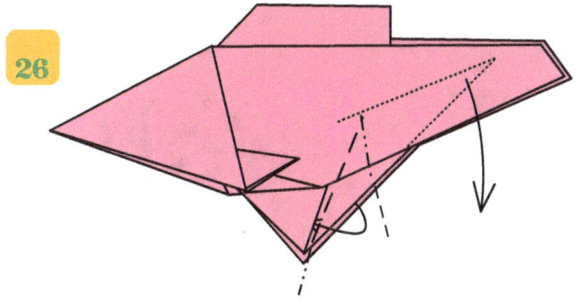

Crimp-fold.

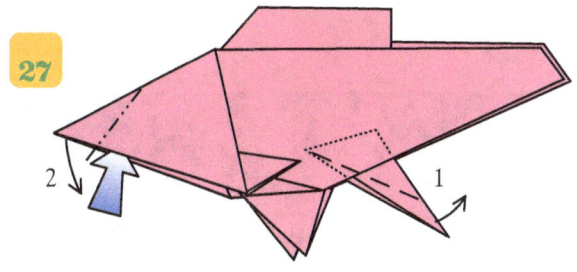

1. Outside-reverse-fold.
2. Reverse-fold.

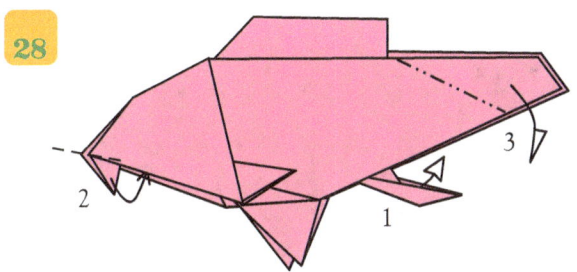

1. Spread and open the fin. Repeat behind.
2. Fold the layers together.
3. Repeat behind.

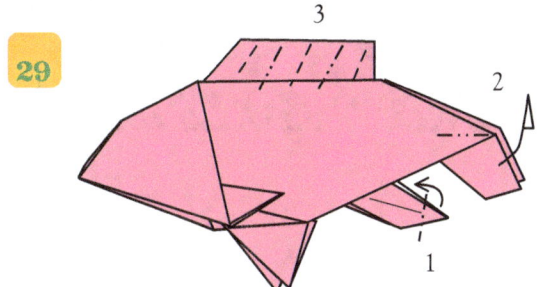

1. Reverse-fold.
2. Fold one layer up.
3. Pleat the fins.

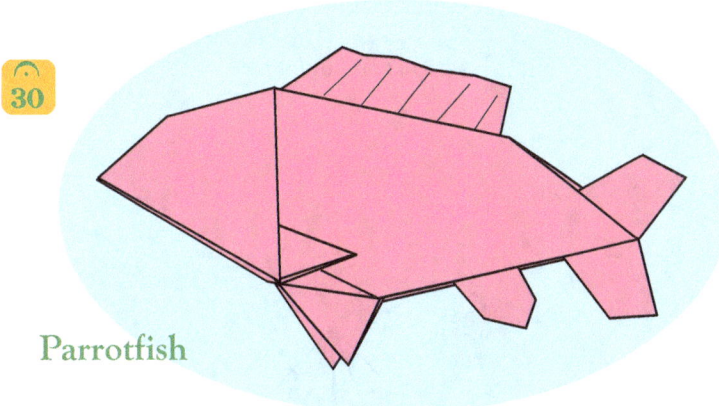

Parrotfish

Perch

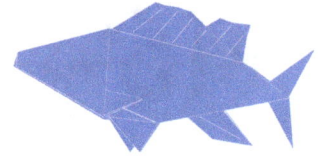

Perch are freshwater fish that live in lakes, ponds, and near the shore. They weigh about one to five pounds. They have rough scales and two dorsal fins. The first dorsal fin is sharp and spiny. They feed on larvae, shrimp, crab, and small fish.

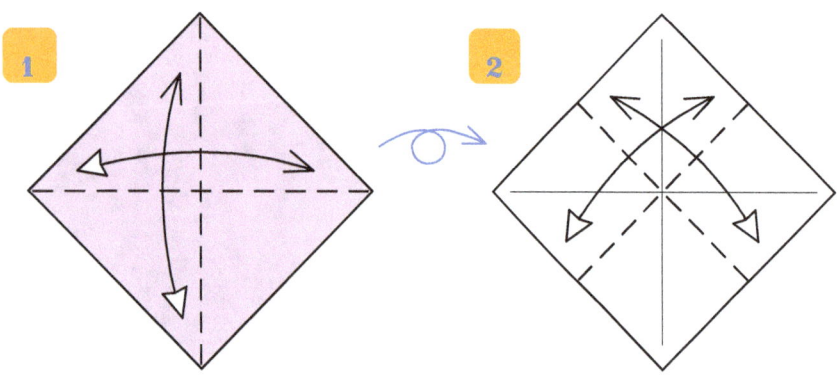

1. Fold and unfold.
2. Fold and unfold.
3. Fold along the creases.

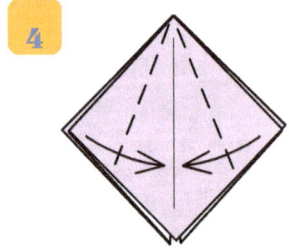
4. Fold to the center.

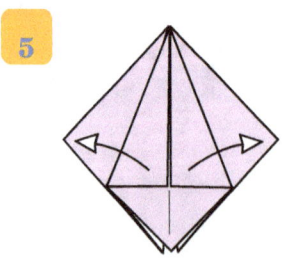
5. Unfold.

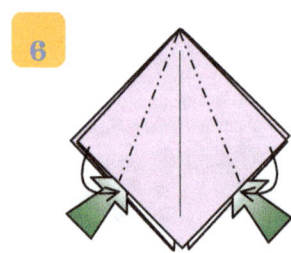
6. Make reverse folds.

62   Origami Symphony No. 8

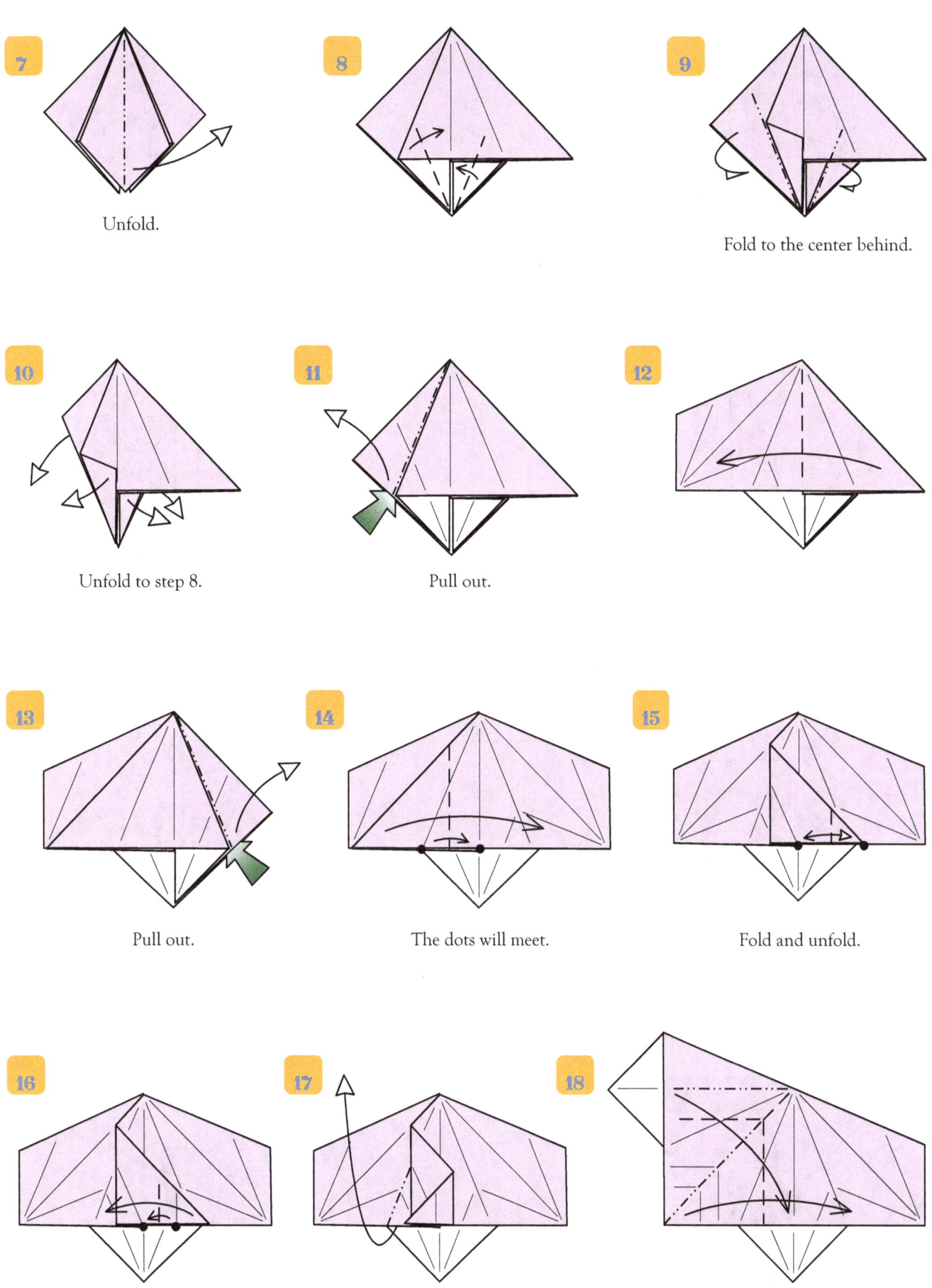

Perch **63**

 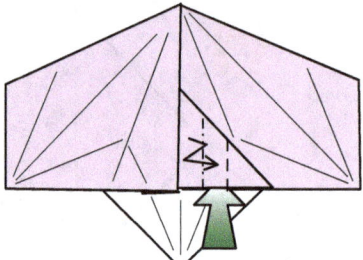

Crimp-fold along the creases.

 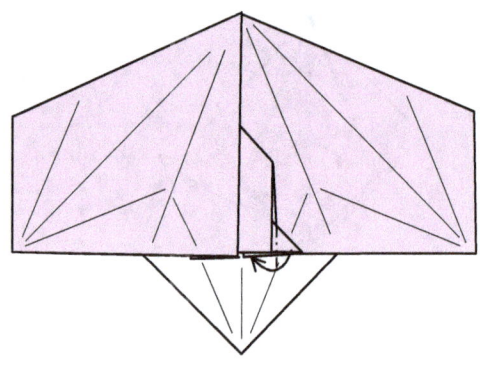

Reverse-fold.

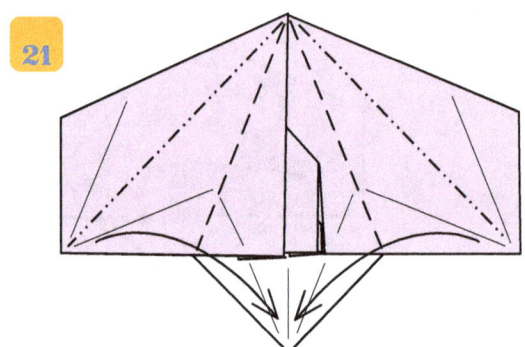

Squash-fold along the creases.
Fold behind the fin on the right.

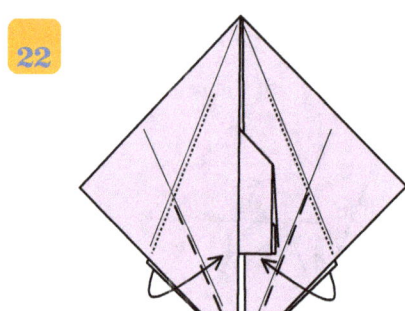

Valley-fold the hidden layers inside.

 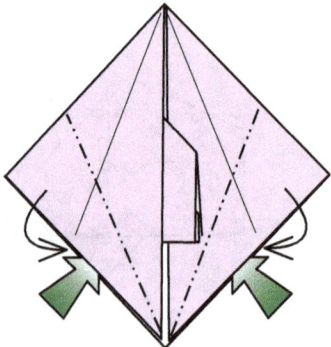

Make reverse folds.

 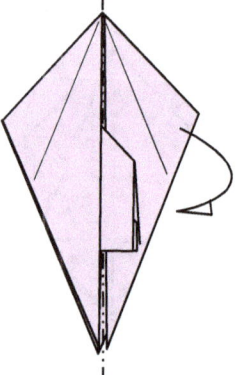

Fold in half and rotate.

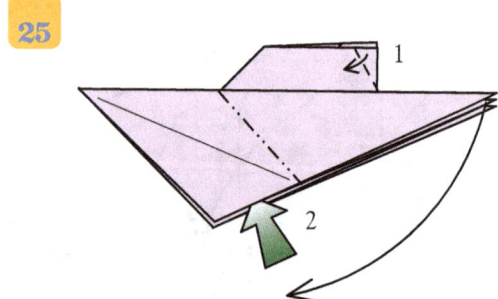

1. Repeat behind.
2. Reverse-fold.

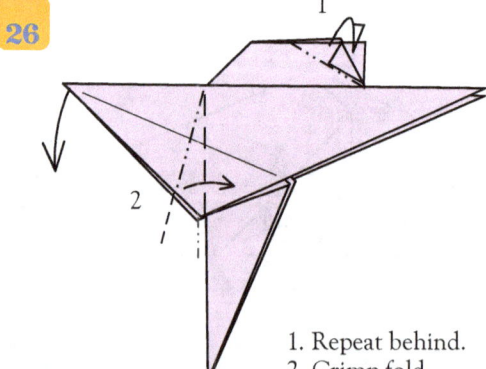

1. Repeat behind.
2. Crimp-fold.

64 *Origami Symphony No. 8*

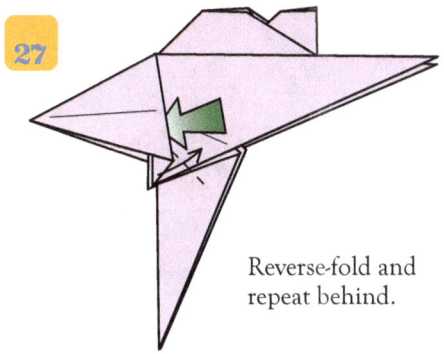

Reverse-fold and repeat behind.

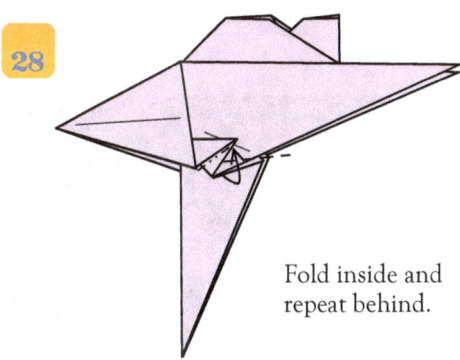

Fold inside and repeat behind.

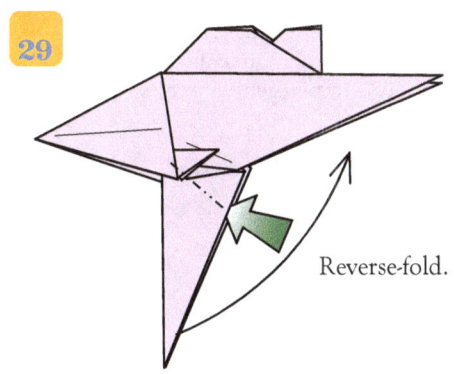

Reverse-fold.

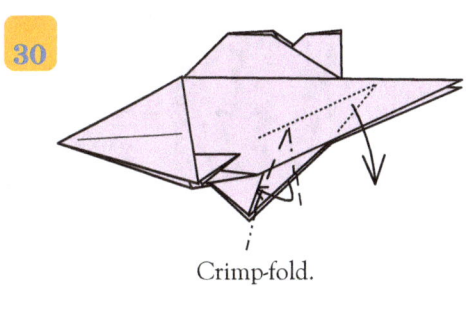

Crimp-fold.

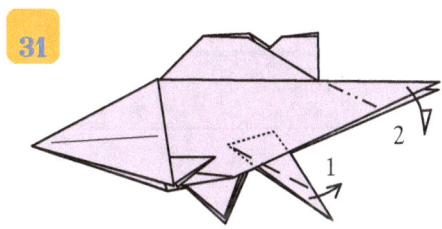

1. Outside-reverse-fold.
2. Repeat behind.

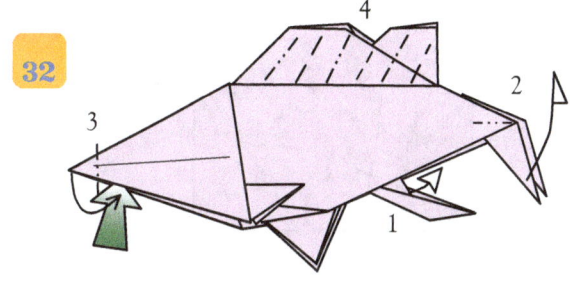

1. Spread and open the fin. Repeat behind.
2. Fold one layer up.
3. Reverse-fold.
4. Pleat the fins.

Perch

Perch **65**

Dolphin

Dolphins are extremely intelligent sea mammals. They might be smarter than us since their brains are larger. Dolphins identify themselves to each other with distinctive whistles, as their names. They have a highly complex social structure. Unlike most animals, they can recognize themselves in a mirror.

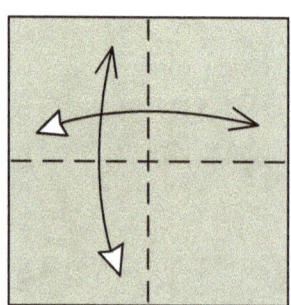

Fold and unfold.

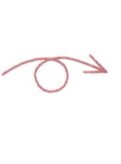 

Fold to the center.

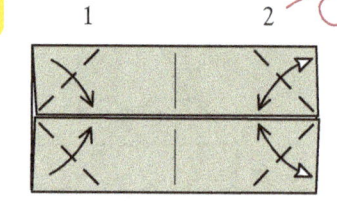

1. Fold to the center.
2. Fold and unfold.

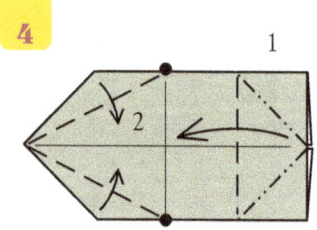

1. Petal-fold.
2. Fold all the layers.

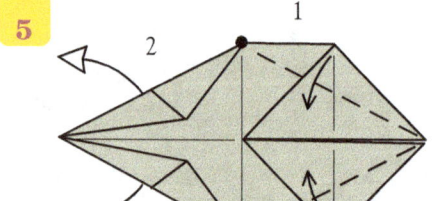

1. Make valley folds.
2. Unfold.

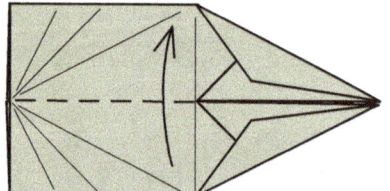

Fold in half.

66 *Origami Symphony No. 8*

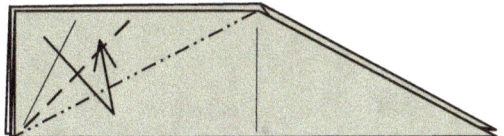 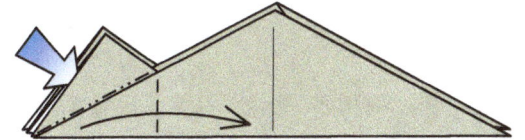

Crimp-fold along the creases. Repeat behind.

Squash-fold, repeat behind.

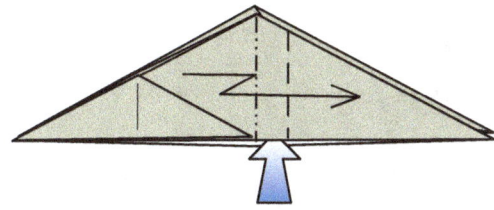 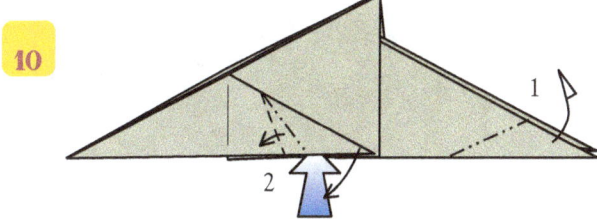

Crimp-fold. Place your finger into the white pocket, the layers are not symmetrical.

1. Mountain-fold.
2. Squash-fold.
Repeat behind.

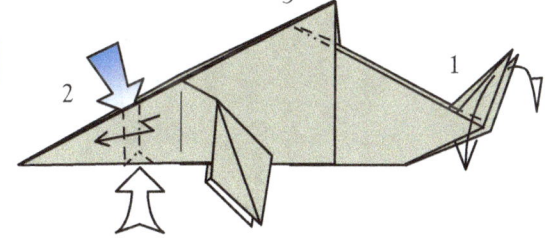 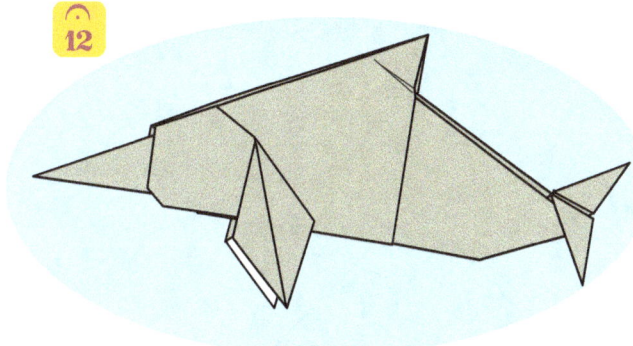

1. Fold part of the way down, repeat behind.
2. Begin by pushing in on the bottom, then crimp-fold on the top.
3. Make a small crimp fold.

Dolphin

Blue Whale

The blue whale is the largest animal to have ever lived on Earth. I hope you have paper that is large enough to make a life-size whale. Their complex sounds are the loudest of any animal and they communicate to each other across large distances. Large as they are, they feed on small krill, eating millions per day.

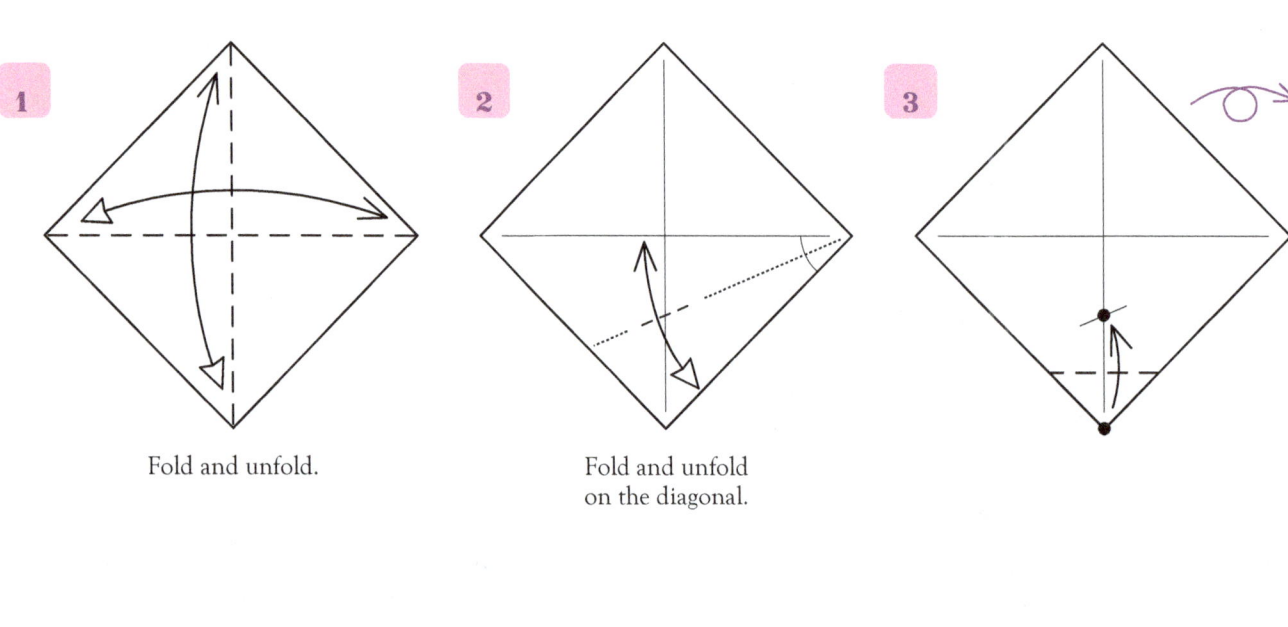

1. Fold and unfold.

2. Fold and unfold on the diagonal.

3.

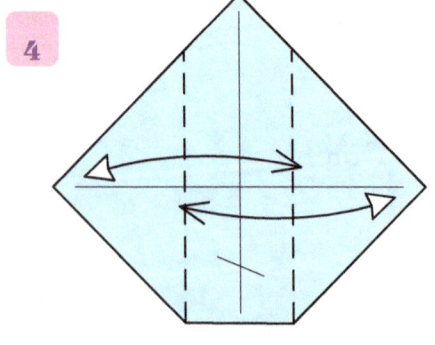
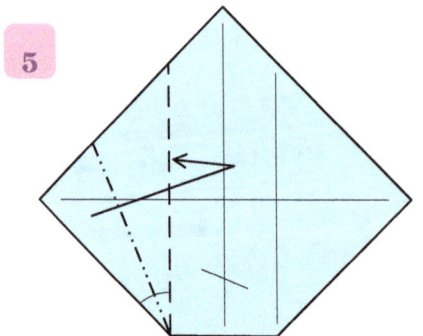
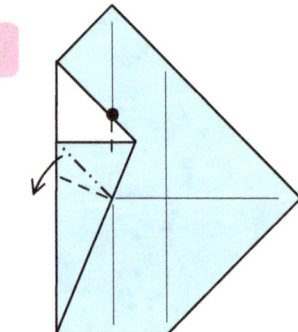

4. Fold and unfold.

5. Pleat-fold.

6. Squash-fold.

68 *Origami Symphony No. 8*

7 Repeat steps 5–6 on the right.

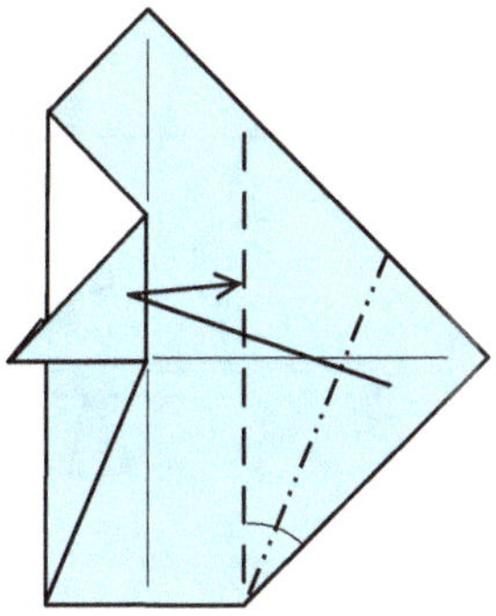

8 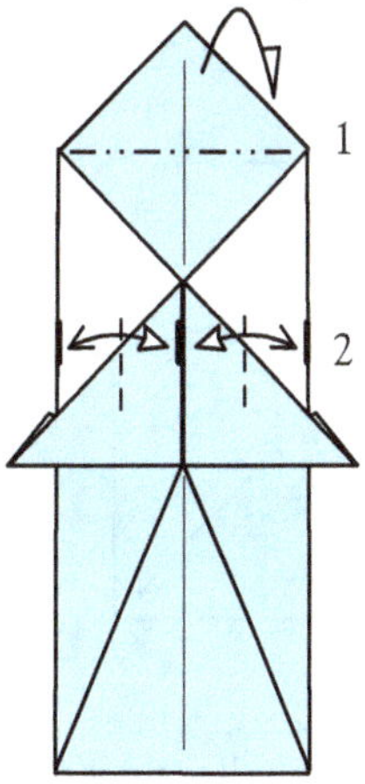
1. Mountain-fold.
2. Fold and unfold.

9 Make squash folds, going to the dotted lines.

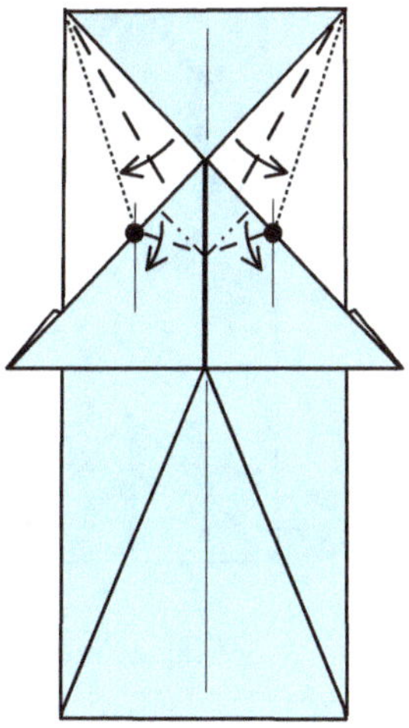

10 Make squash folds.

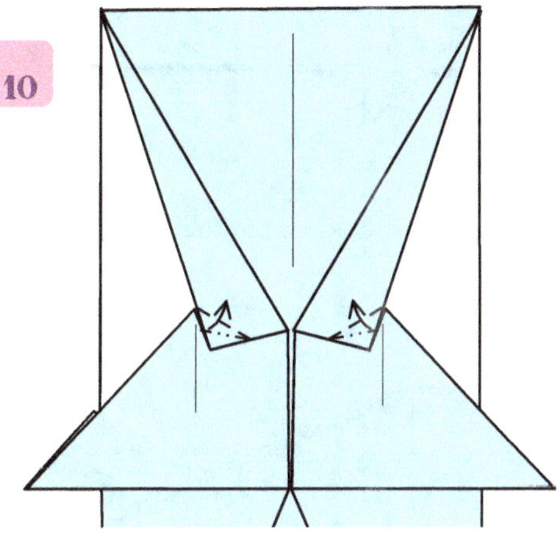

11 Fold and unfold.

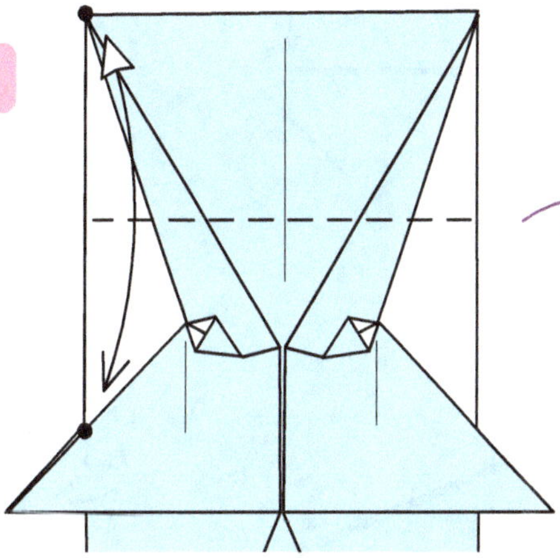

12 Fold and unfold.

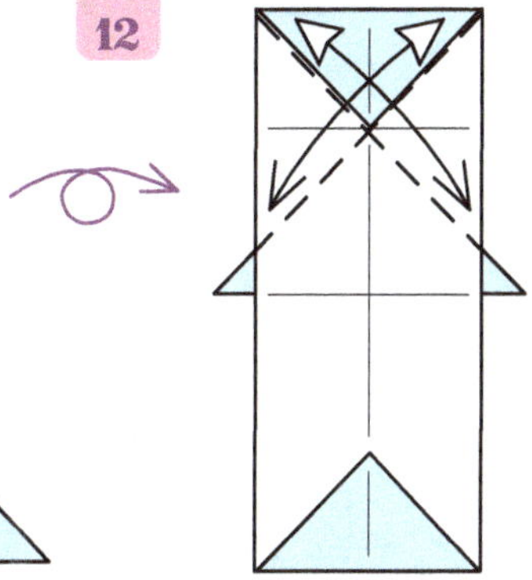

13 Fold and unfold.

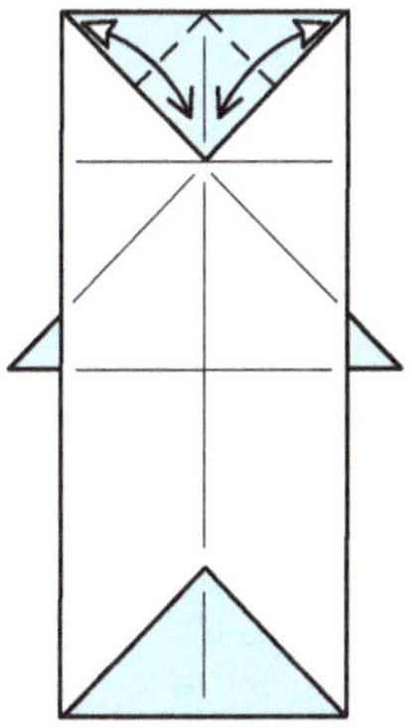

14 Unfold.

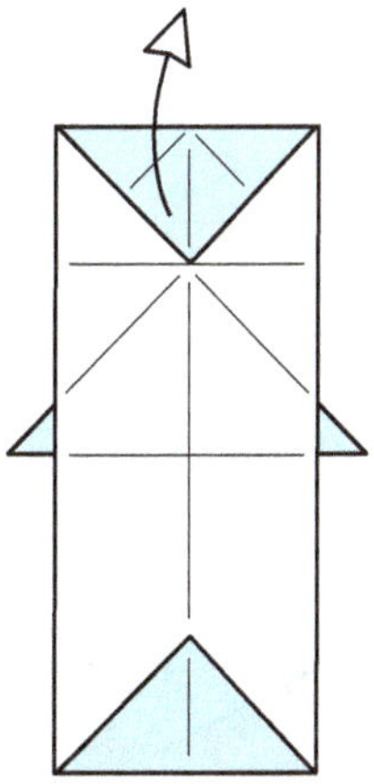

15 Fold along the creases.

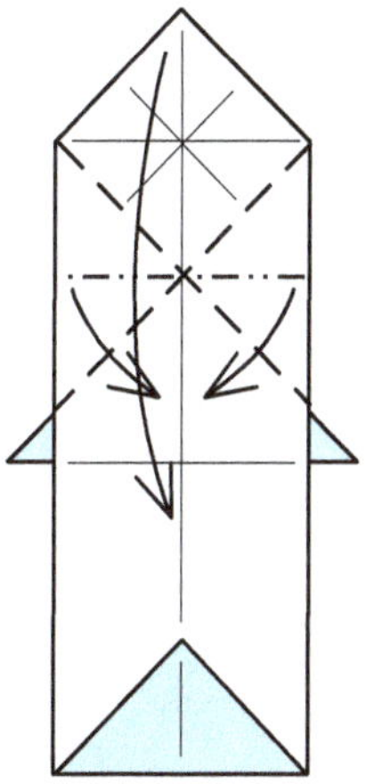

Blue Whale **69**

16 Wrap around.

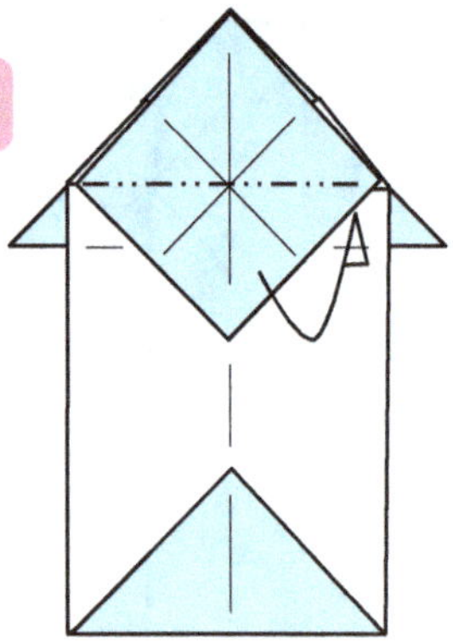

17 Lift up at the top while folding in half. Rotate 90°.

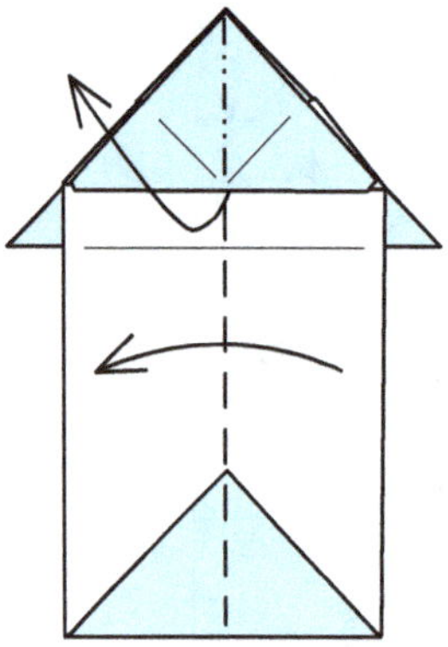

18 Reverse-fold.

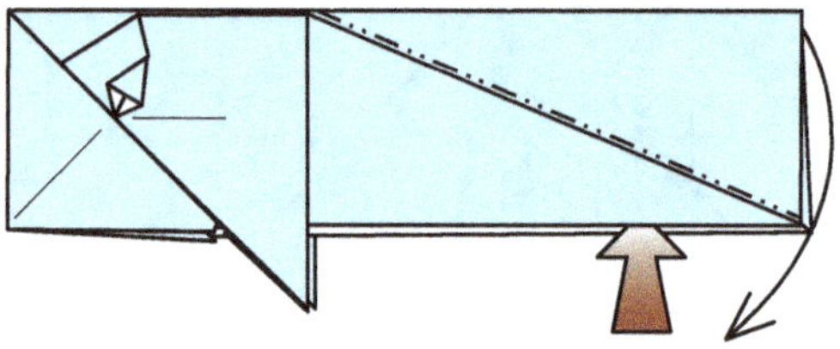

19 Reverse-fold.

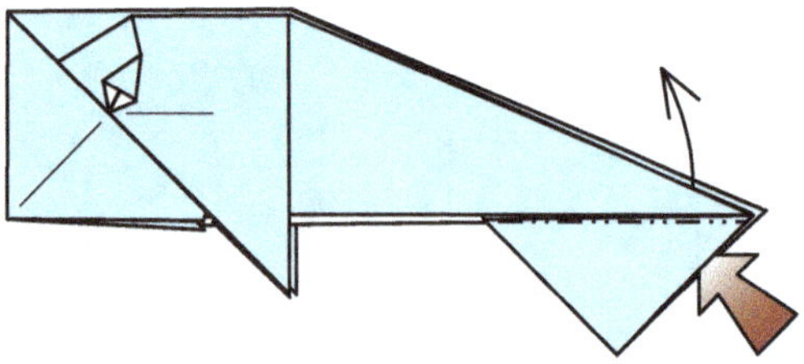

20 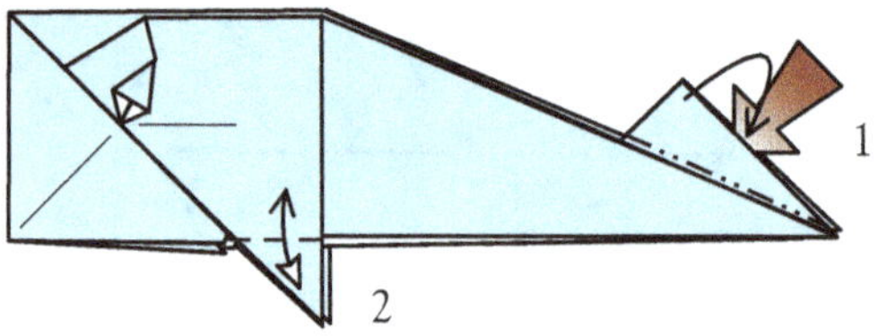
1. Reverse-fold.
2. Fold and unfold.

21 Squash-fold, repeat behind.

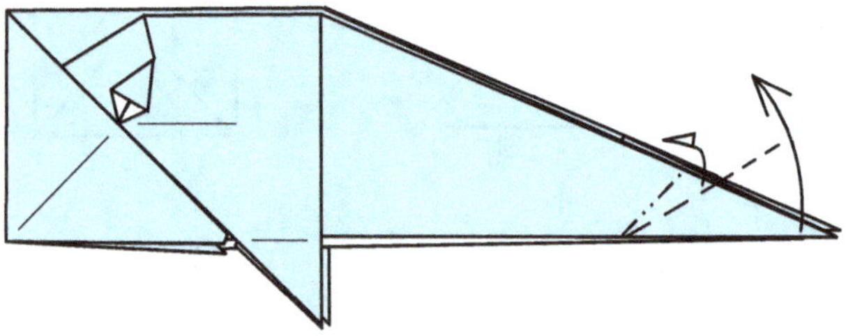

22 The whale will be 3D.
1. Fold down part of the way, repeat behind.
2. Fold up part of the way, repeat behind.
3. Push in and shape the head.

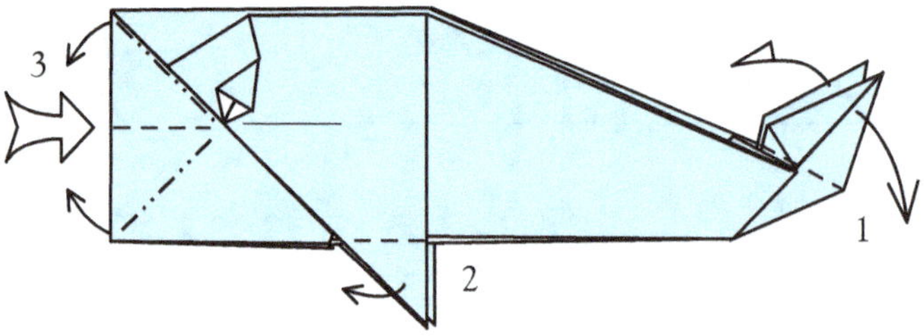

23

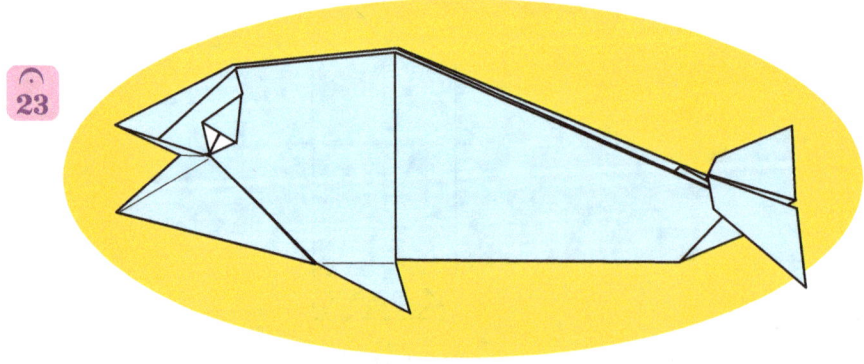

Blue Whale

70 *Origami Symphony No. 8*

Third Movement

Minuet of Tall Prisms with a Trio of Spherical Shapes

 Here is a collection of tall prisms, from a triangular to an octagonal base. Each prism has identical rectangular sides with a polygon base at the top and bottom. These shapes progress from relatively simple to more complex and make for perfect stands for the cats and circus animals. The complex spherical shapes will enhance a circus scene.

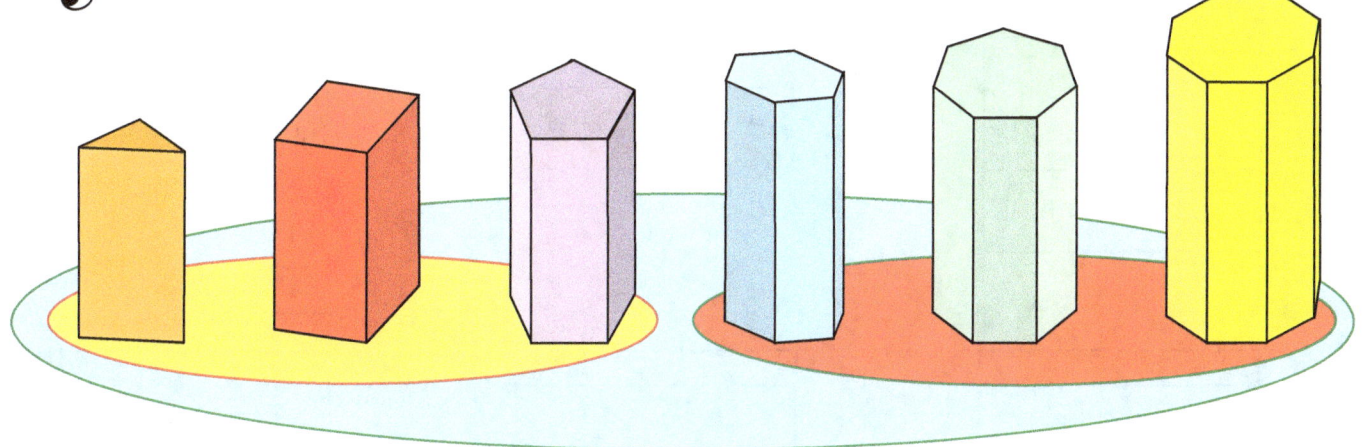

Tall Triangular Prism

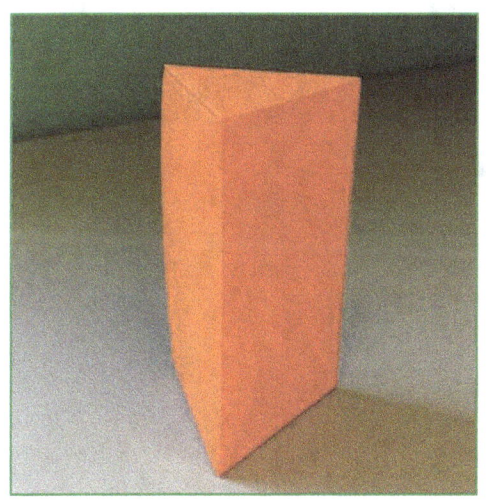

The length of this triangular prism is double the height of the triangle as shown by the dotted lines. If each triangle has sides of 1, 1, and 1, then each rectangle is $1 \times \sqrt{3}$.

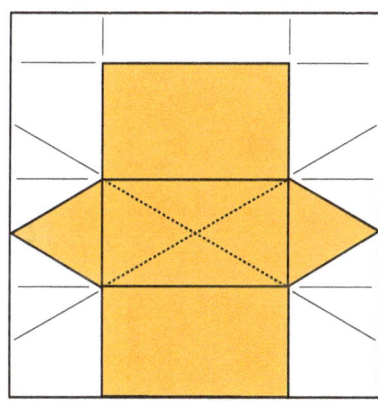

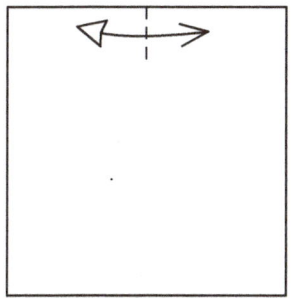

Fold and unfold at the top.

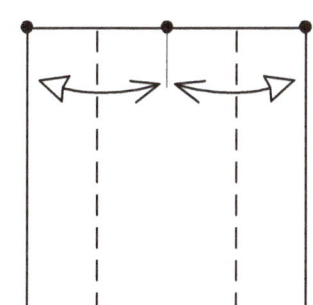

Fold to the center and unfold.

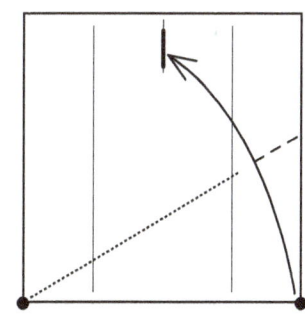

Crease on the right.

Tall Triangular Prism **71**

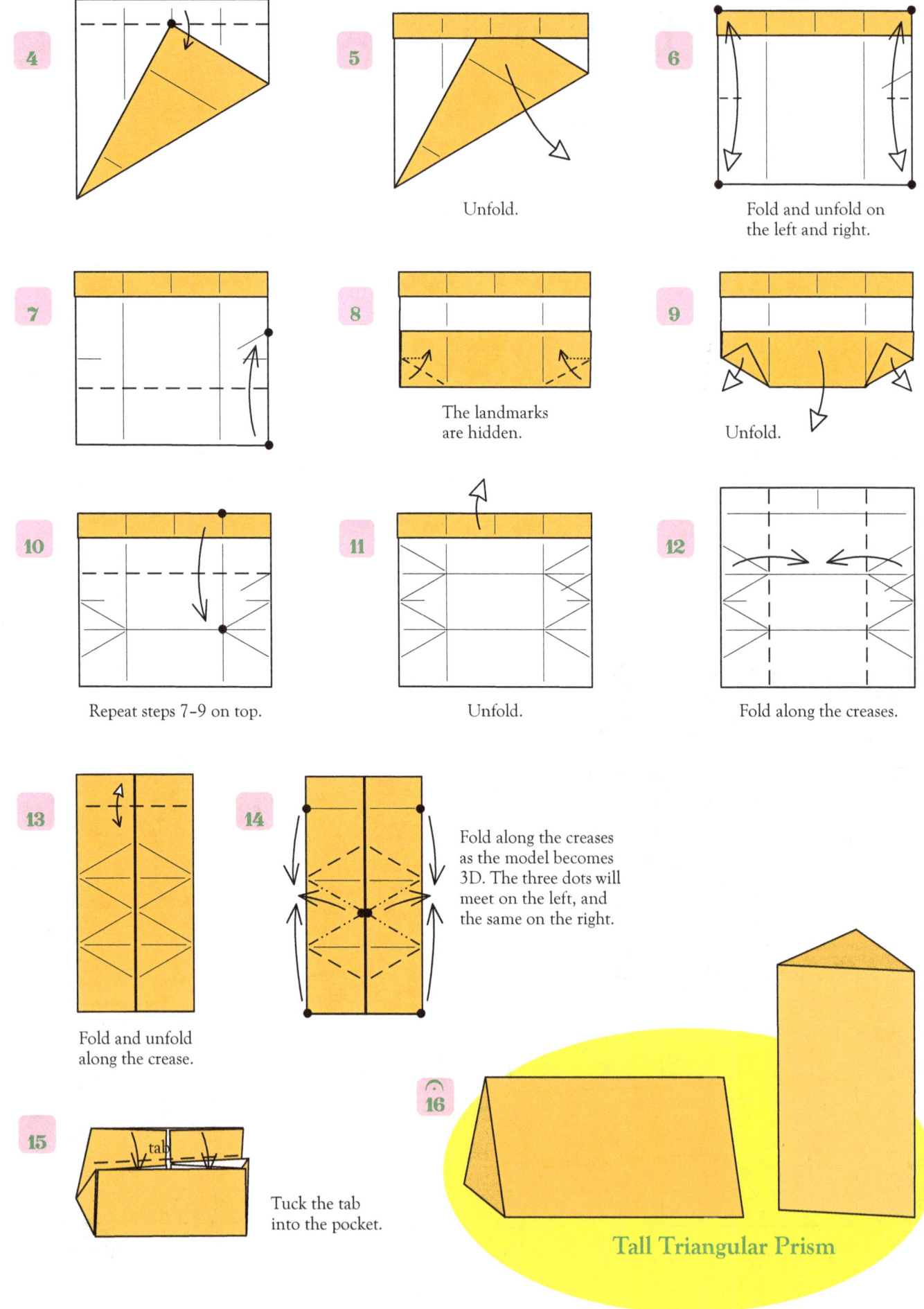

Tall Rectangular Prism

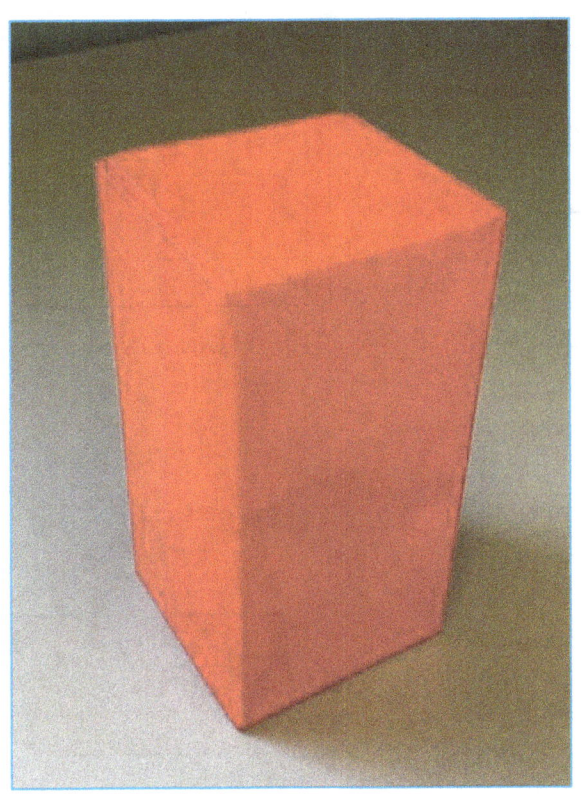
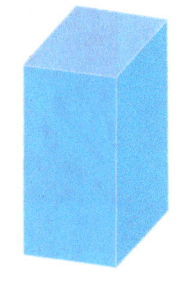
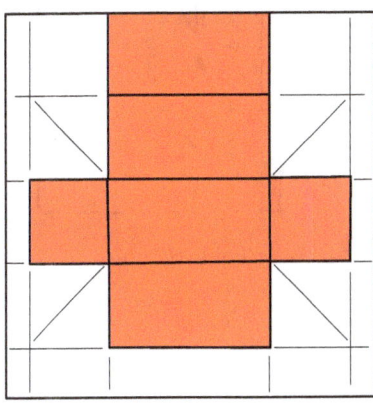

This tall rectangular prism has dimensions 1 x 1 x 2. It can be placed upright or on its side.

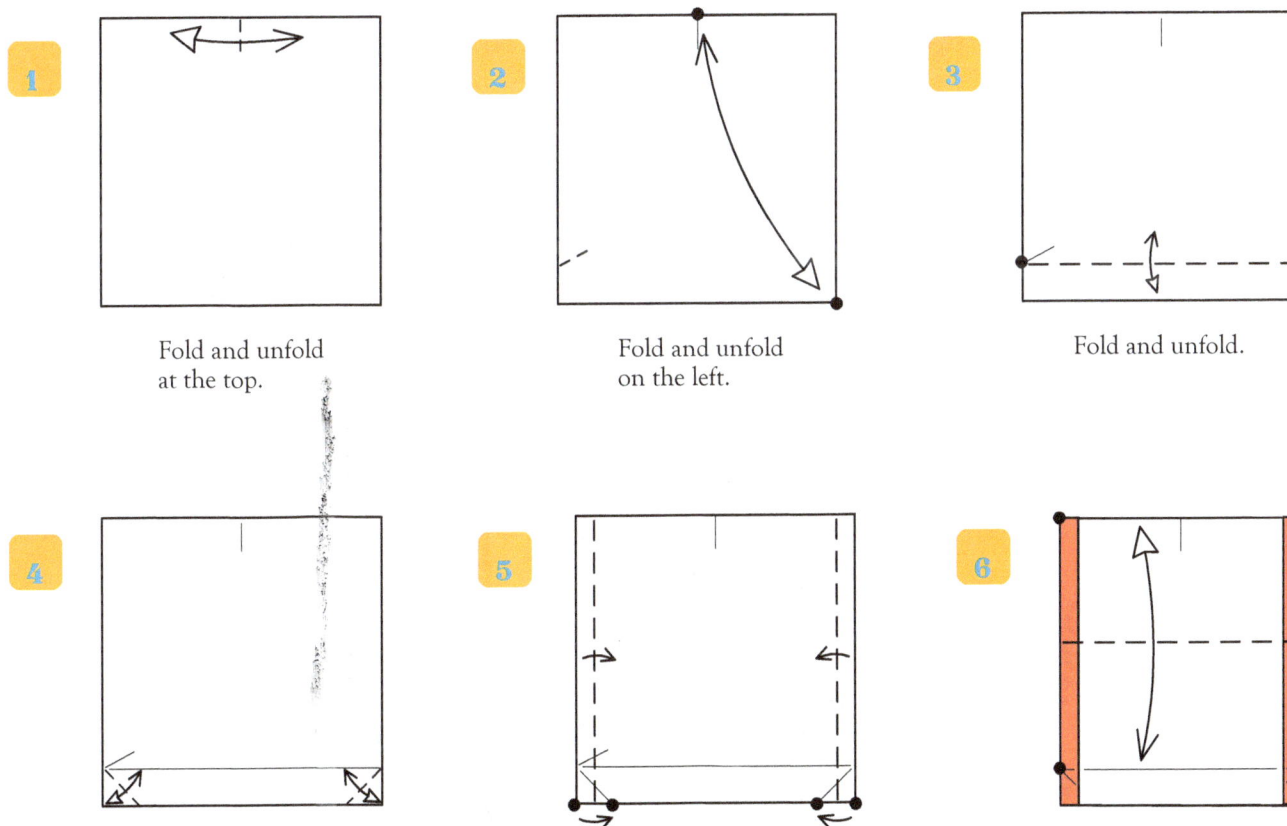

1. Fold and unfold at the top.
2. Fold and unfold on the left.
3. Fold and unfold.
4. Fold and unfold.
5. The dots will meet.
6. Fold and unfold.

Tall Rectangular Prism **73**

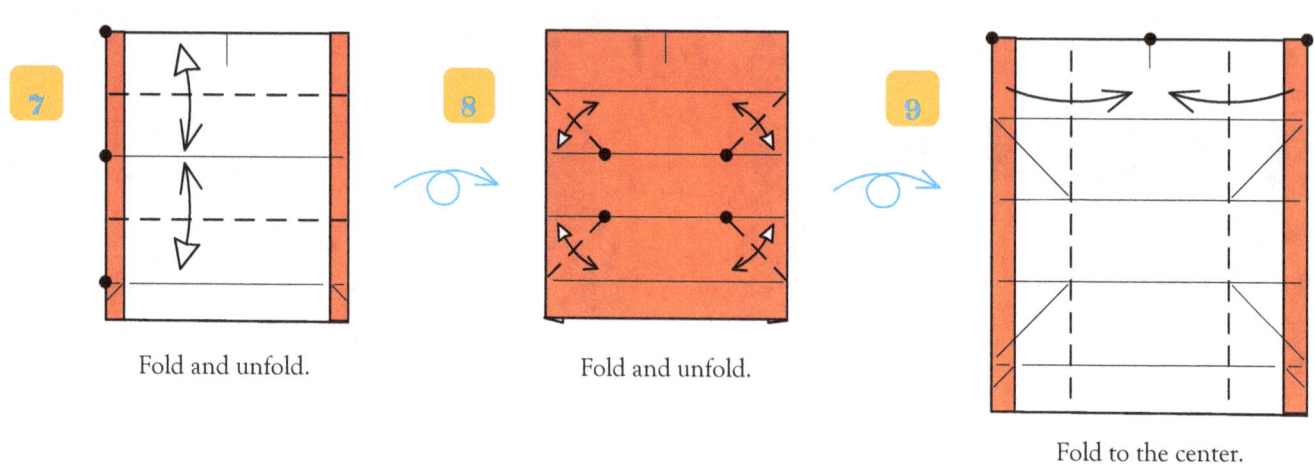

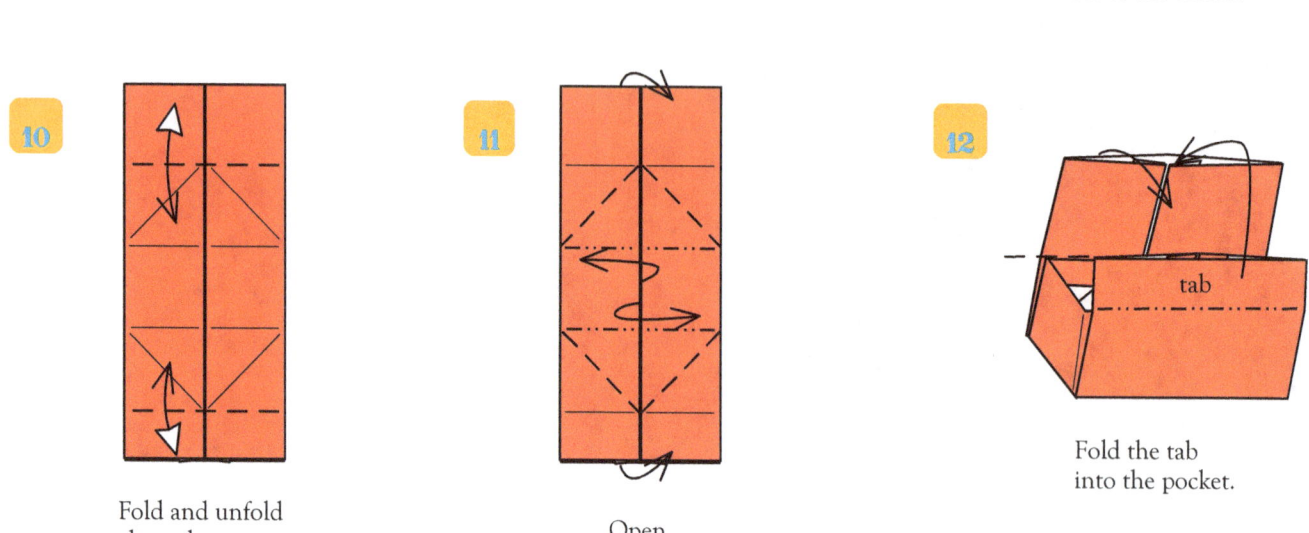

Tall Rectangular Prism

74 Origami Symphony No. 8

Tall Pentagonal Prism

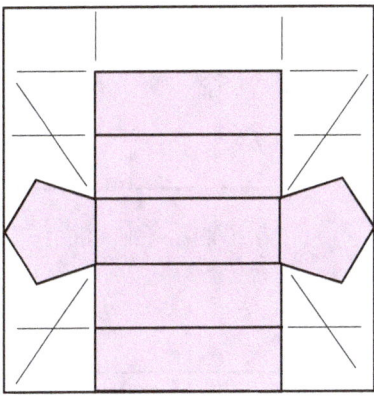

This pentagonal prism is composed of two pentagons and five long rectangles. The paper is divided into six strips (formed in step 10) and pentagons are formed on the left and right. Interesting geometry is used to form the pentagons.

1.

1. Fold and unfold.
2, 3. Fold and unfold on the edges.

2.

Fold and unfold on the right.

3.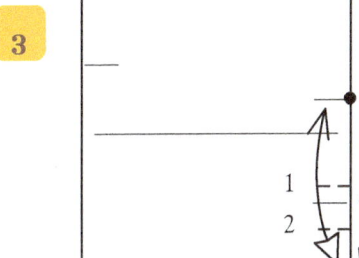

Fold and unfold on the right.

4.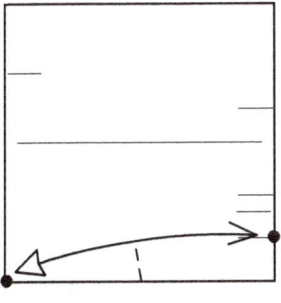

Fold and unfold on the bottom.

5.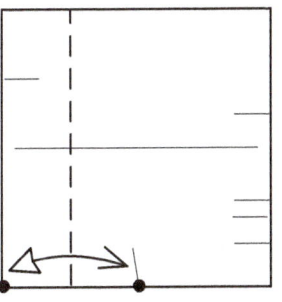

Fold and unfold. Rotate 180°.

6.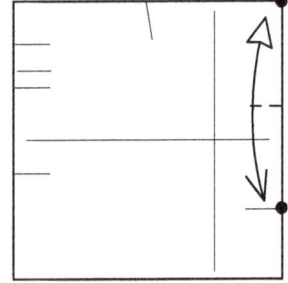

Repeat steps 2–5.

Tall Pentagonal Prism **75**

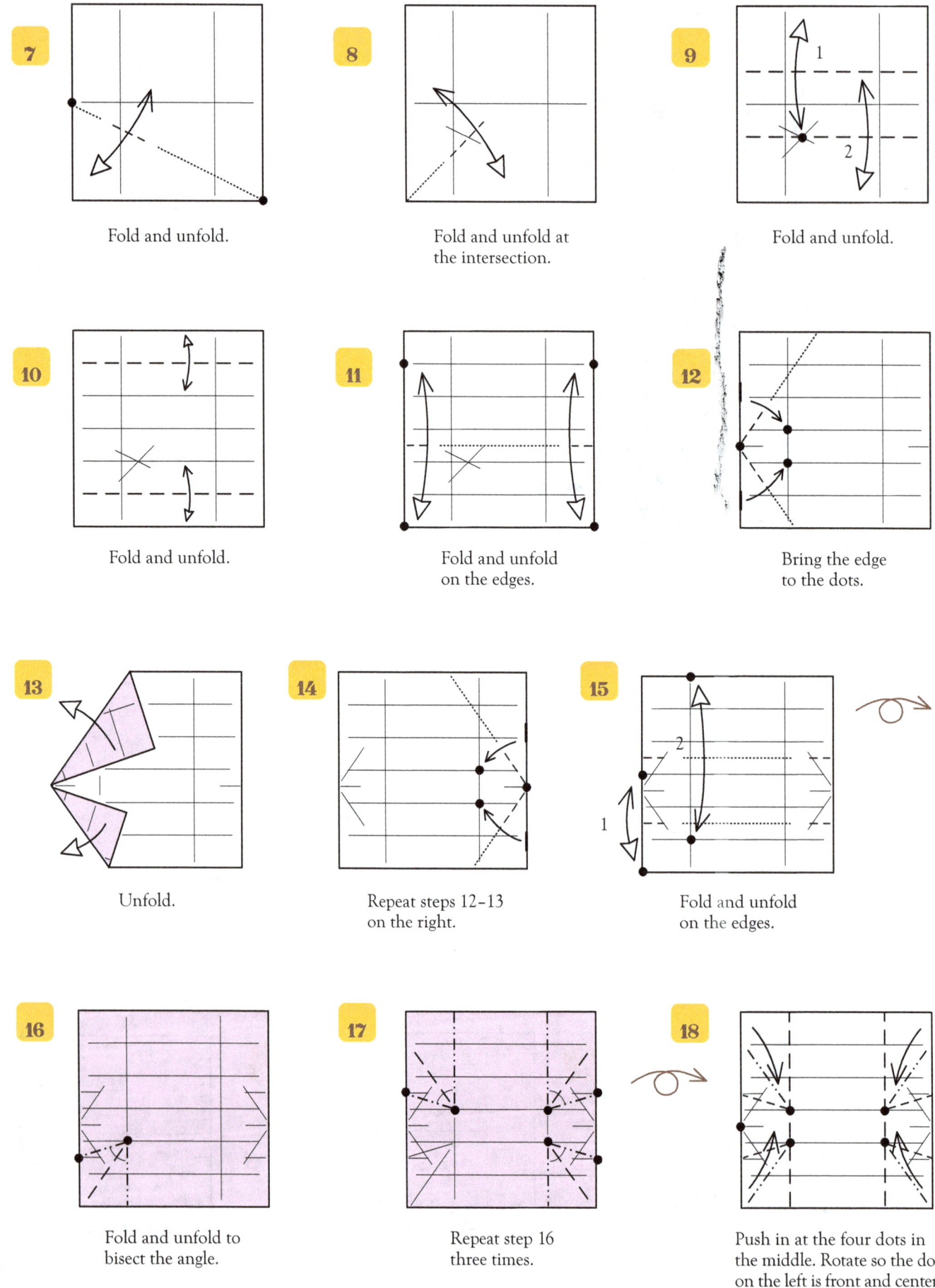

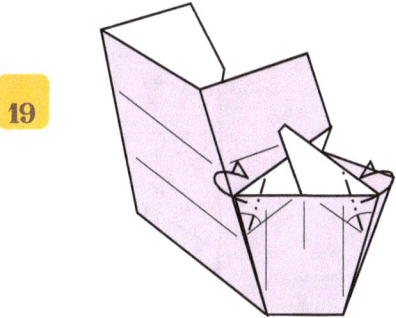

Repeat behind.

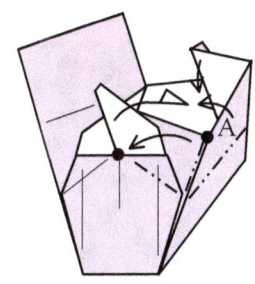

Fold side A inward so the dots meet. Repeat behind.

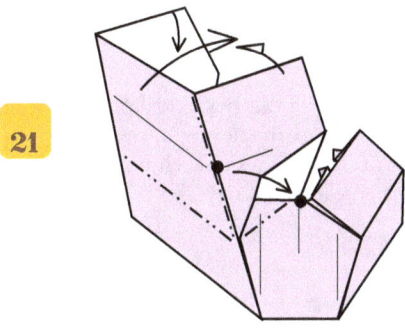

Repeat step 20 on the left.

Tuck the tab inside the pocket.

Tall Pentagonal Prism

Tall Pentagonal Prism **77**

Tall Hexagonal Prism

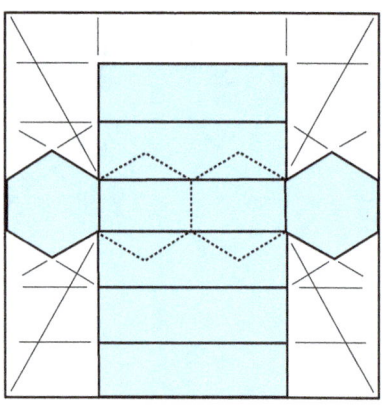

The length of this hexagonal prism is double the height of the hexagon, as shown in the layout. If the sides of each hexagon are all 1, then each rectangle is $1 \times 2\sqrt{3}$.

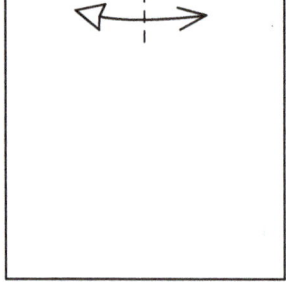

1. Fold and unfold at the top.

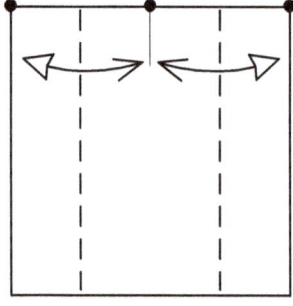

2. Fold to the center and unfold.

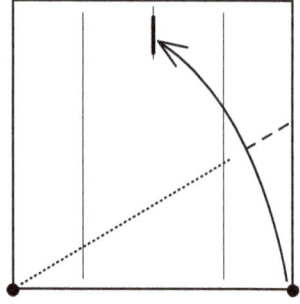

3. Crease on the right.

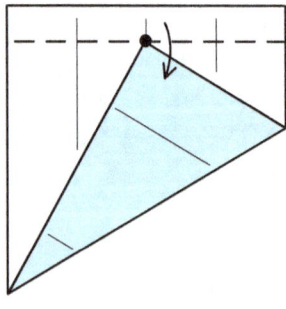

4.

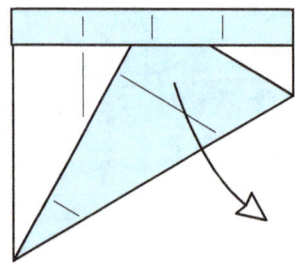

5. Unfold.

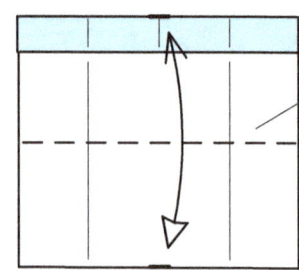

6. Fold and unfold.

78 Origami Symphony No. 8

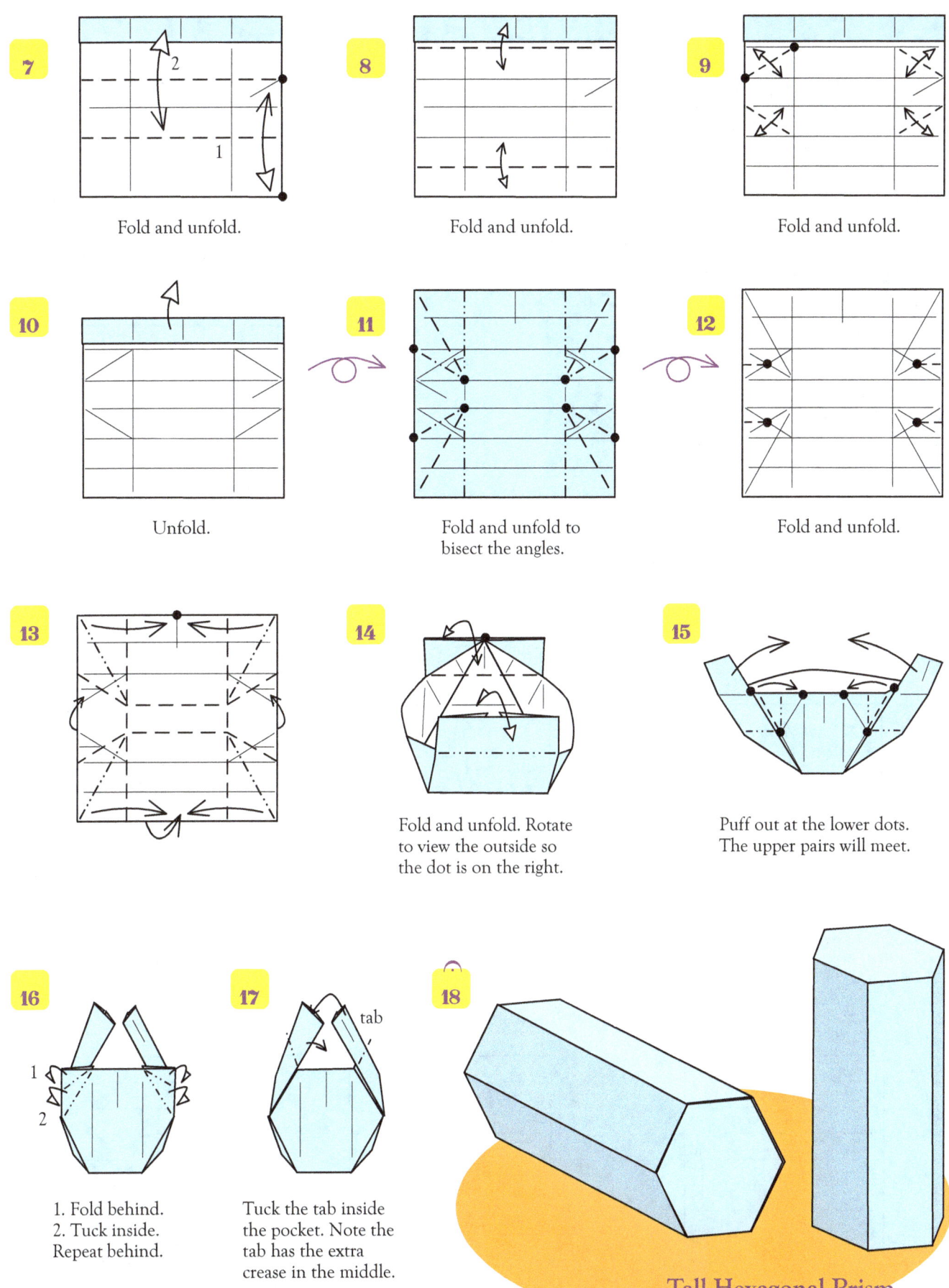

Tall Hexagonal Prism

Tall Heptagonal Prism

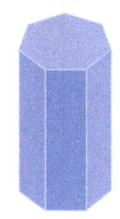

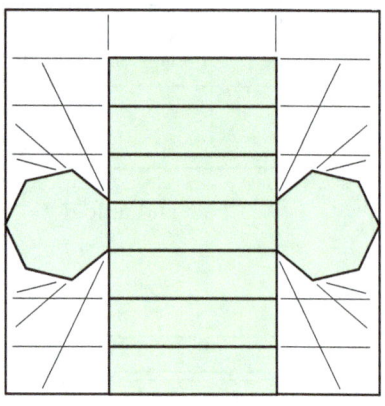

This heptagonal prism is composed of two heptagons and seven long rectangles. The paper is divided into eighths. Interesting geometry is used to form the heptagons on each side.

 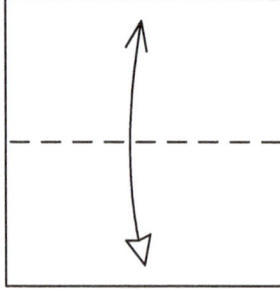

Fold and unfold.

 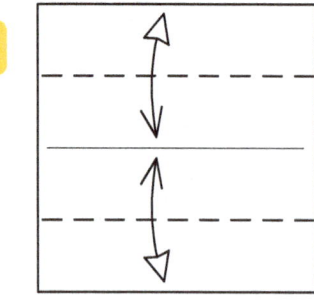

Fold and unfold.

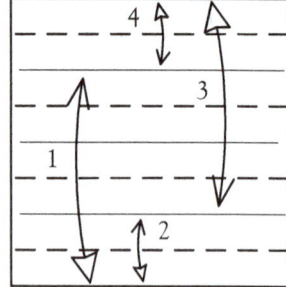

Fold and unfold to divide into eighths.

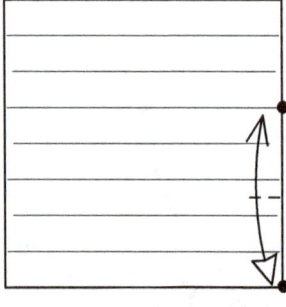

Fold and unfold on the right.

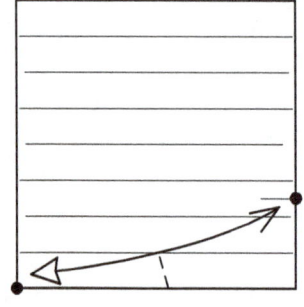

Fold and unfold on the bottom.

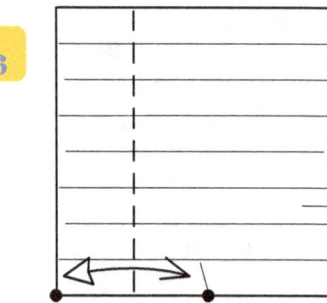

Fold and unfold. Rotate 180°.

80 Origami Symphony No. 8

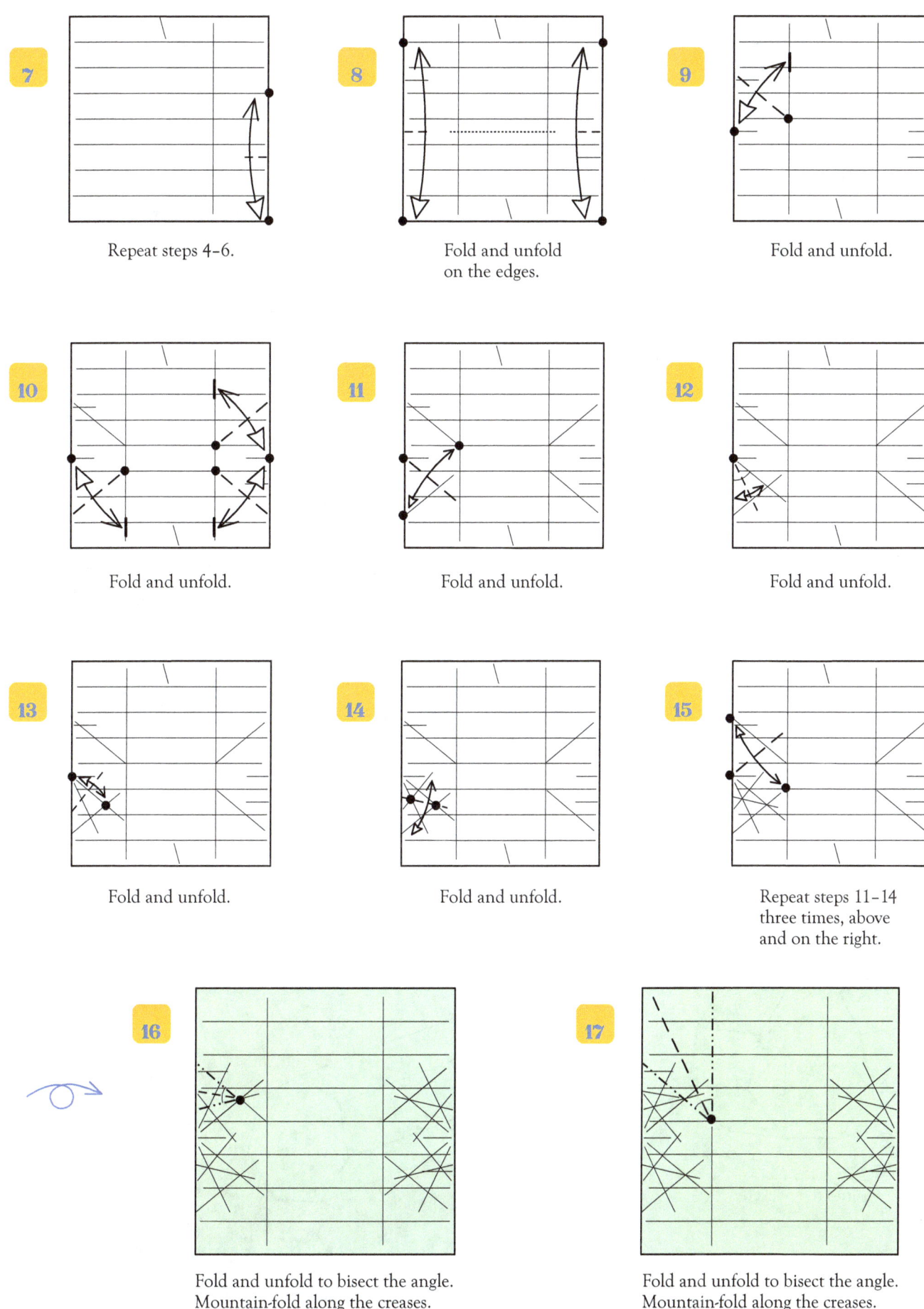

Tall Heptagonal Prism 81

18
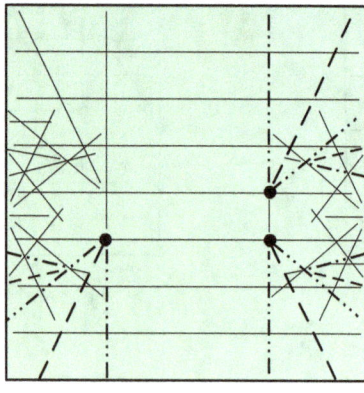
Repeat steps 16–17 three times.

19
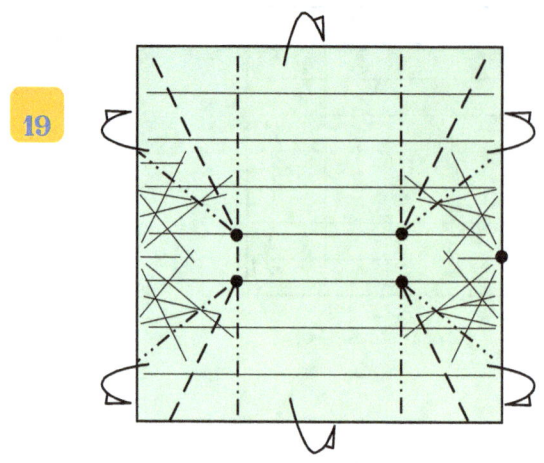
Puff out at the dots in the middle. Rotate so the dot on the right goes to the front.

20
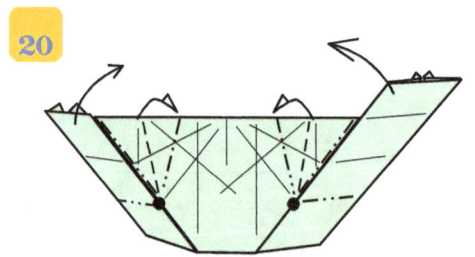
Puff out at the dots. Repeat behind.

21

Repeat behind.

22

Fold and unfold.

23
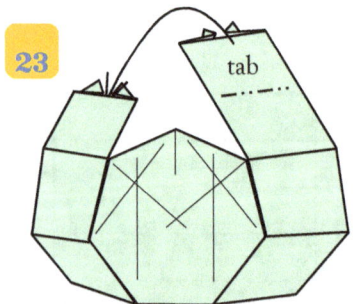
Tuck the tab into the pocket.

24
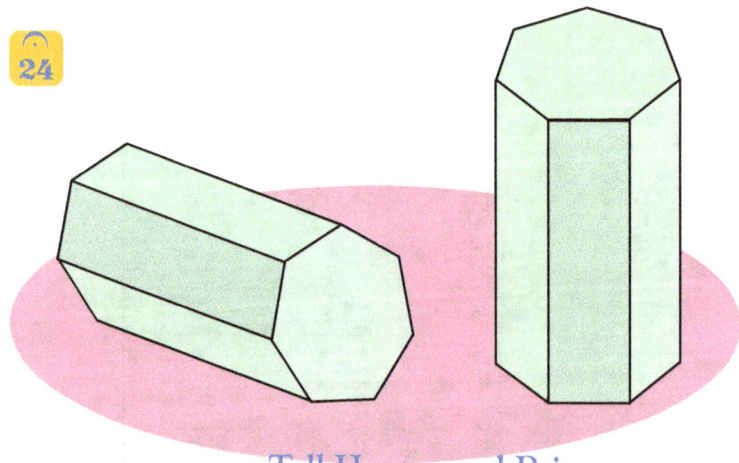
Tall Heptagonal Prism

82 Origami Symphony No. 8

Tall Octagonal Prism

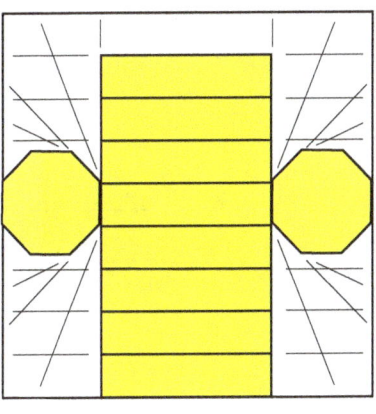

This octagonal prism is composed of two octagons and eight long rectangles. By step 7, the paper is divided into nineths.

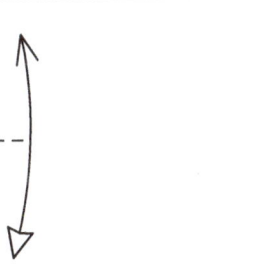

1

Fold and unfold on the left.

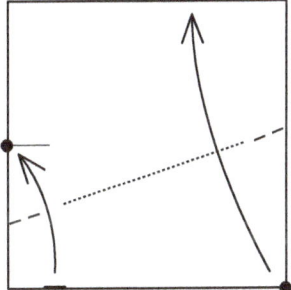

2

Bring the bottom edge to the left dot and the bottom right corner to the top. Crease on the edges.

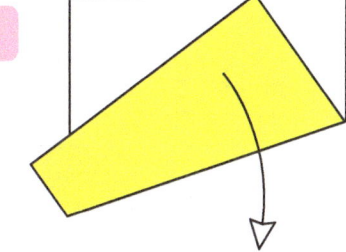

3

Unfold.

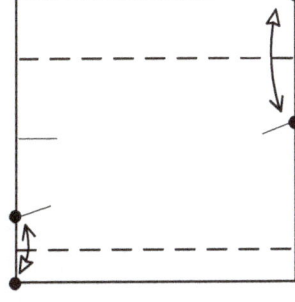

4

Fold and unfold.

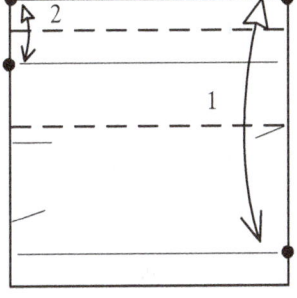

5

Fold and unfold.

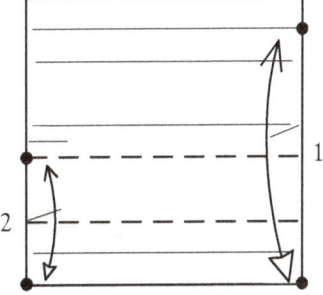

6

Fold and unfold.

Tall Octagonal Prism **83**

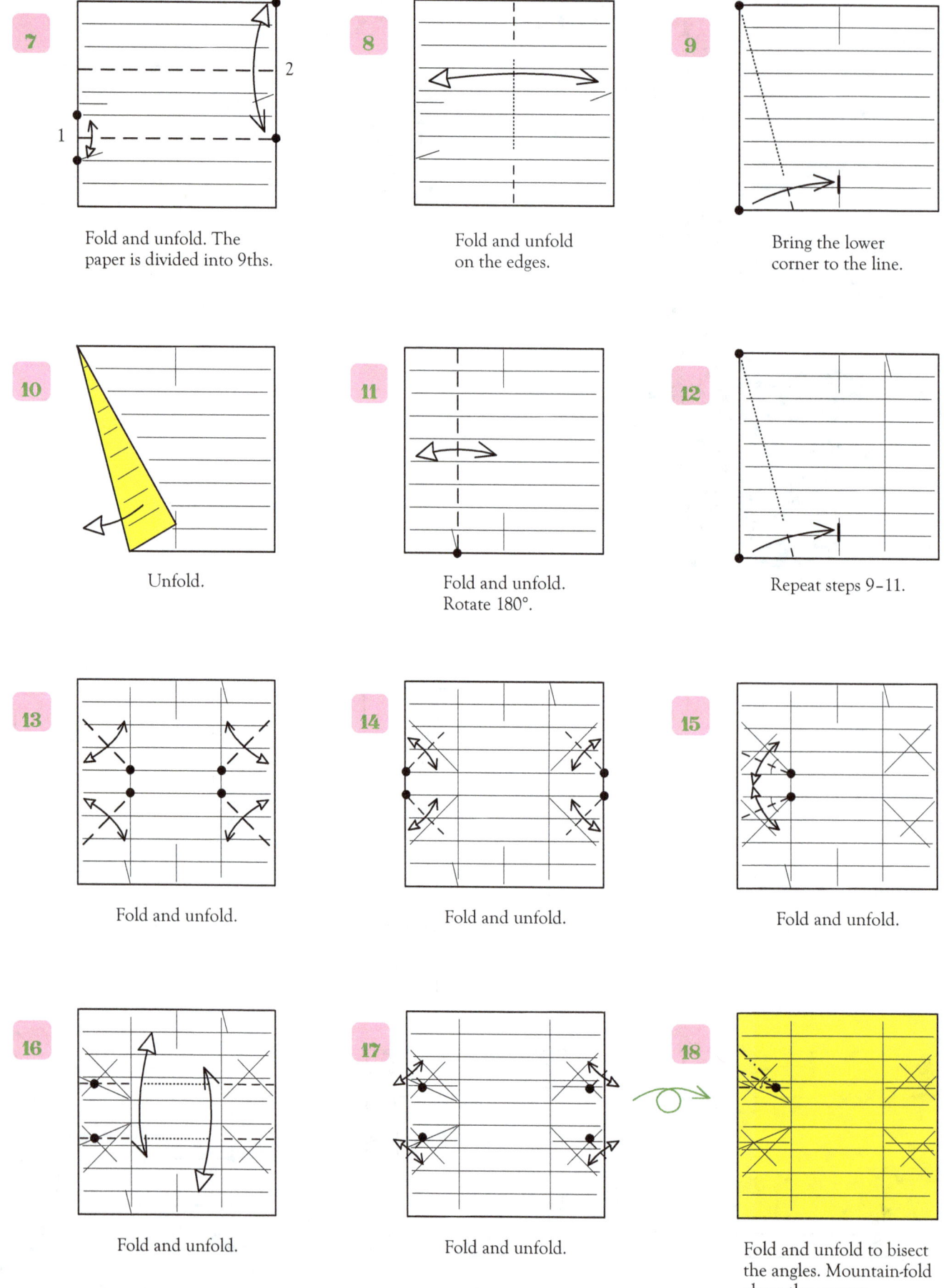

84 Origami Symphony No. 8

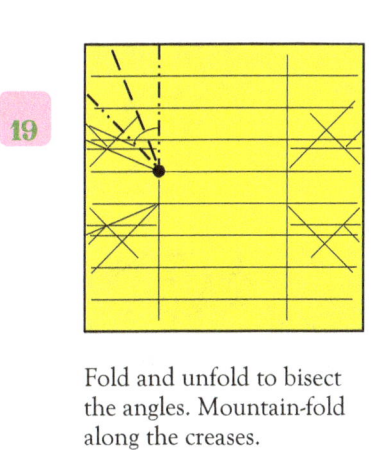

19

Fold and unfold to bisect the angles. Mountain-fold along the creases.

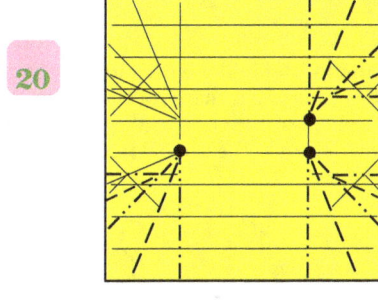

20

Repeat steps 18–19 three times.

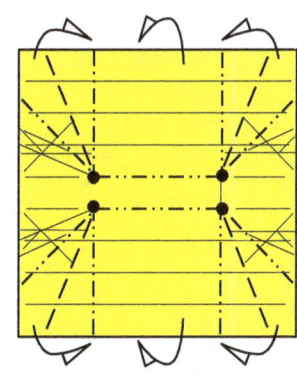

21

Puff out at the dots and rotate.

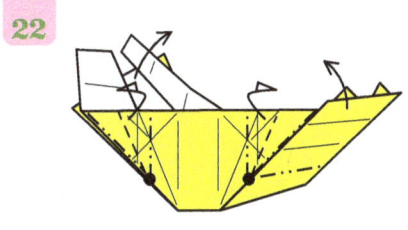

22

Puff out at the dots. Repeat behind.

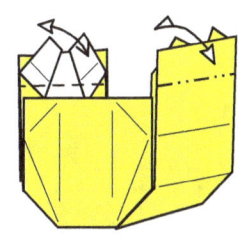

23

Fold and unfold along the creases.

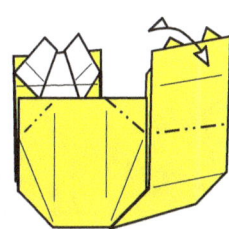

24

Fold and unfold along the creases. Repeat behind.

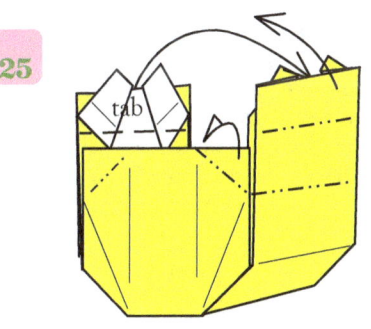

25

Tuck the tab inside the pocket.

26

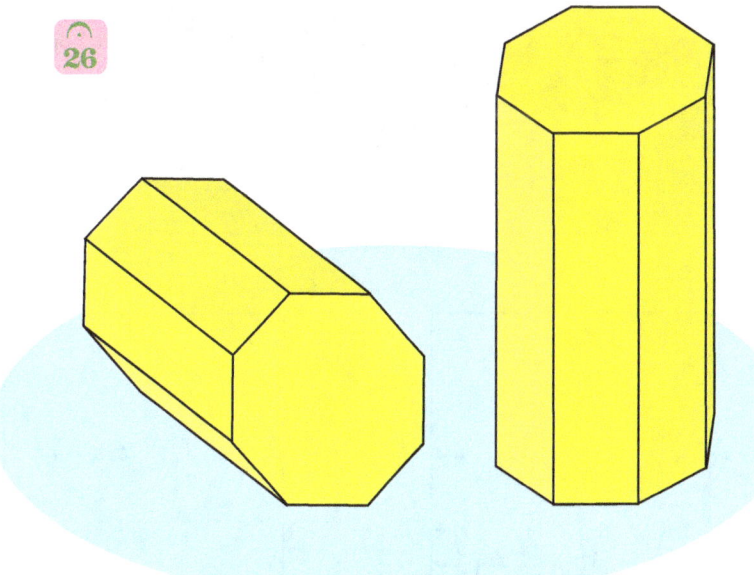

Tall Octagonal Prism

Tall Octagonal Prism **85**

Trio of Spherical Shapes

This trio of complex polyhedra will challenge the folder with stunning shapes. The icosahedron uses odd symmetry, which means when the layout is rotate 180°, it will be the same. The dimpled great rhomicuboctahedron and dimpled snub cube both use square symmetry. For these, the layout is the same when rotated 90°.

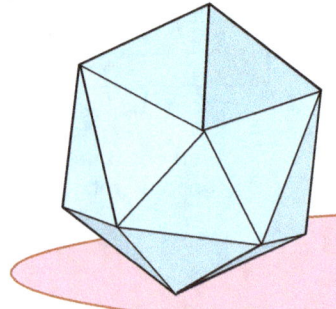 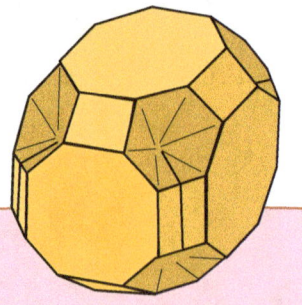 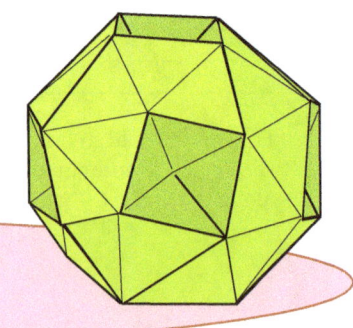

Icosahedron

The icosahedron is composed of 20 equilateral triangles. Plato attributed this model to water because if its ability to roll. The layout shows a band of ten triangles on the diagonal with five triangles on each side. Odd symmetry is used which means the layout is the same when rotated 180°. This version is diagrammed in only 24 steps.

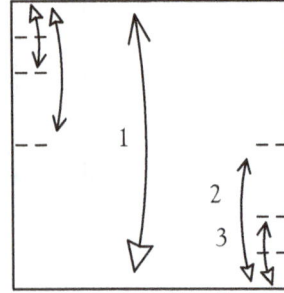

Make small marks by folding and unfolding in half three times, on the left and right.

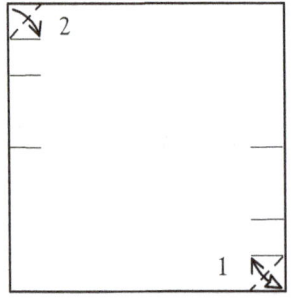

1. Fold and unfold.
2. Fold to the line.
Rotate 45°.

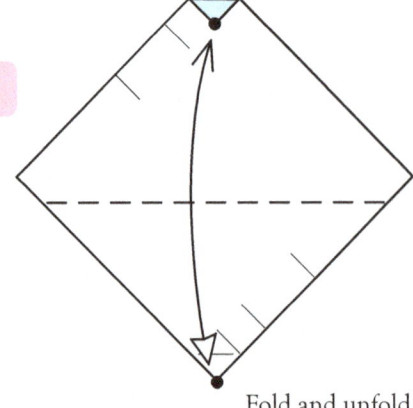

Fold and unfold.
Rotate 180°.

86   *Origami Symphony No. 8*

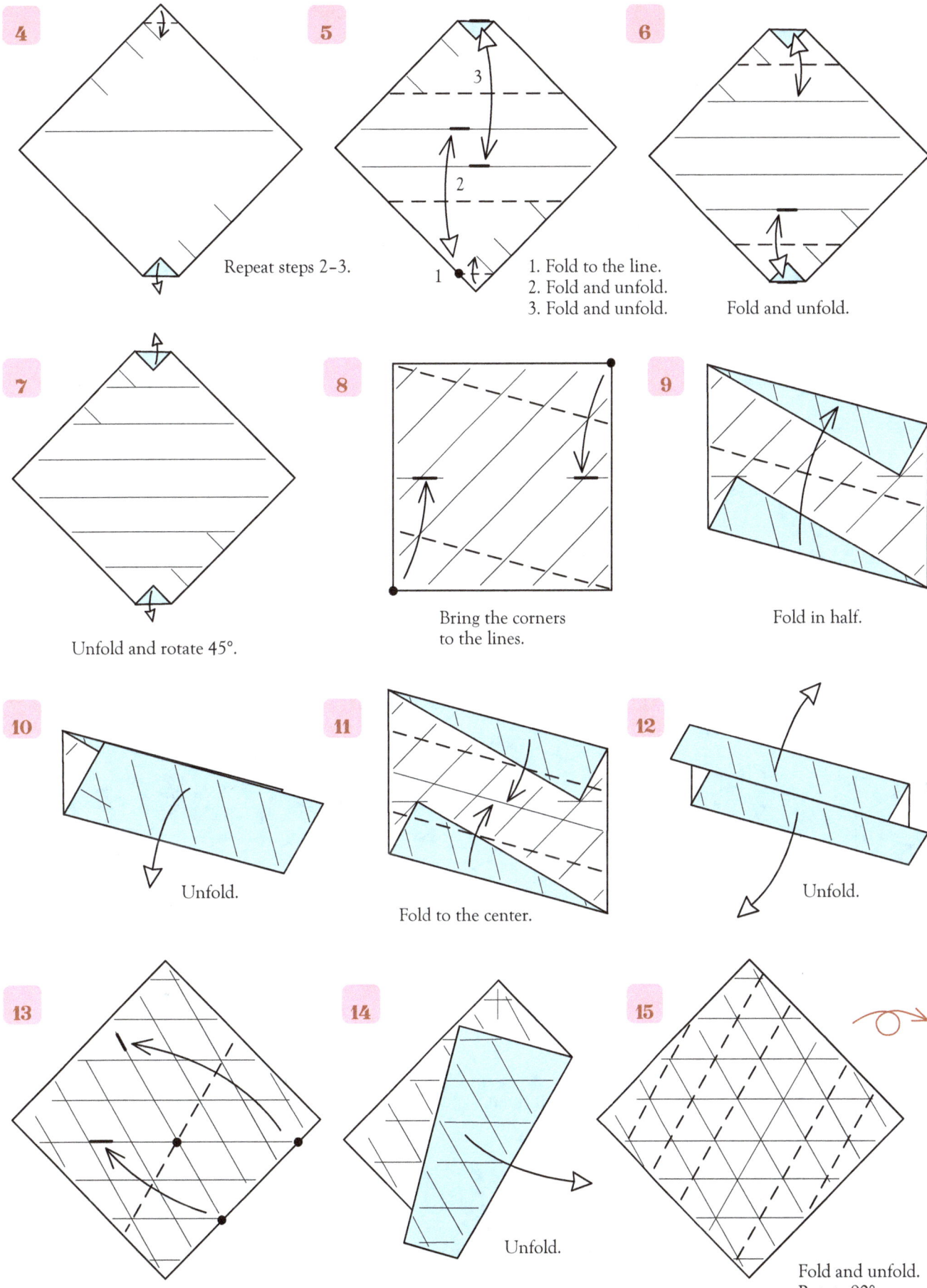

Icosahedron 87

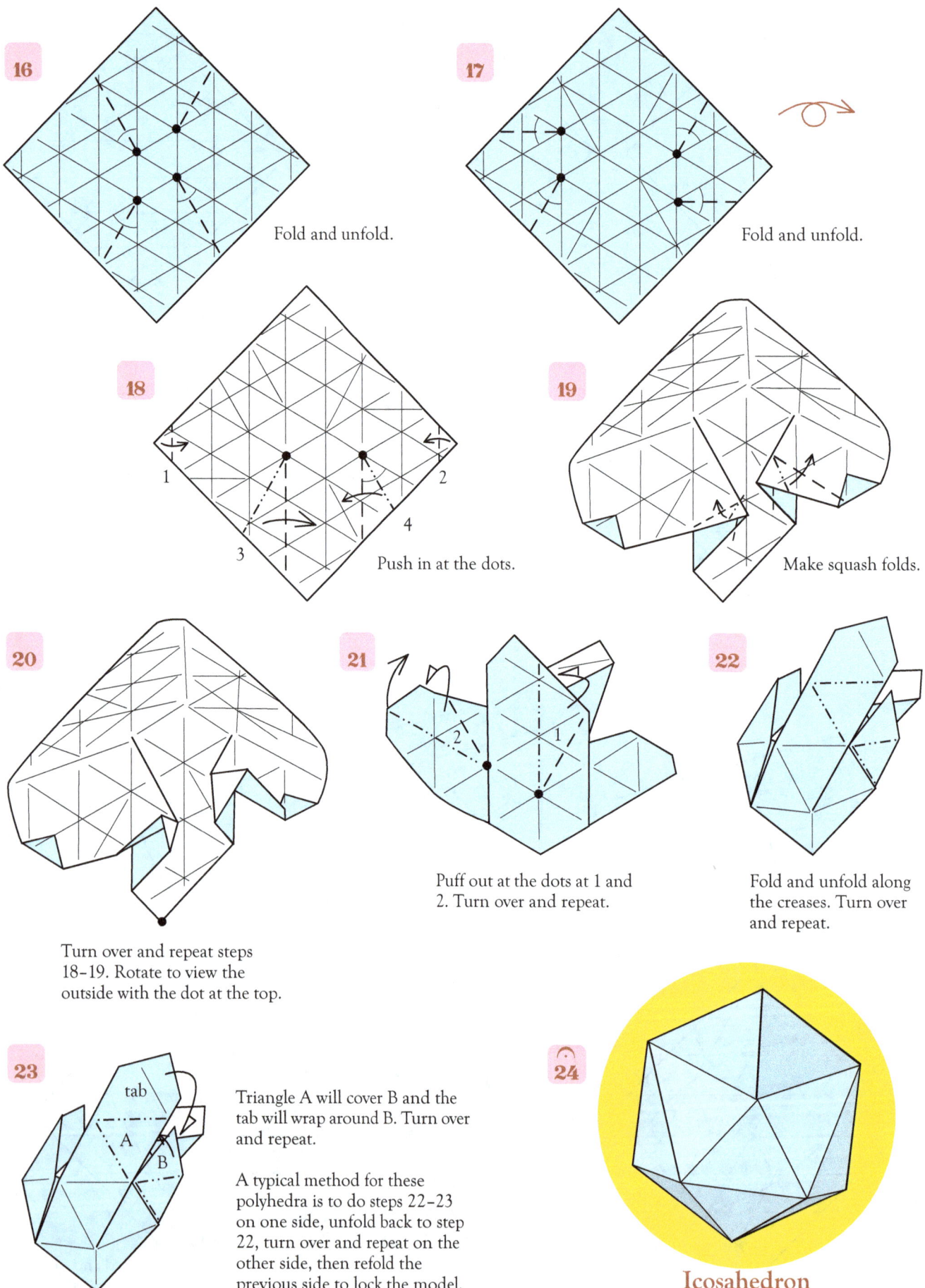

Icosahedron

88　*Origami Symphony No. 8*

Dimpled Great Rhombicuboctahedron

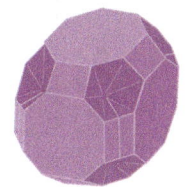
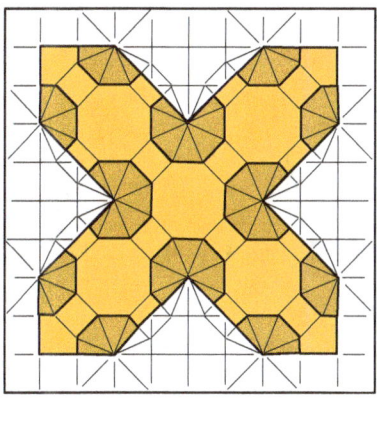

The great rhombicuboctahedron resembles a shaved cube. It has six octahedrons, eight hexagons, and twelve squares. For this dimpled one, the hexagons are sunken. The darker part of the crease pattern shows the sunken hexagons. This model develops as an ornamented cube.

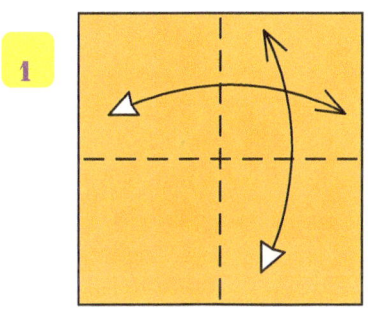

1. Fold and unfold.

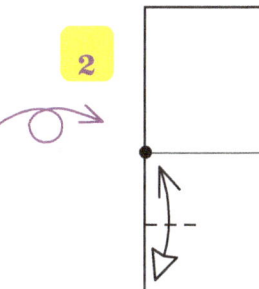

2. Fold and unfold on the left.

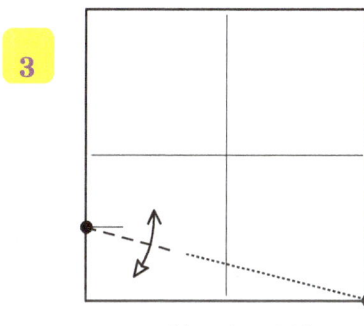

3. Fold and unfold on the left.

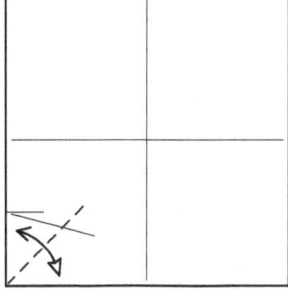

4. Fold and unfold along the diagonal at the bottom.

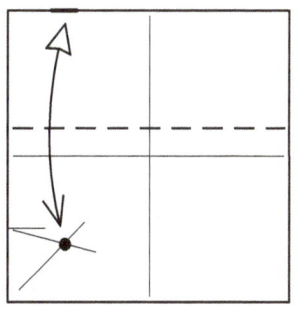

5. Fold and unfold.

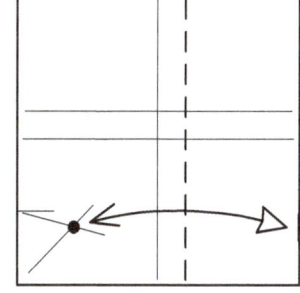

6. Fold and unfold.

Dimpled Great Rhombicuboctahedron 89

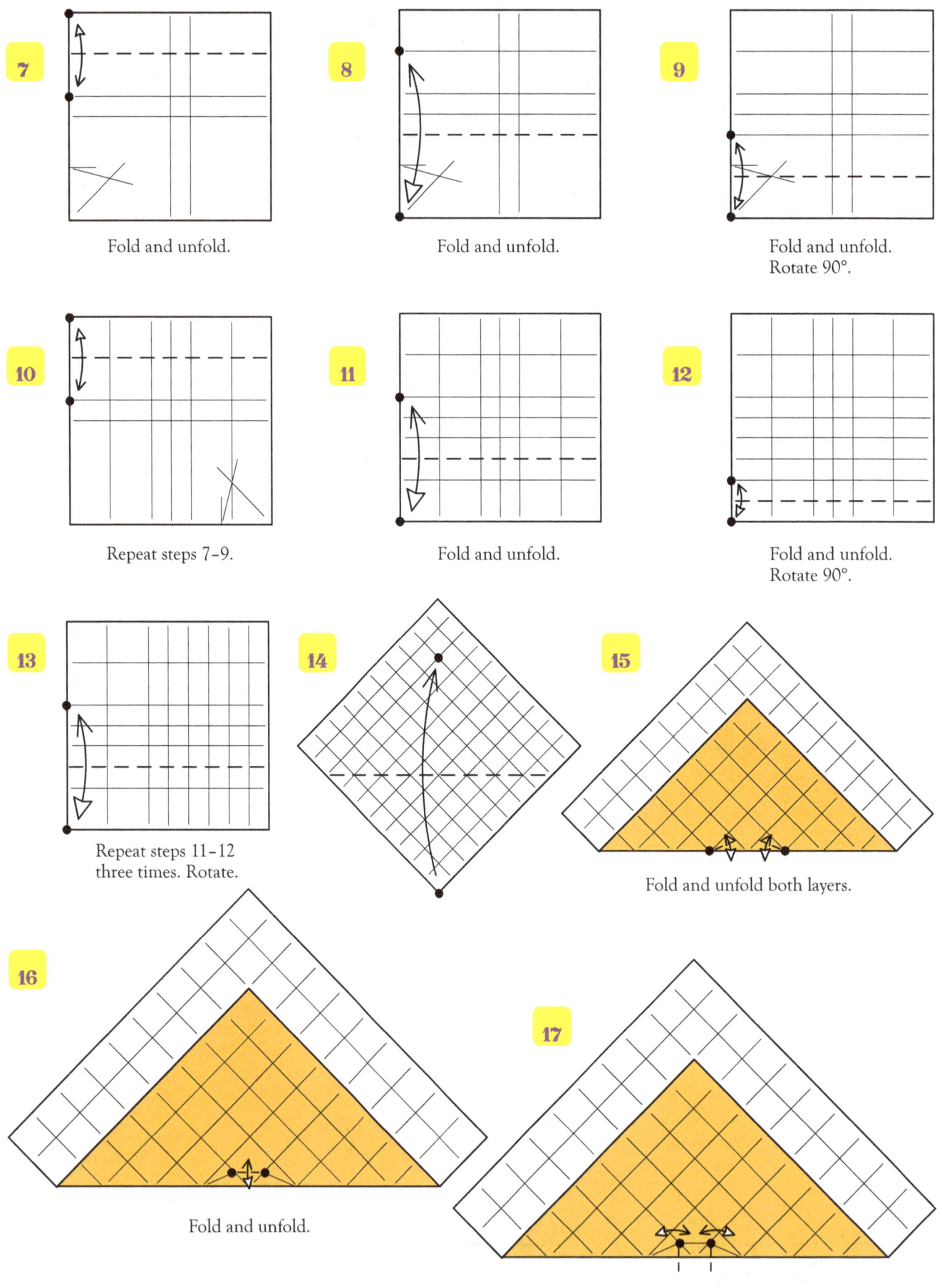

90   Origami Symphony No. 8

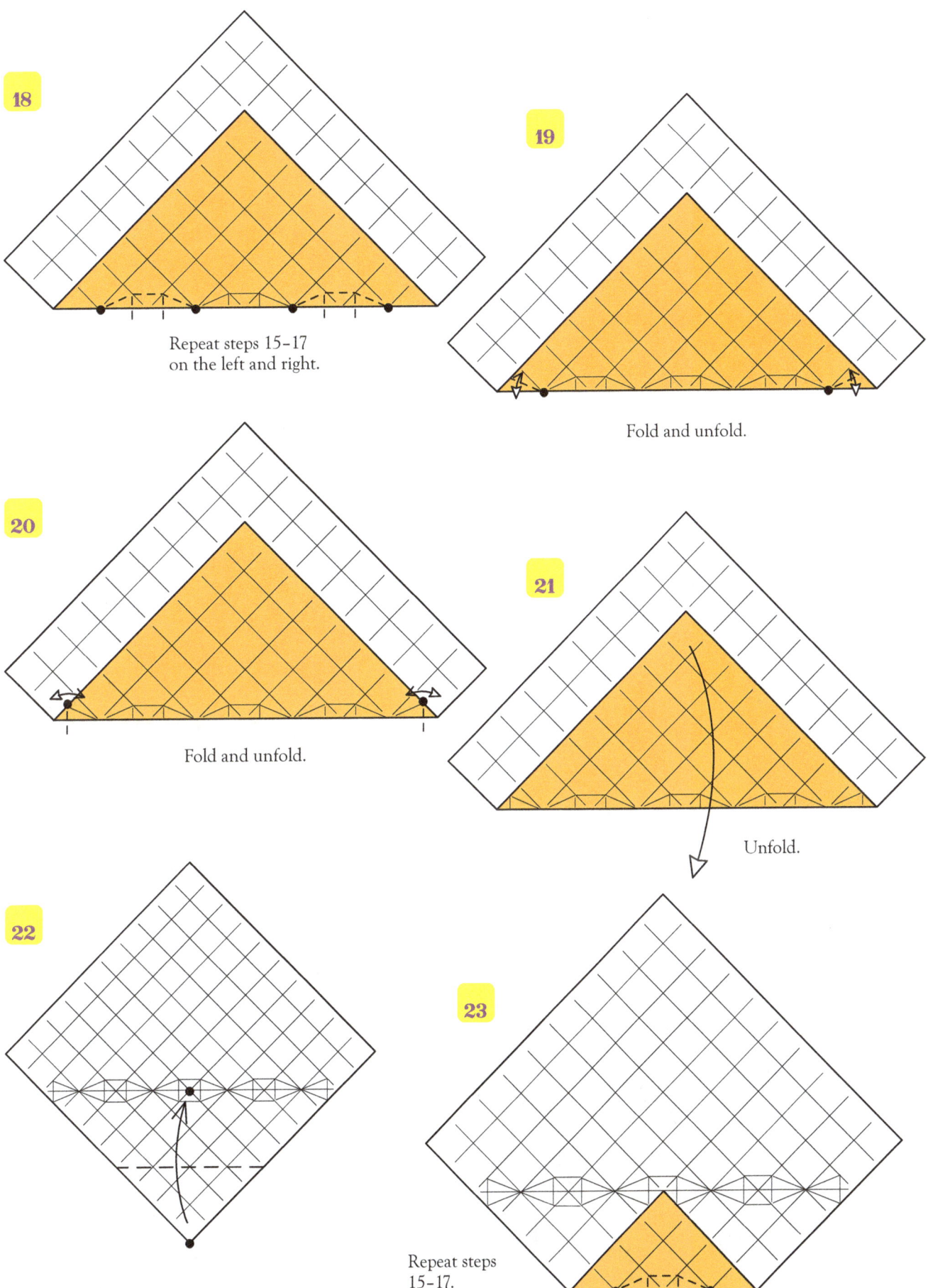

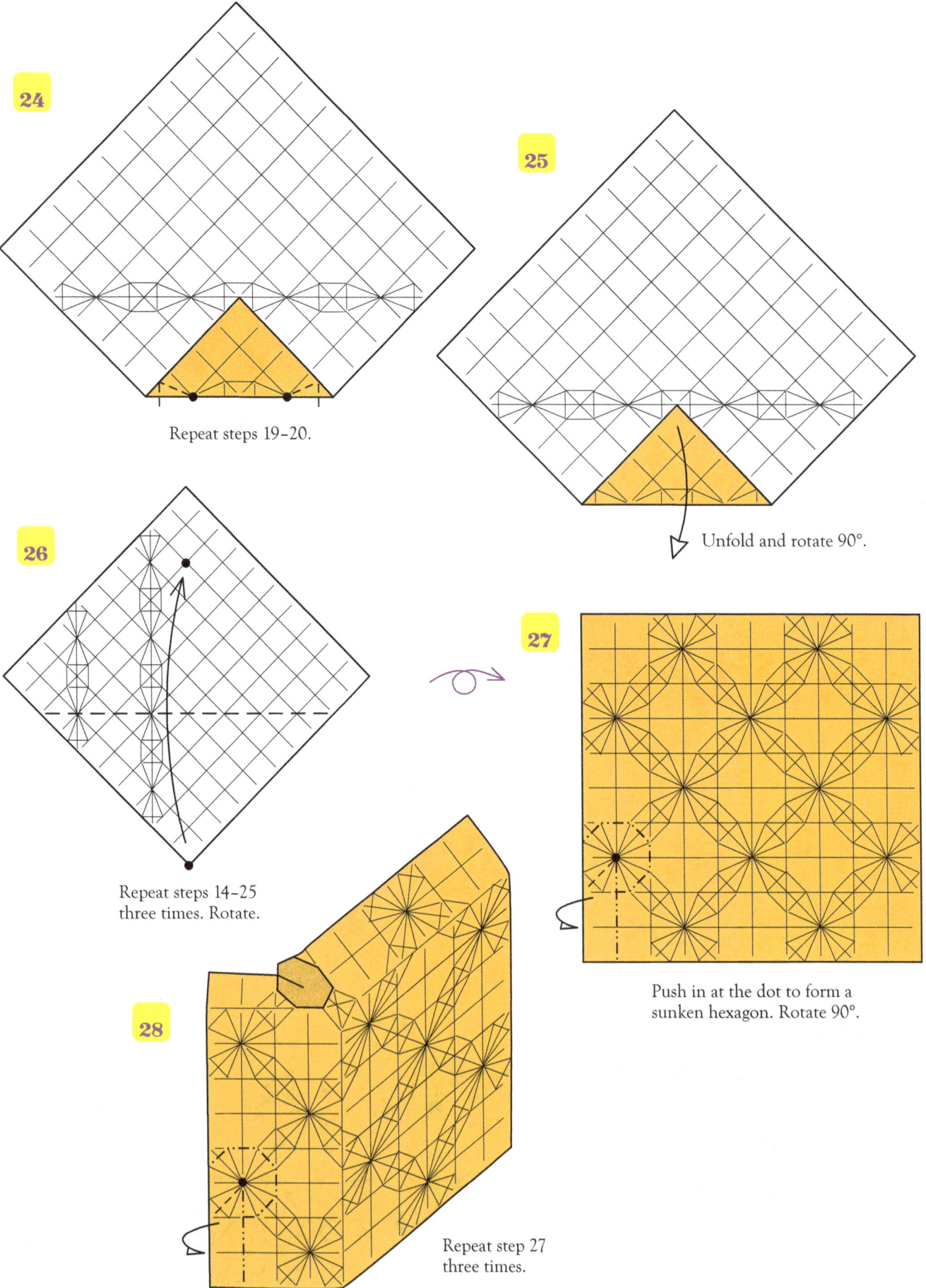

92   Origami Symphony No. 8

29

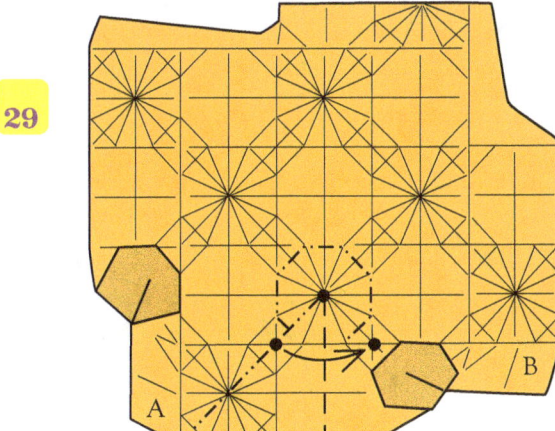

Push in at the upper dot. The other two dots will meet to form a sunken hexagon. Rotate the top to the bottom. Follow A and B into the next step.

30

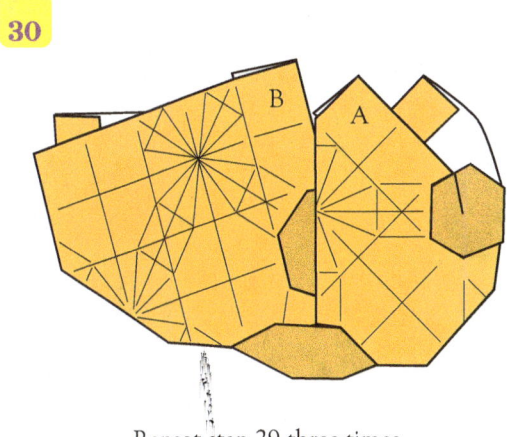

Repeat step 29 three times.

31

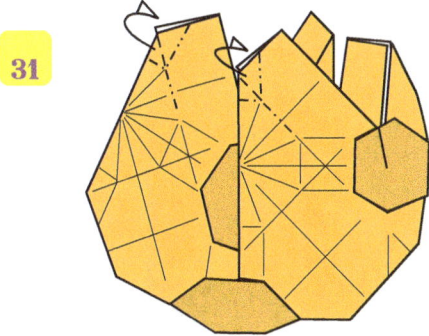

Make four small 3D reverse folds. Two of the four are shown.

32

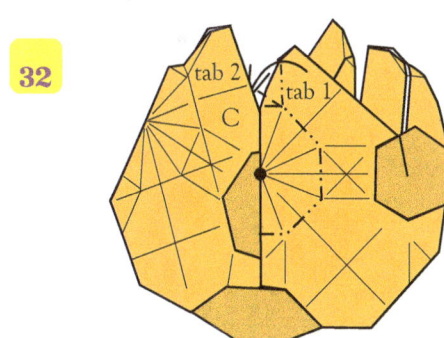

There are four tabs at the top, two are shown. Tuck tab 1 under C and push in at the dot. Continue all around.

33

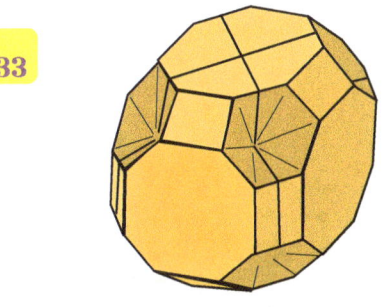

Rotate the top to the bottom.

34

Dimpled Great Rhombicuboctahedron

Dimpled Great Rhombicuboctahedron

Dimpled Snub Cube

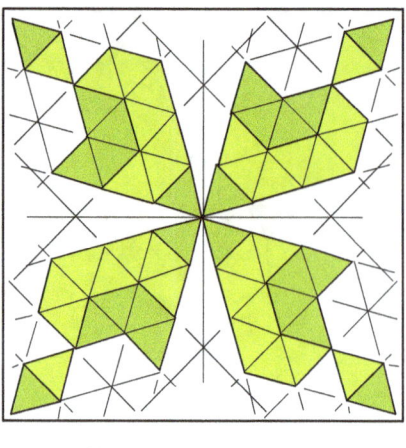

The snub cube is one of thirteen Archimedean Solids. It comes in a left and right handed form. This polyhedron has six dimpled square sides and 32 equilateral triangles. Square symmetry is used. The darker areas refer to the sunken squares.

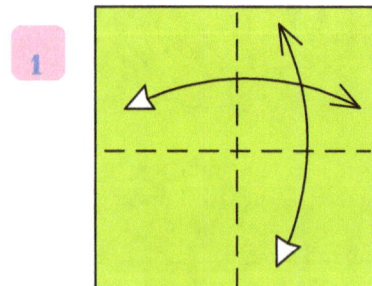

1. Fold and unfold.

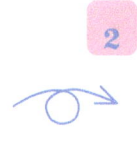
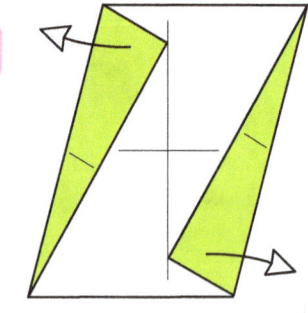

2. Bring the corners to the lines. Crease at the top and bottom.

3. Unfold.

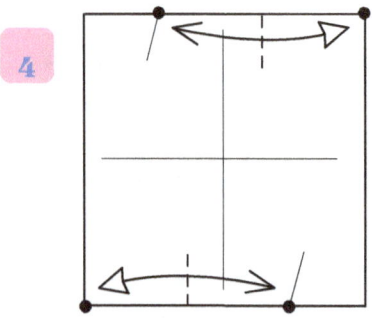
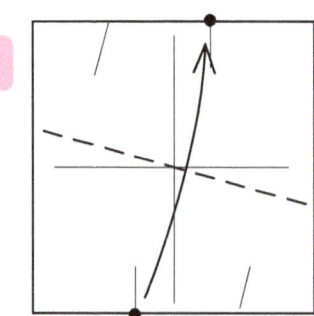
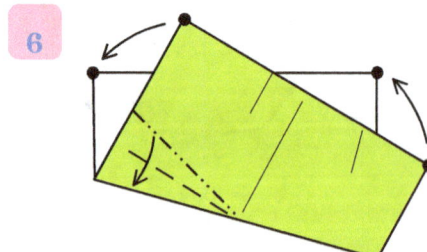

4. Fold and unfold at the top and bottom.

5.

6. Valley-fold along the crease. Turn over and repeat.

94 Origami Symphony No. 8

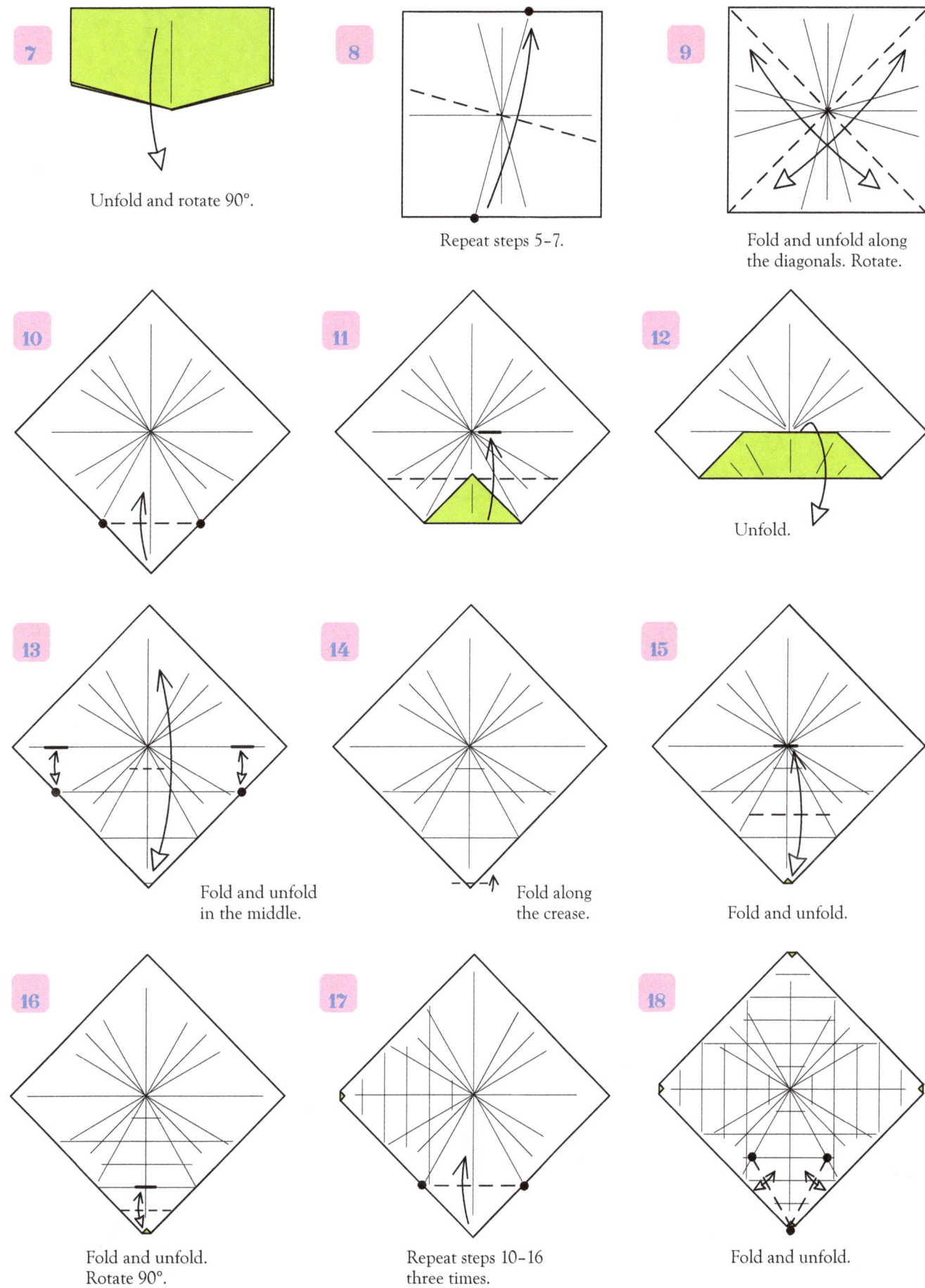

Dimpled Snub Cube

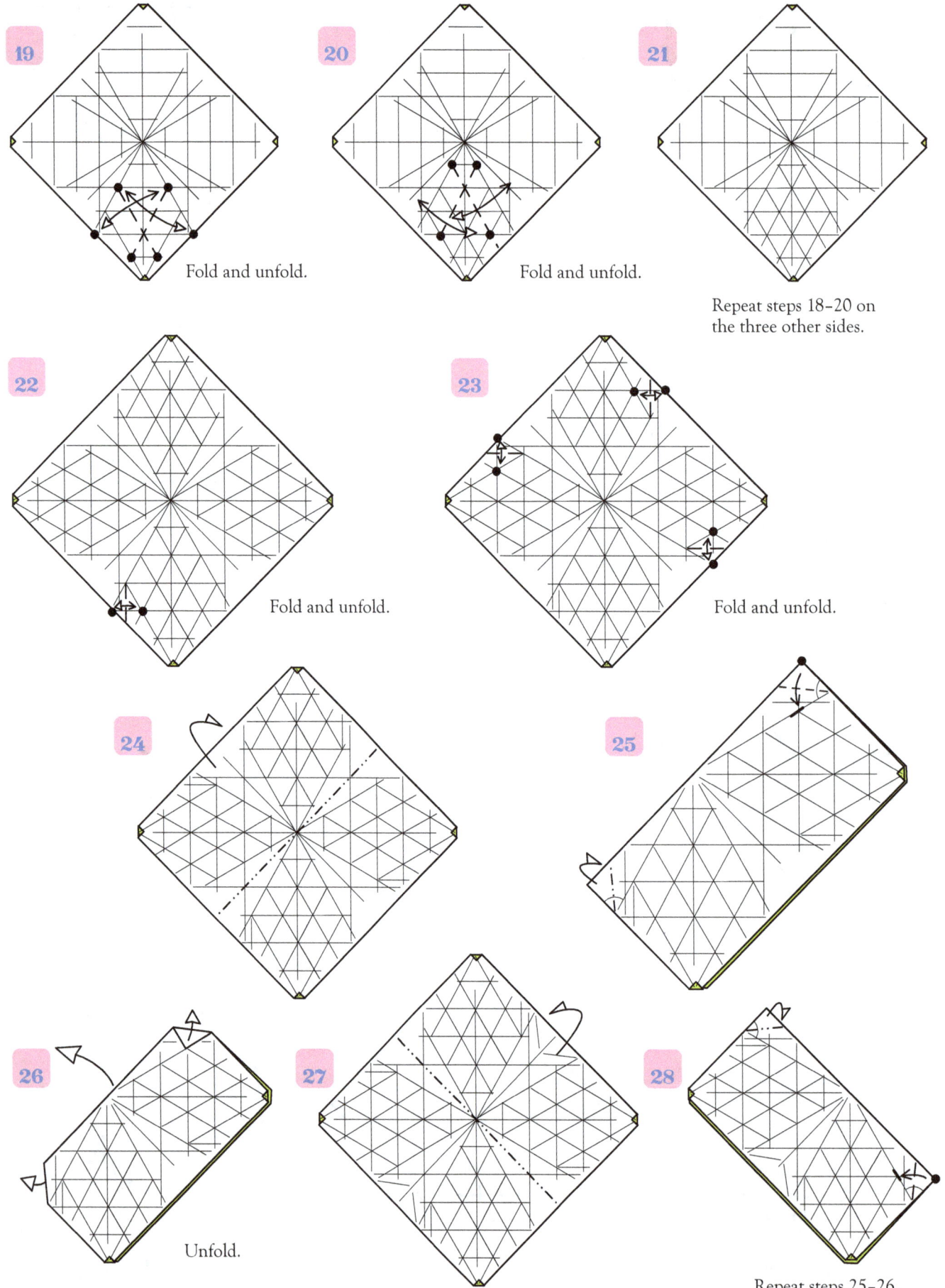

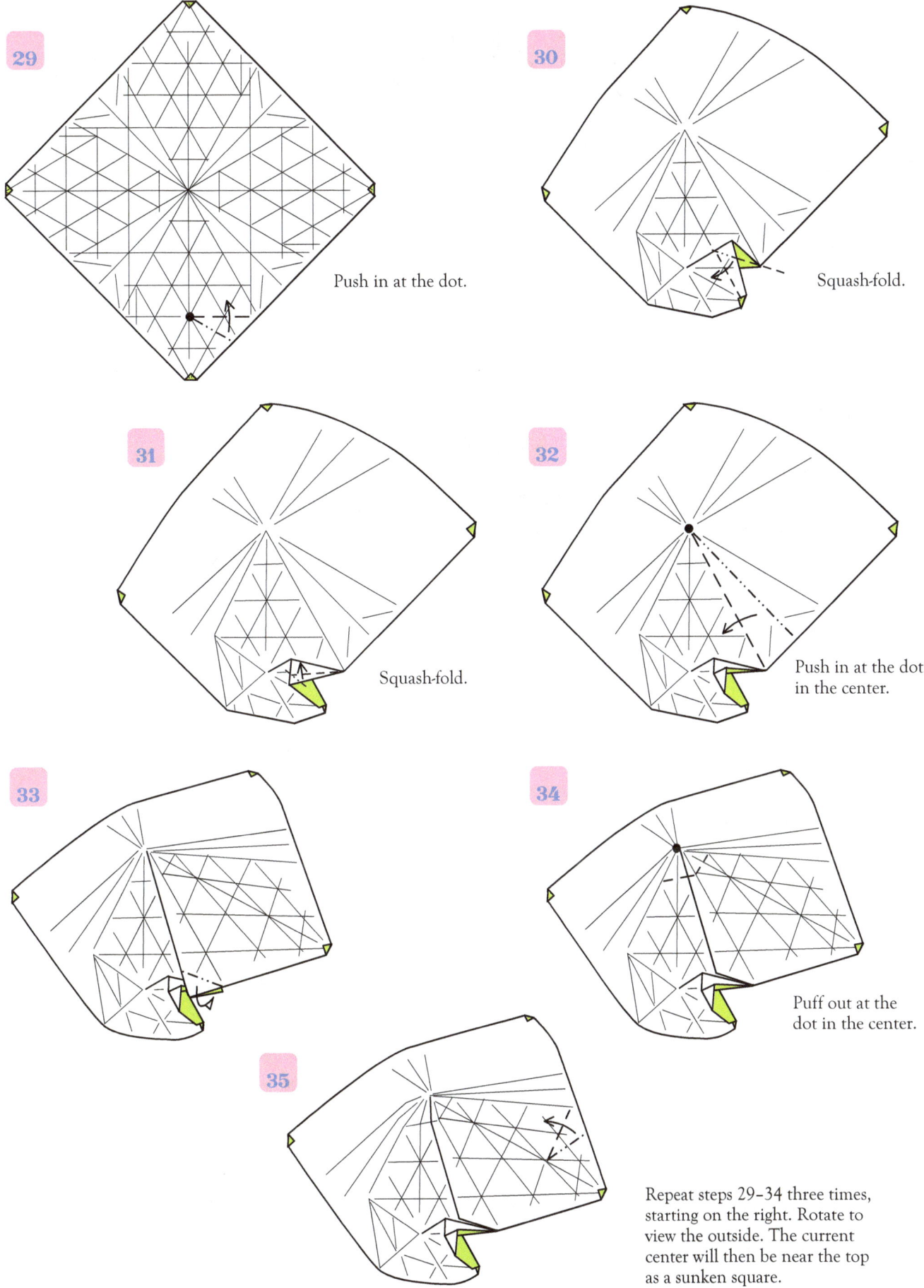

Dimpled Snub Cube

36
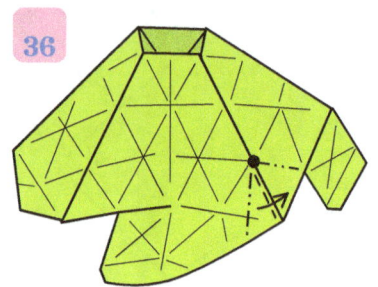
Puff out at the dot.

37
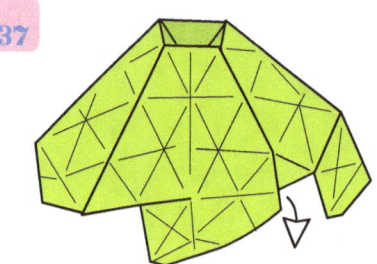
Unfold.

38
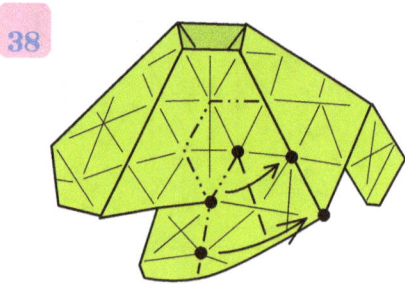
Push in at the upper dot to form a sunken square.

39
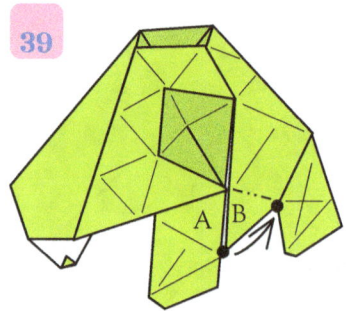
Repeat step 36 on the hidden layers so triangle A will cover triangle B.

40
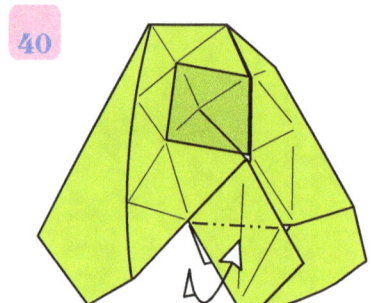
Fold and unfold.

41
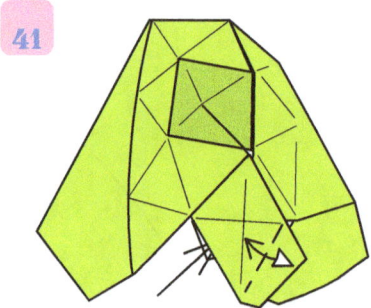
Fold and unfold. Note the pocket.

42

Repeat steps 36–41 three times.

43
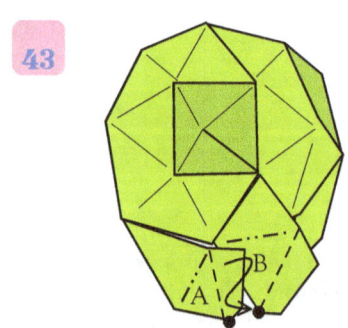
Triangles A and B are two of the four that will form the bottom sunken square. Tuck each of the flaps inside the pockets to close the model.

44
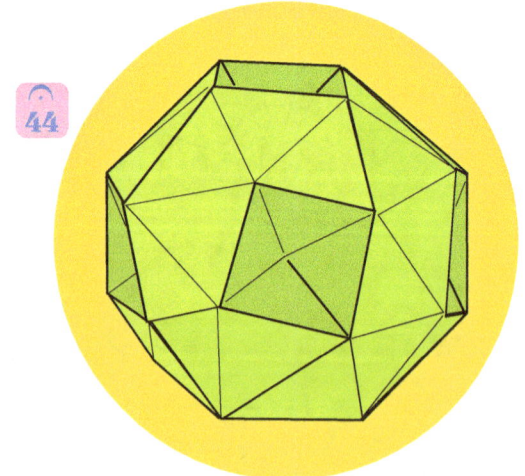
Dimpled Snub Cube

98 Origami Symphony No. 8

Fourth Movement

March of the Circus Animals

𝄢 The modern circus began in the 18th century as a way to demonstrate horse riding tricks. Clowns and acrobats were included. In time, large cats, elephants, and other exotic animals were added along with a variety of skillful acts. For this movement, no animals were harmed. Prisms and spherical shapes will enhance the origami circus display. The large cats shown here are united in structure by the cats from the first movement. Enjoy the best show on Earth.

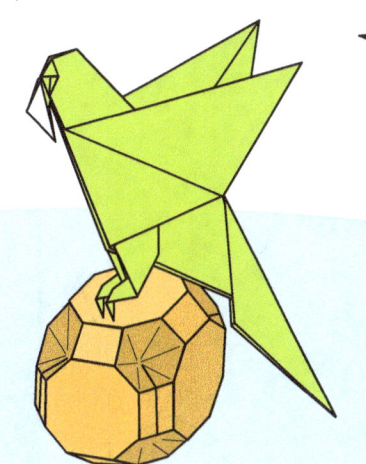

Seal

Circus seals can do amazing tricks. They can spin balls on their noses while dancing or play with hola hoops on their face. Zoos and large aquariums offer plenty of space for them as they swim and do antics.

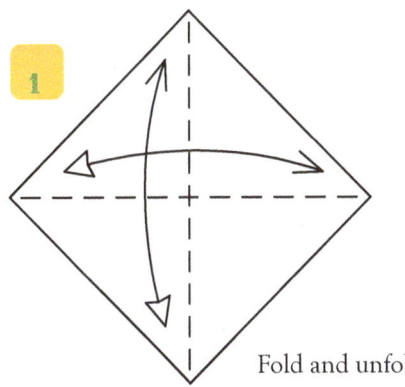

1 Fold and unfold.

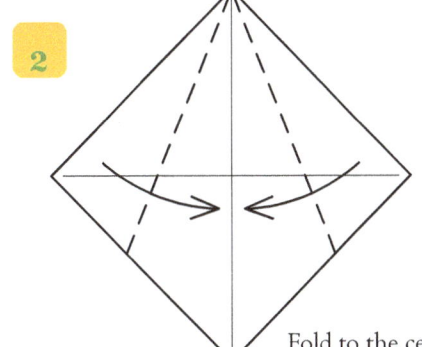

2 Fold to the center.

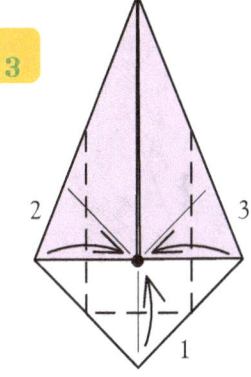

3

Seal

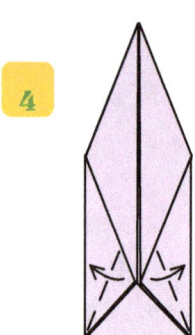

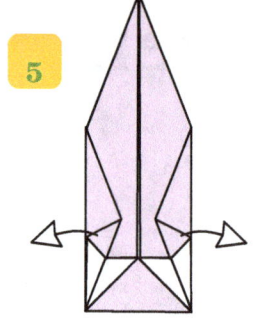

Unfold.

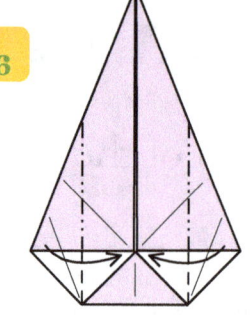

Make reverse folds.

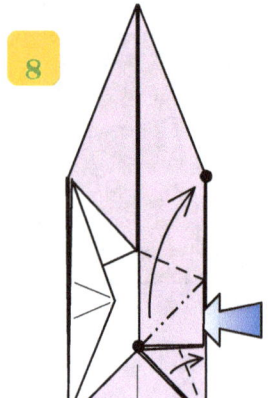

This is a combination of squash folds.

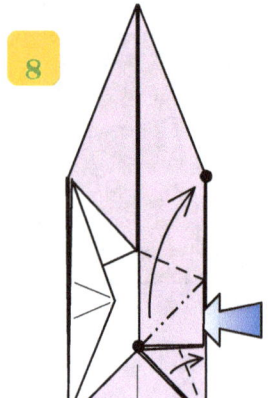

Repeat step 7 on the right.

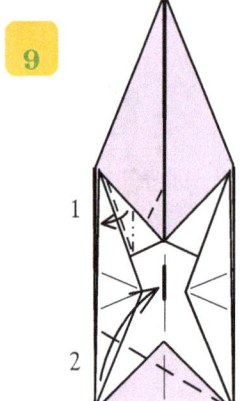

1. Squash-fold.
2. Bring the corner to the line.

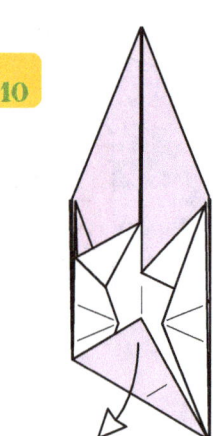

Unfold.

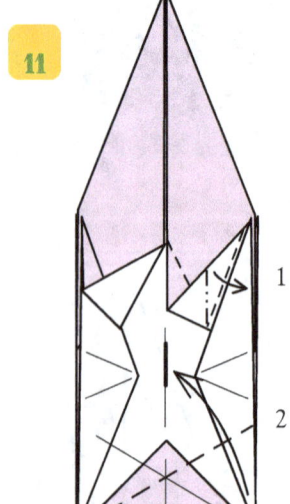

Repeat steps 9–10 on the right.

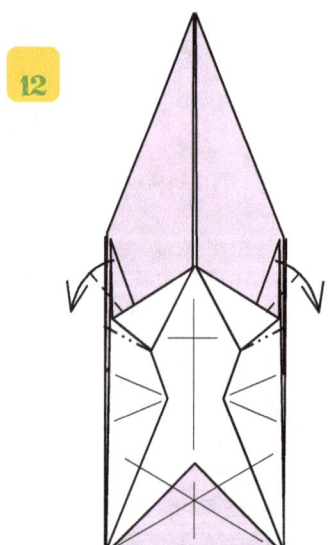

Make squash folds.

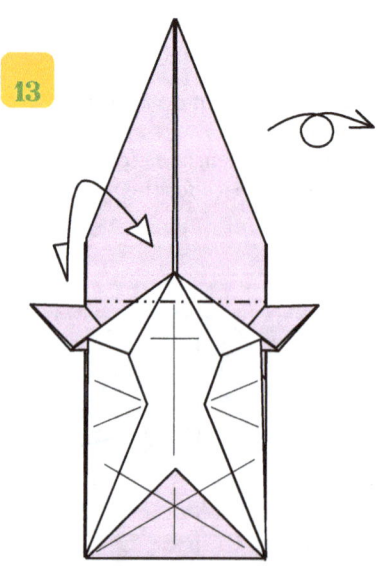

Fold and unfold.

Origami Symphony No. 8

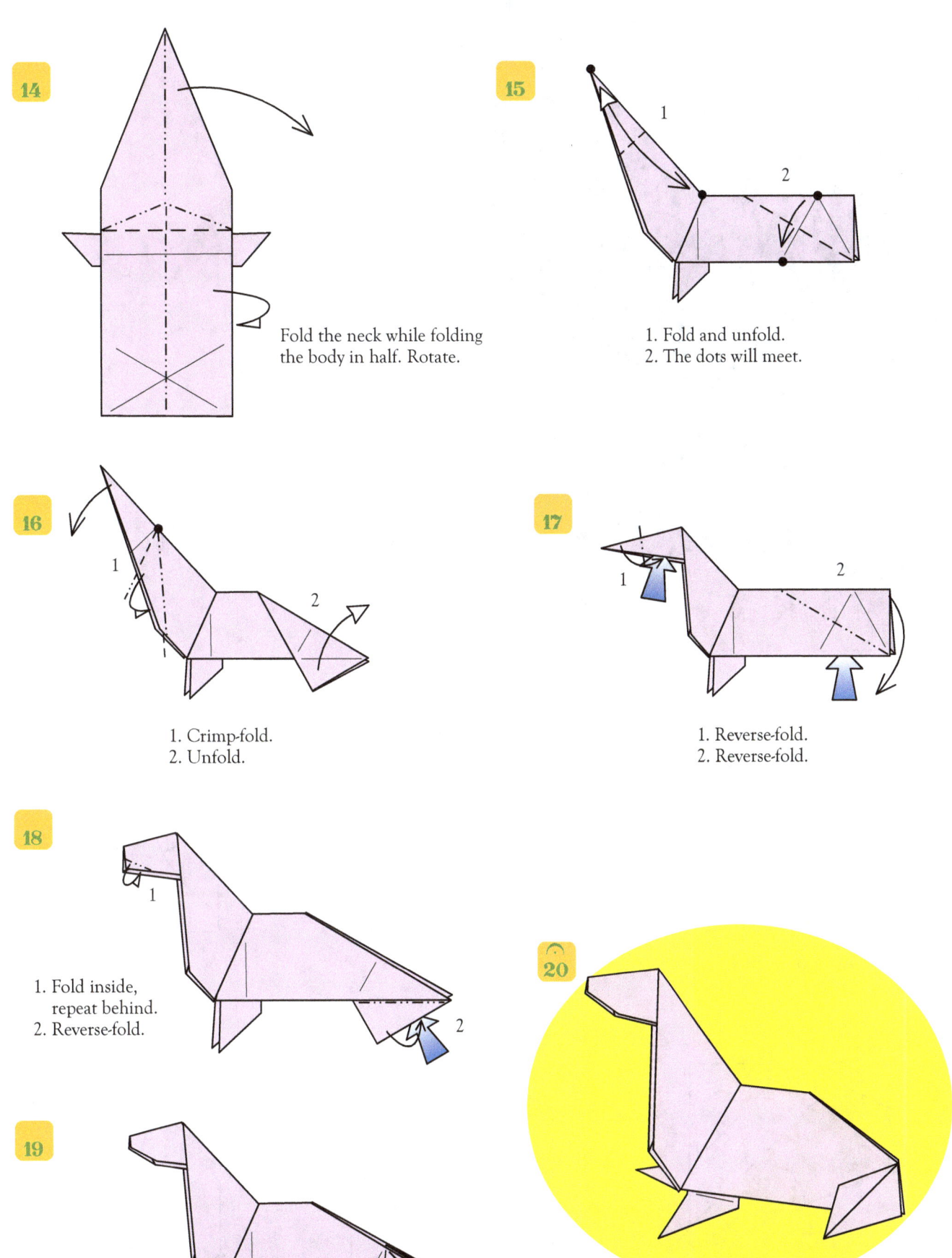

14 Fold the neck while folding the body in half. Rotate.

15
1. Fold and unfold.
2. The dots will meet.

16
1. Crimp-fold.
2. Unfold.

17
1. Reverse-fold.
2. Reverse-fold.

18
1. Fold inside, repeat behind.
2. Reverse-fold.

19
1. Fold up.
2. Squash-fold. Repeat behind.

20 Seal

Seal 101

Parrot

Parrots are very intelligent birds. They can speak and learn all kinds of tricks. These tropical and colorful birds like attention. A group of parrots is a pandemonium. Parrots use their feet as arms as they feed themselves.

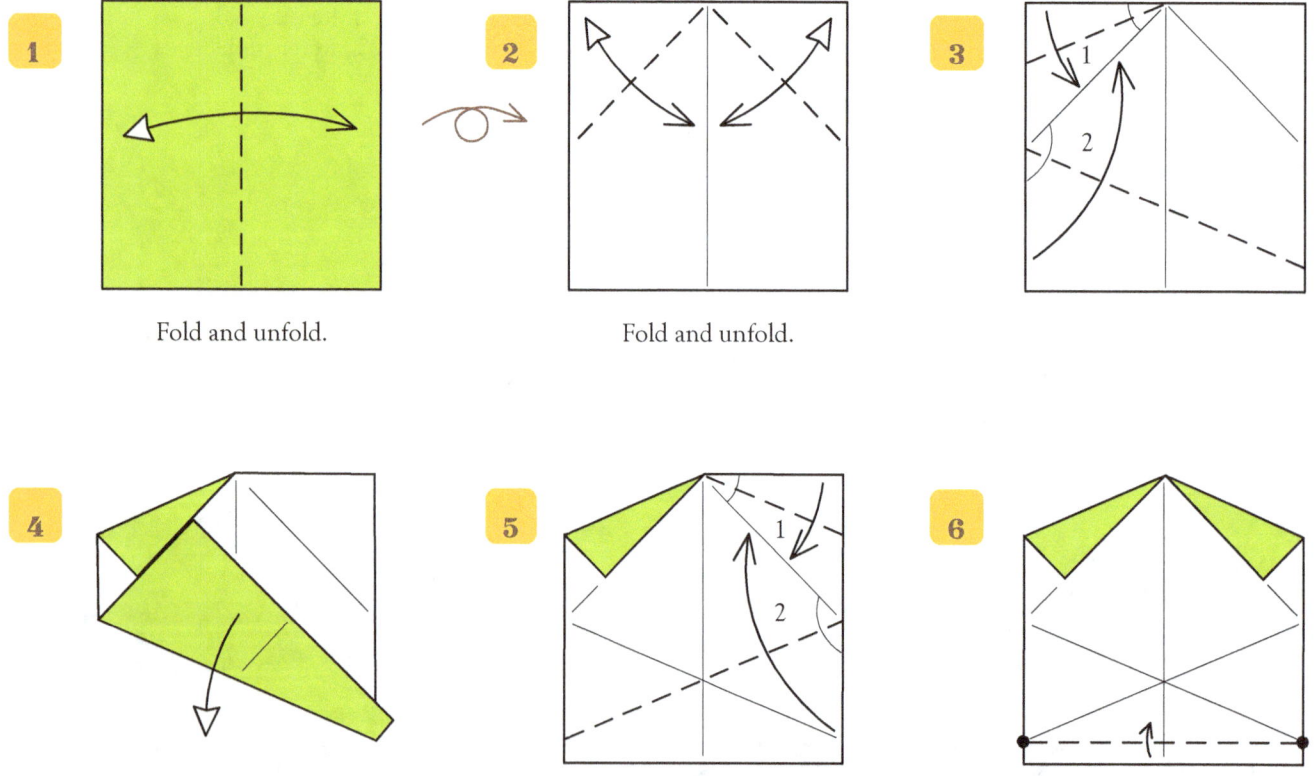

1. Fold and unfold.
2. Fold and unfold.
3.
4. Unfold.
5. Repeat steps 3-4 on the right.
6.

102 Origami Symphony No. 8

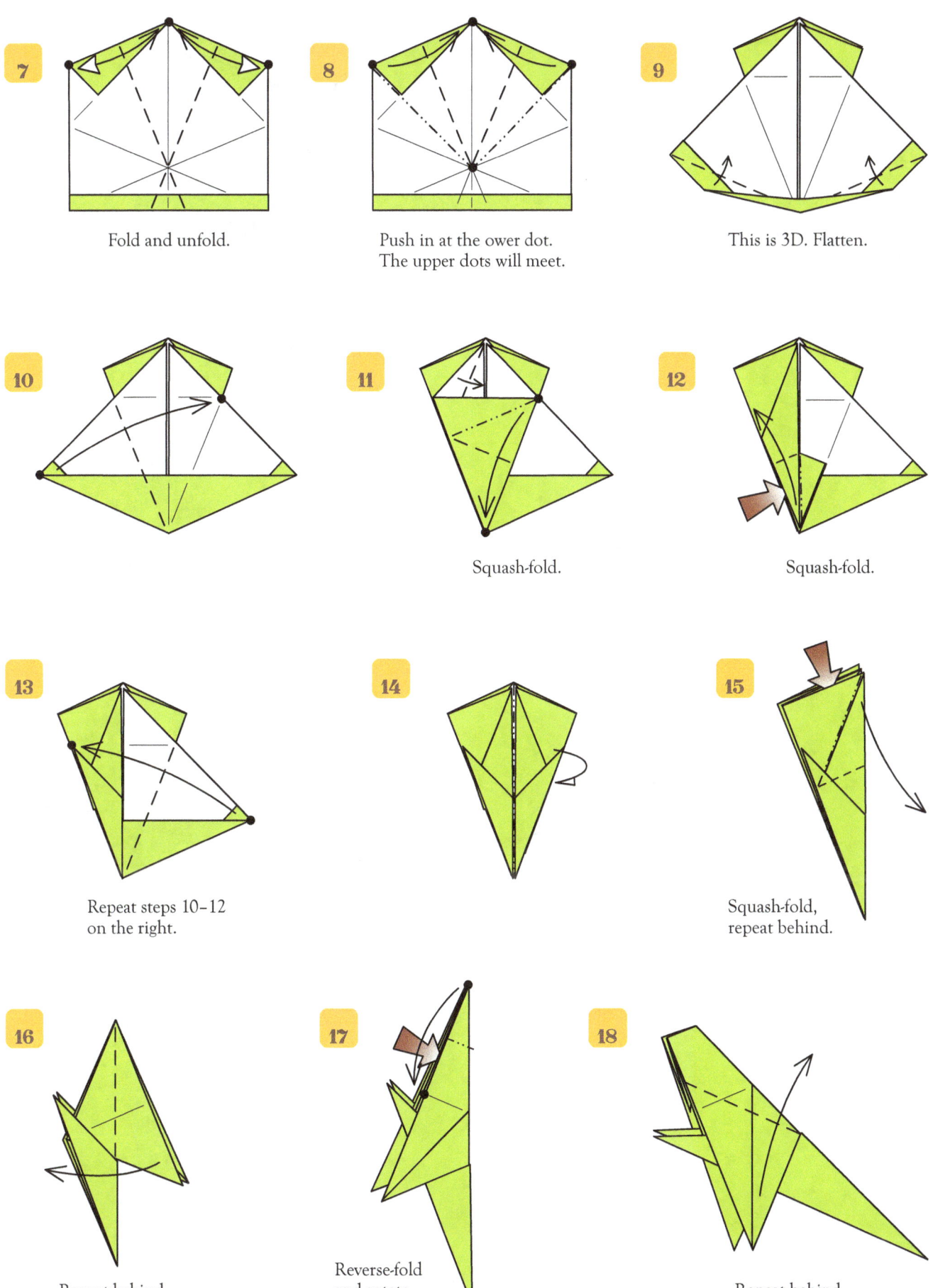

Parrot **103**

19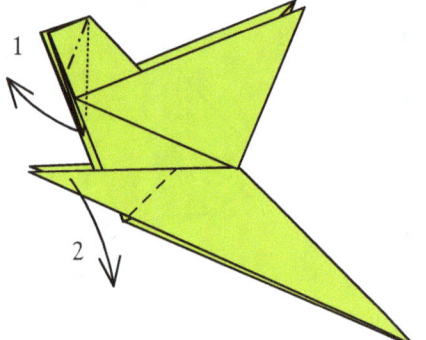

1. Reverse-fold.
2. Repeat behind.

20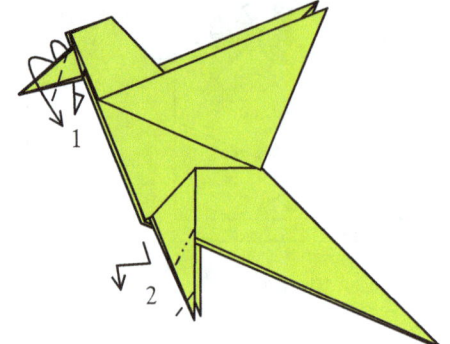

1. Outside-reverse-fold.
2. Make reverse folds, repeat behind.

21

1. Squash-fold, repeat behind.
2. Tuck under region A, repeat behind.
3. Crimp-fold.
4. Spread the wings.

22

Parrot

104 Origami Symphony No. 8

Bear

Bears are good at standing up and can walk for short distances. They are among the most intelligent land animals found in North America. There are stories of abandoned bear cubs that were taken care of by humans. As the bears grew, they continued to be tame and believed the humans to be part of their family.

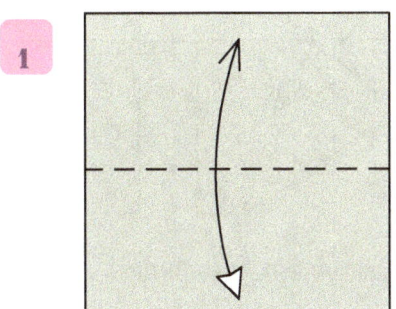

Fold and unfold.

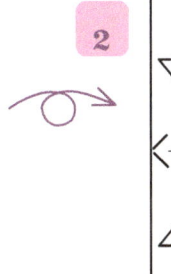

Fold to the center and unfold.

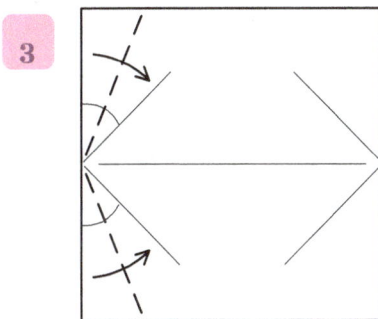

Fold to the lines.

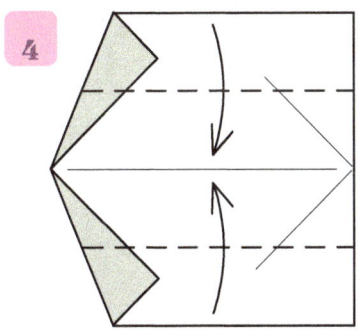

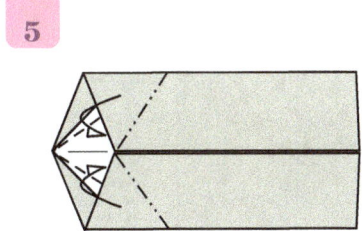

Make reverse folds.

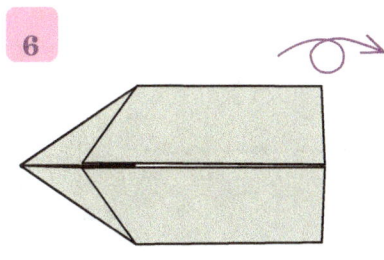

Bear **105**

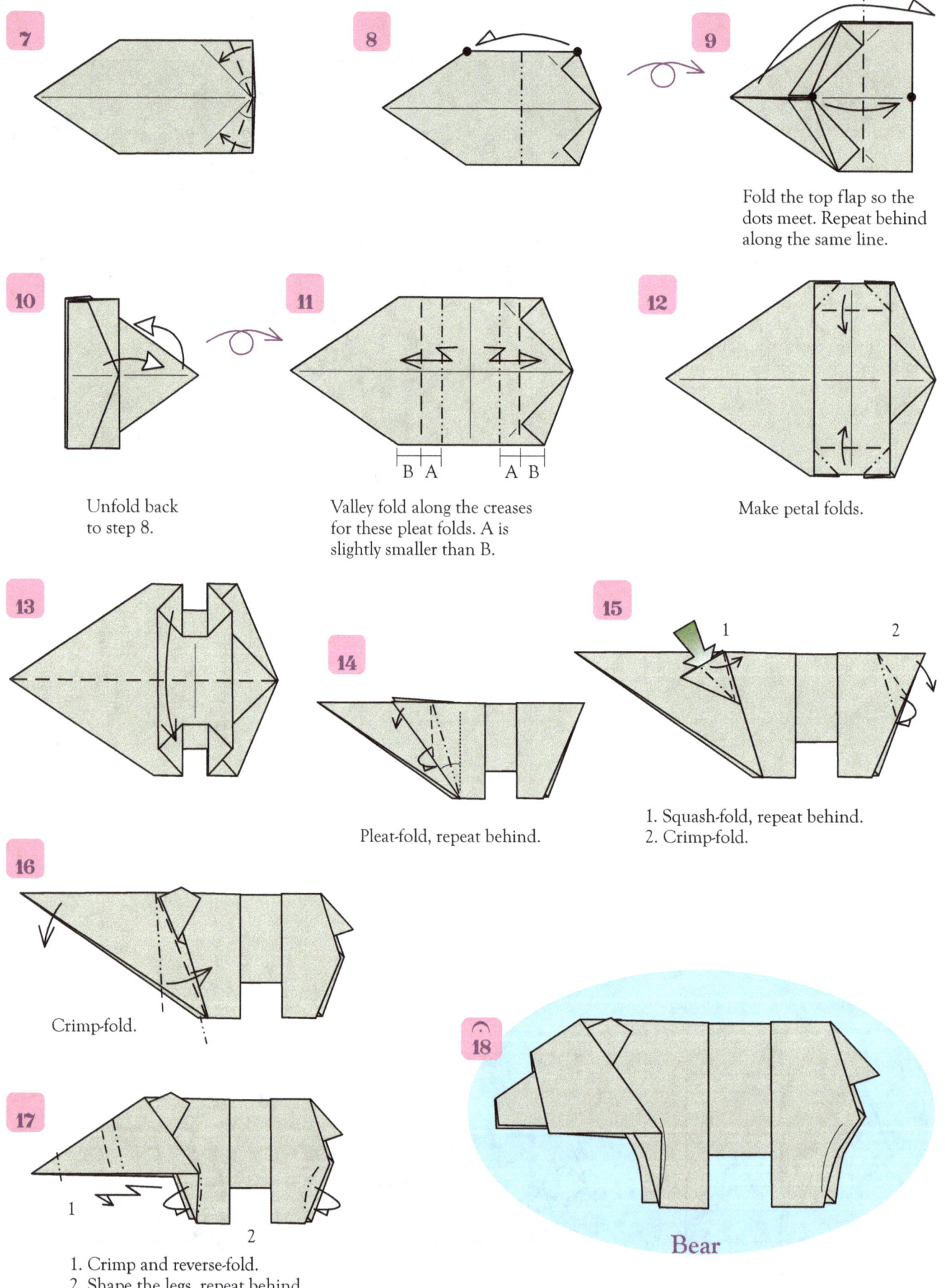

9. Fold the top flap so the dots meet. Repeat behind along the same line.

10. Unfold back to step 8.

11. Valley fold along the creases for these pleat folds. A is slightly smaller than B.

12. Make petal folds.

14. Pleat-fold, repeat behind.

15. 1. Squash-fold, repeat behind. 2. Crimp-fold.

16. Crimp-fold.

17. 1. Crimp and reverse-fold. 2. Shape the legs, repeat behind.

Bear

106 Origami Symphony No. 8

Lion

Lions live in green plains, grasslands, and deserts, but not in the jungle. They spend most of the day resting and sleeping. A lion's roar can be heard a few miles away. As a hunting strategy, lions often hunt during storms since prey cannot detect them very well.

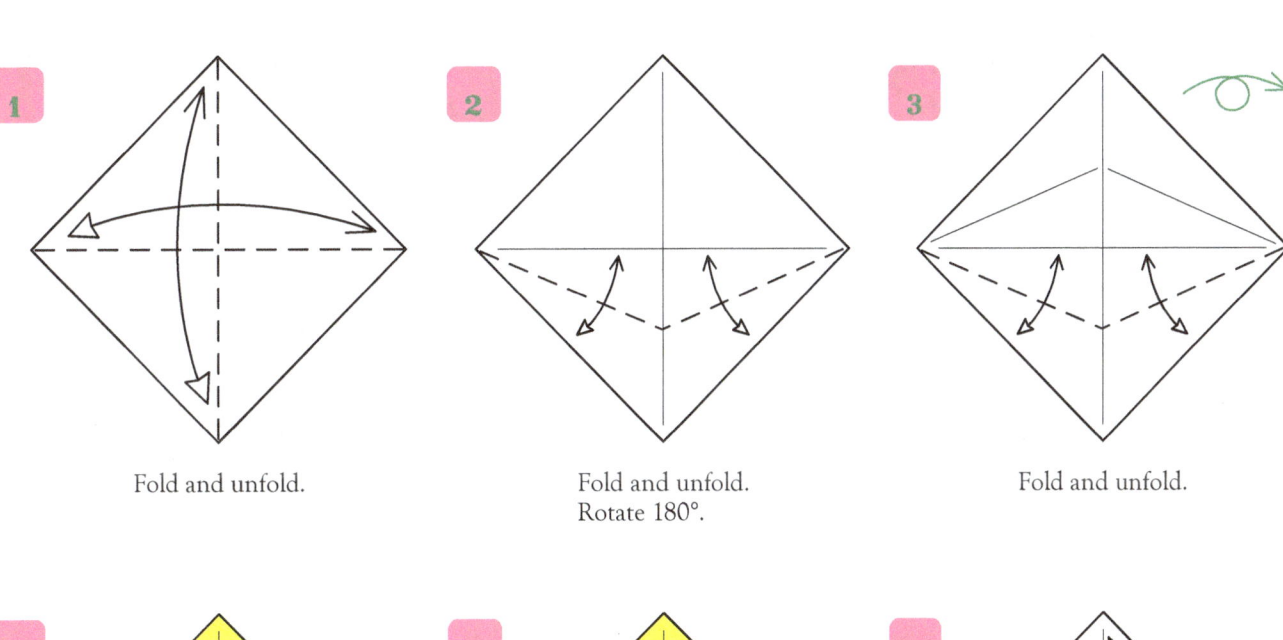

1. Fold and unfold.
2. Fold and unfold. Rotate 180°.
3. Fold and unfold.

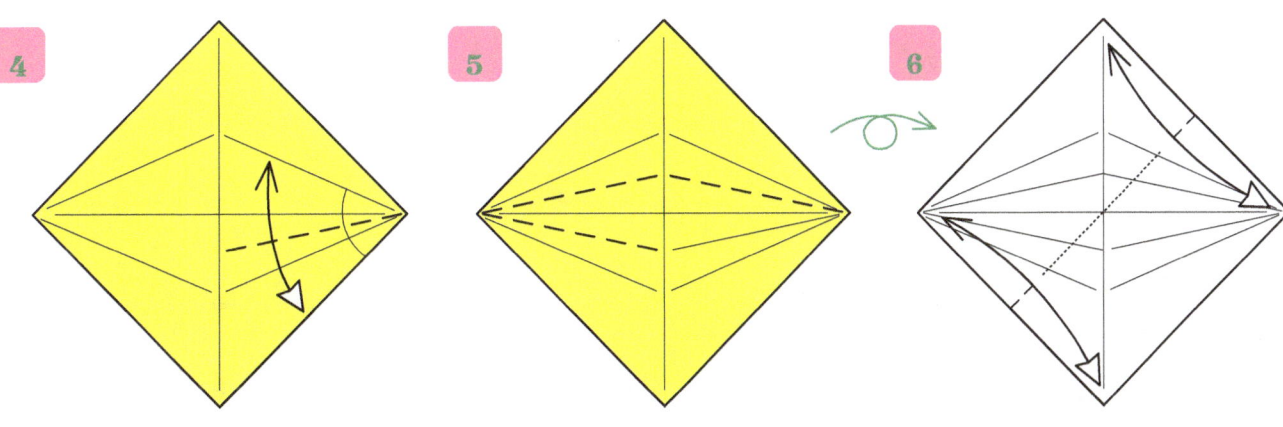

4. Fold and unfold.
5. Repeat step 4 three times, on the left and above.
6. Fold and unfold on the edges.

Lion **107**

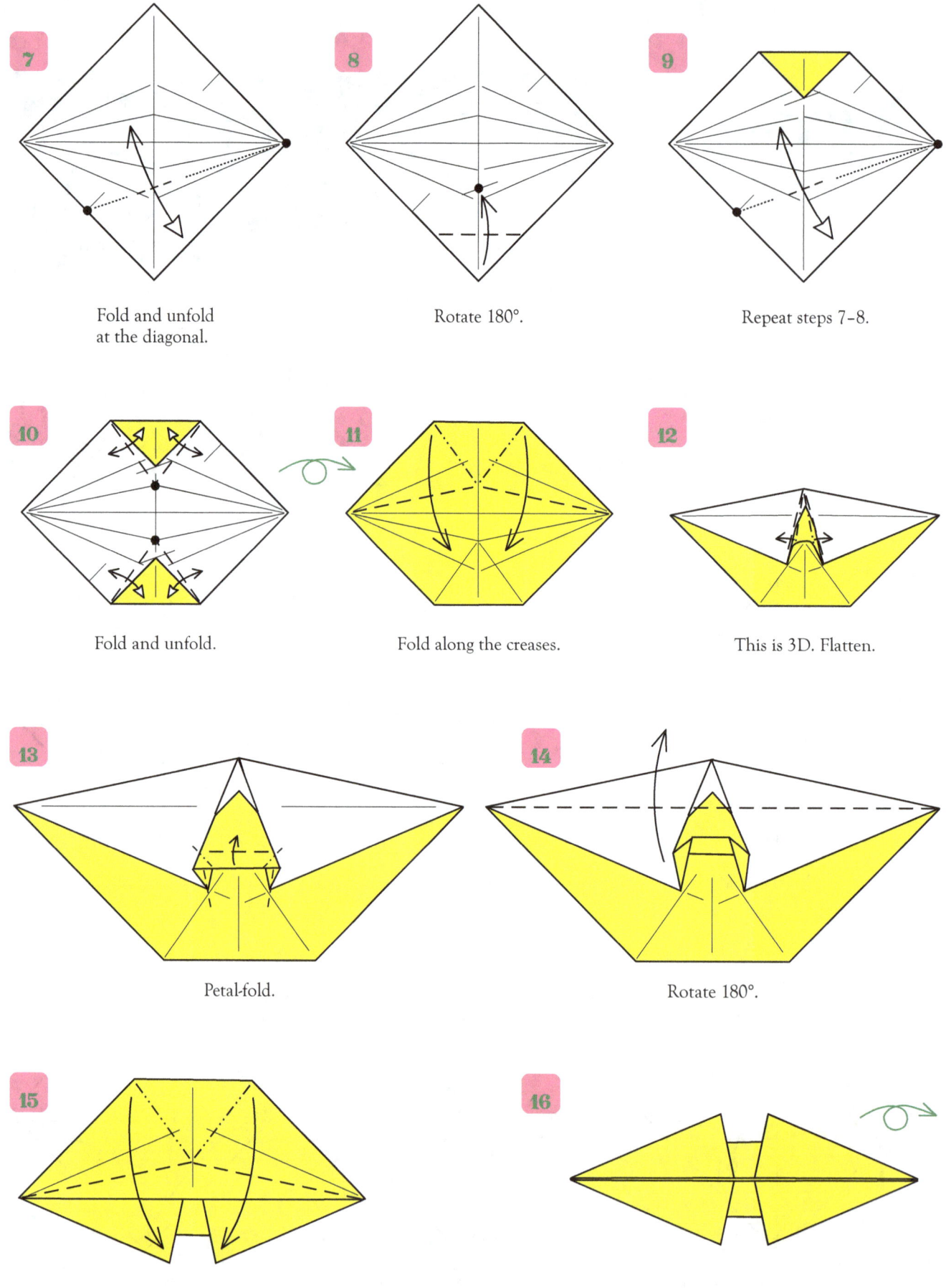

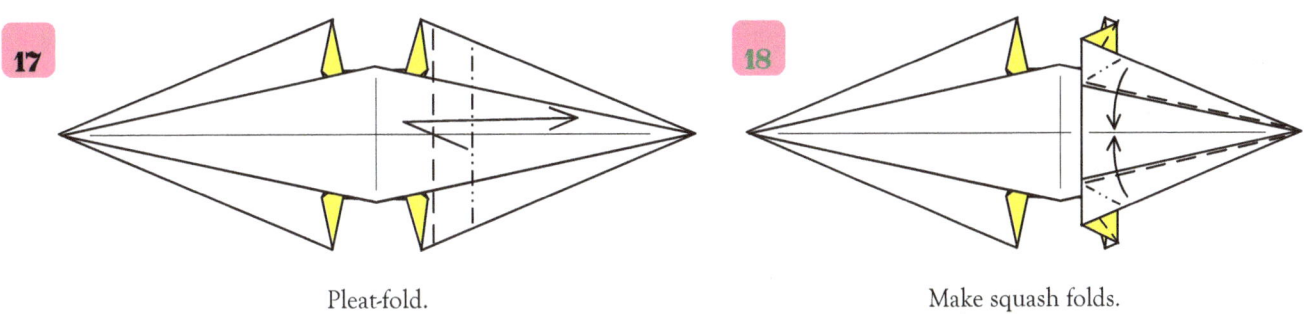

17 Pleat-fold.

18 Make squash folds.

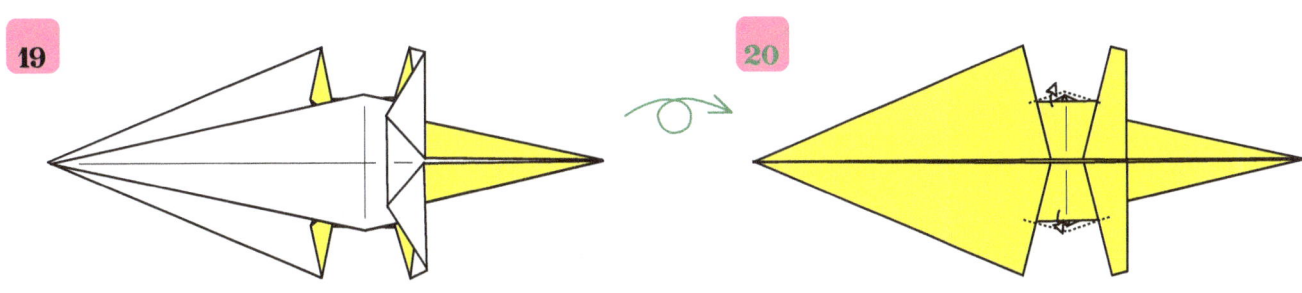

19

20 Spread from underneath to the dotted lines.

21 Pleat-fold.

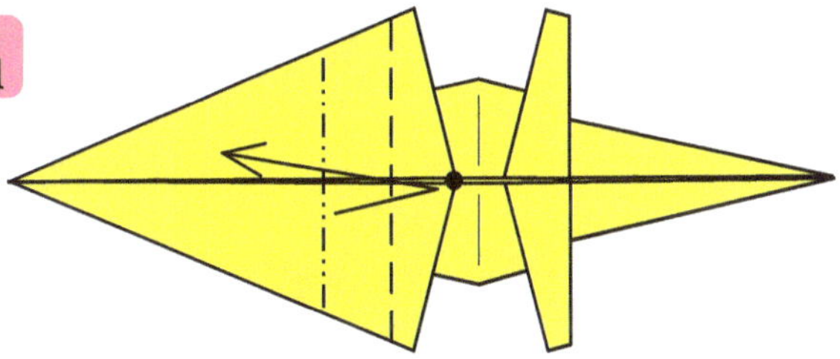

22

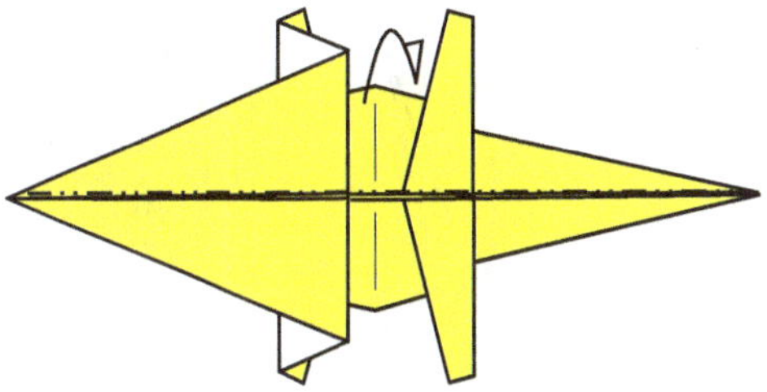

23
1. Pivot at the dot. 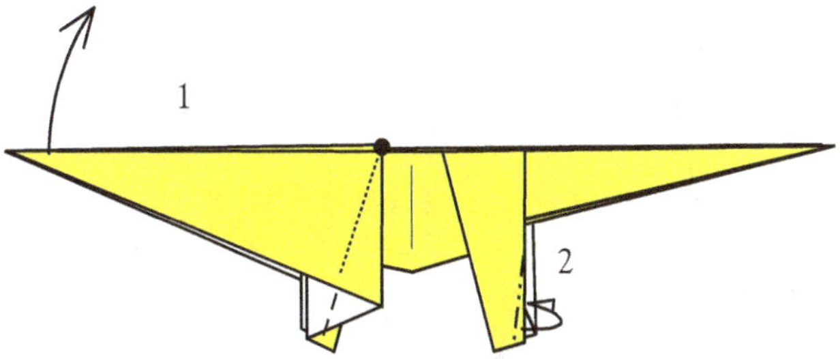
2. Repeat behind.

24 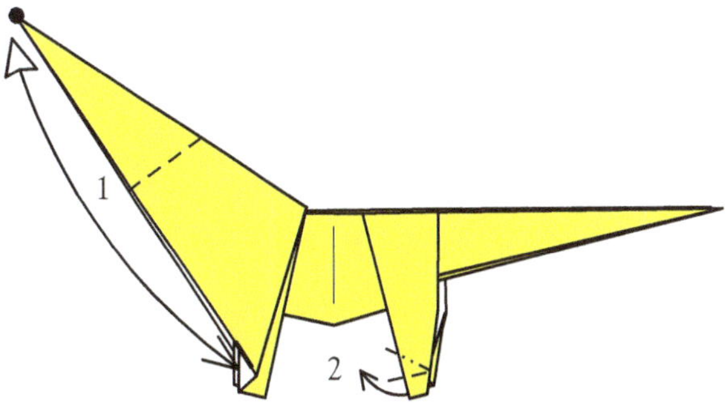
1. Fold and unfold.
2. Pleat-fold, repeat behind.

Lion 109

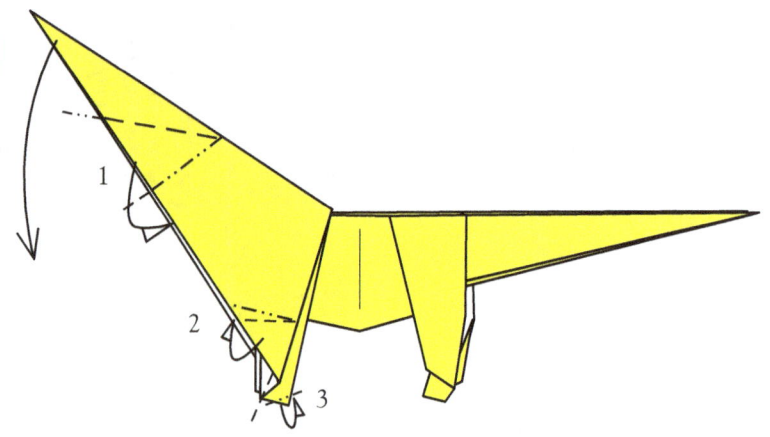

1. Mountain-fold along the crease for this crimp fold.
2. Shape the mane, repeat behind.
3. Repeat behind.

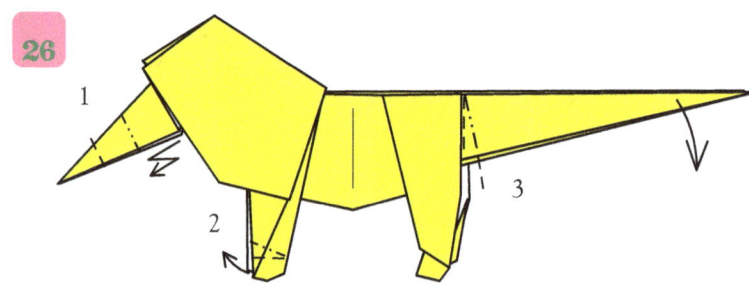

1. Crimp-fold.
2. Pleat-fold, repeat behind.
3. Crimp-fold.

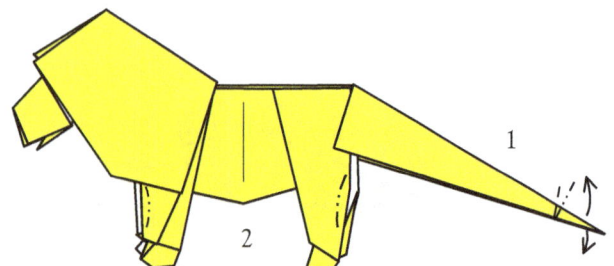

1. Spread the tip of the tail.
2. Shape the legs, repeat behind.

Lion

Panther

A panther is defined as a black or dark large cat, which can be a tiger, jaguar, or leopard. Panthers are nocturnal and hunt at night. Stealth, camouflage, and excellent night vision give them the advantage when hunting. They are some of the best large cats at climbing trees.

Begin with step 21 of the Lion on page 107.

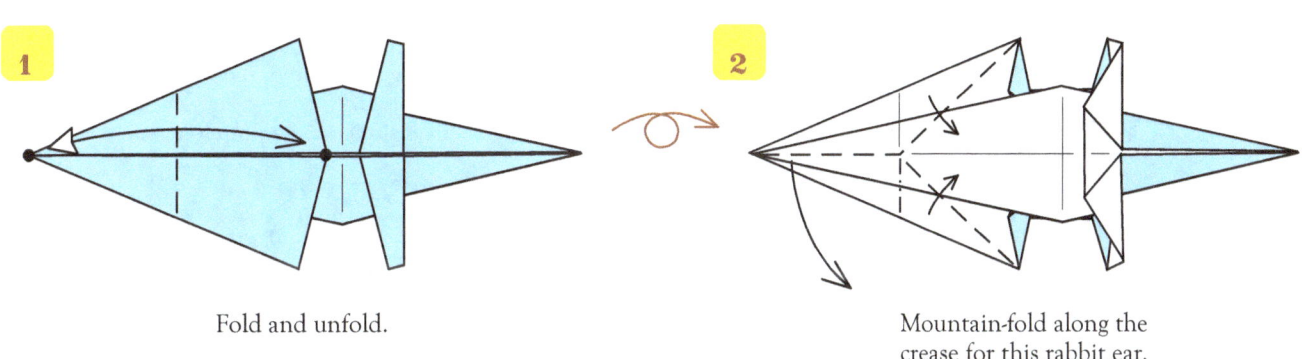

1. Fold and unfold.

2. Mountain-fold along the crease for this rabbit ear.

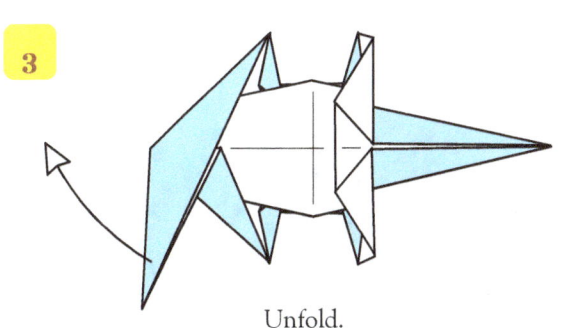

3. Unfold.

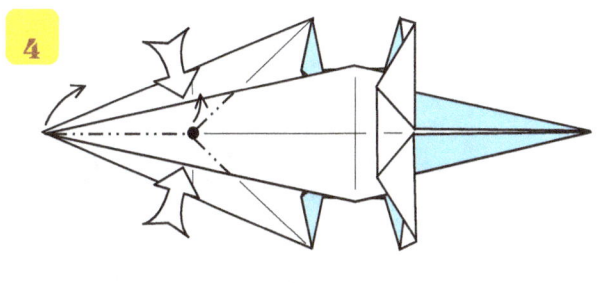

4. Puff out at the dot.

Panther **111**

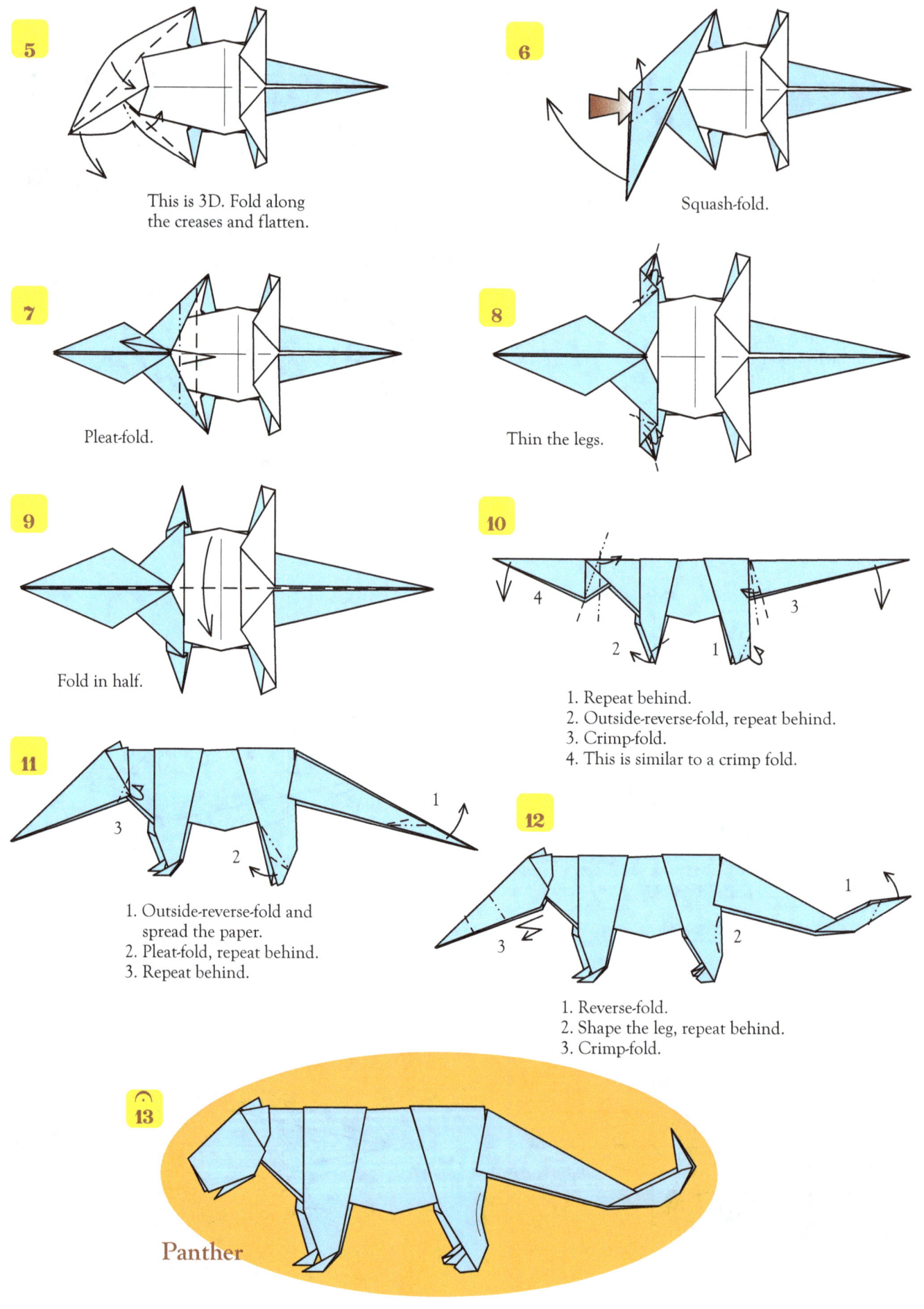

Dog

Of all the circus animals, dogs can continue to perform and do tricks. Dogs enjoy learning new tricks while pleasing their owners. Dogs jump through hoops, dance as they run around each other, push shopping carts, and much more. Their wagging tails say it all.

Begin with step 18 of the Lion on page 107.

1

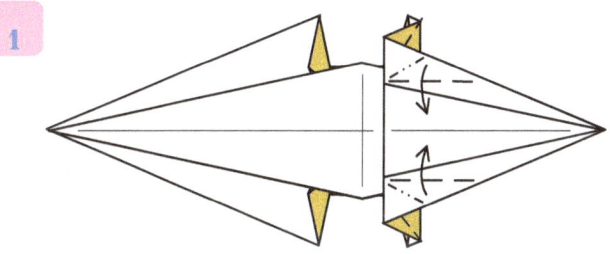

Make squash folds.

2

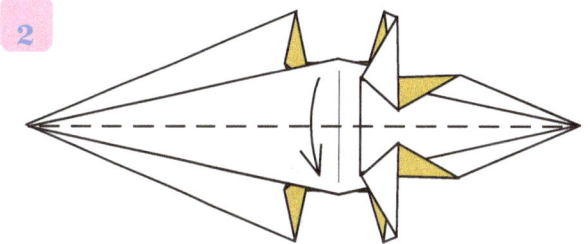

Fold in half.

3

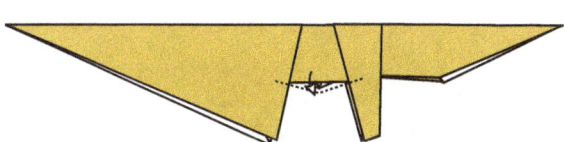

Spread from underneath to the dotted lines. Repeat behind.

4

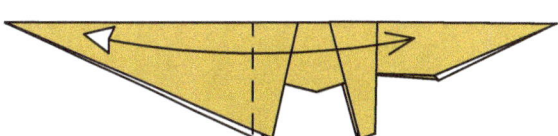

Fold and unfold.

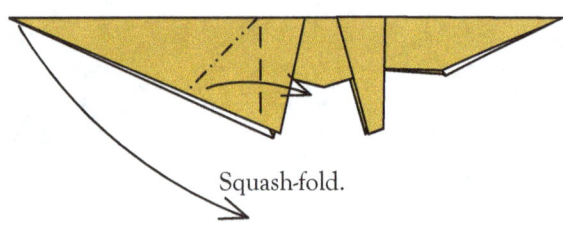

5. Squash-fold.

6. Wrap around and petal-fold.

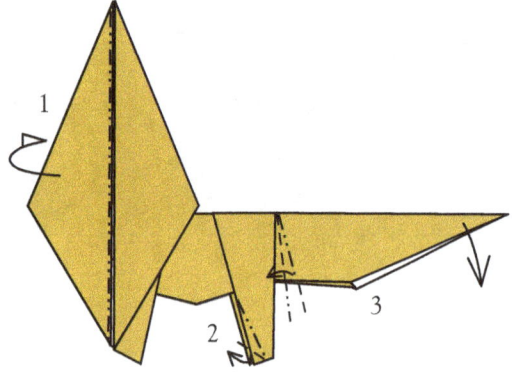

7.
1. Fold behind.
2. Pleat-fold, repeat behind.
3. Crimp-fold.

8.
1. Outside-reverse-fold.
2. Repeat behind.
3. Reverse-fold.

9.
1. Reverse-fold, repeat behind.
2. Crimp-fold.

10.
1. Make reverse folds.
2. Pleat-fold, repeat behind.
3. Shape the leg, repeat behind.

11. Dog

114 Origami Symphony No. 8

Horse

The horse is a favorite circus animal. Some time ago when the circus was new, horses played an important role. Prior to the opening of the circus, horses would parade through towns to advertise the show. Horses performed many acrobatic tricks. From the early circus, a circular course for the horses with a 42 foot ring diameter shaped the development of the circus performance space.

1

1. Fold and unfold.
2. Fold and unfold on the edge.

2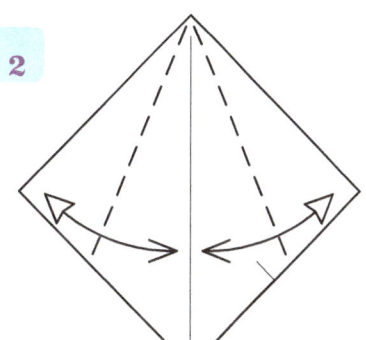

Fold to the center and unfold.

3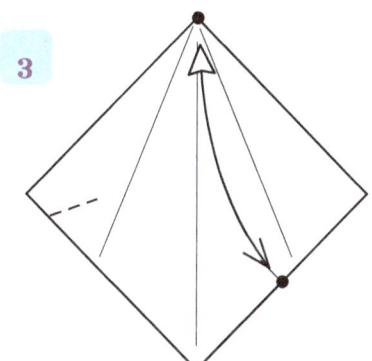

Fold and unfold on the edge.

4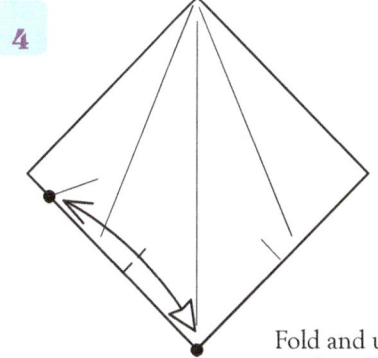

Fold and unfold on the edge.

5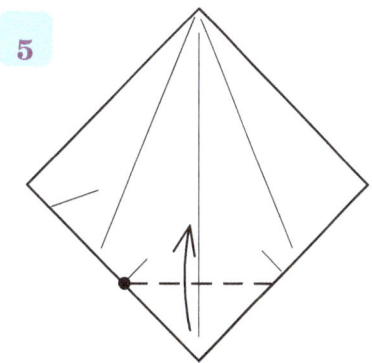

6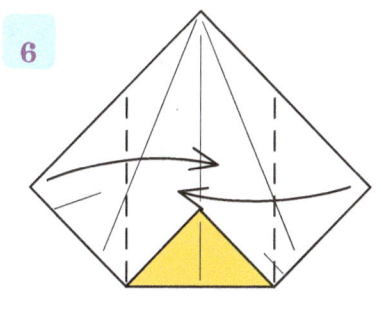

Horse **115**

7

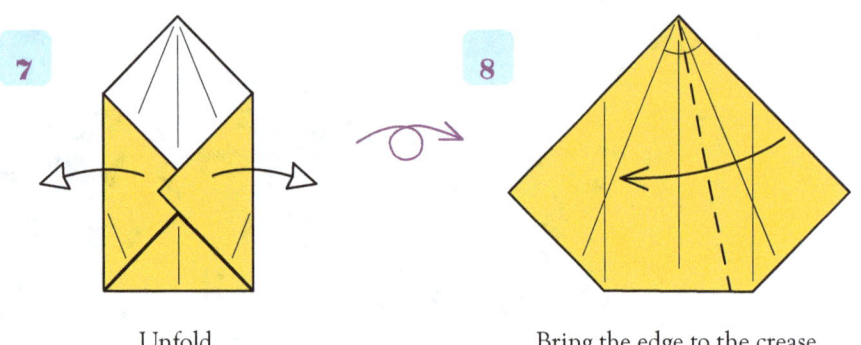

Unfold.

8

Bring the edge to the crease.

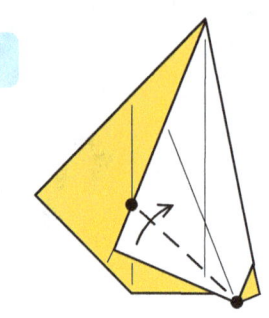

9

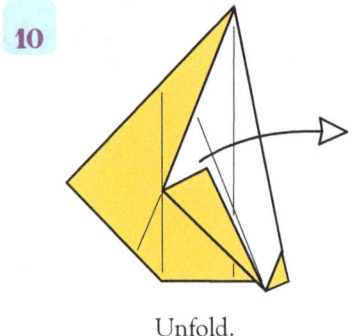

10

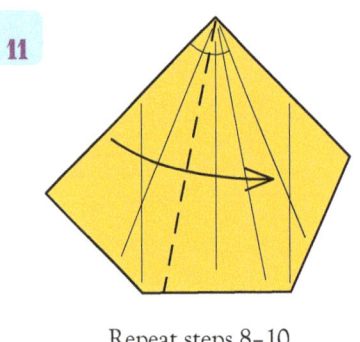

Unfold.

11

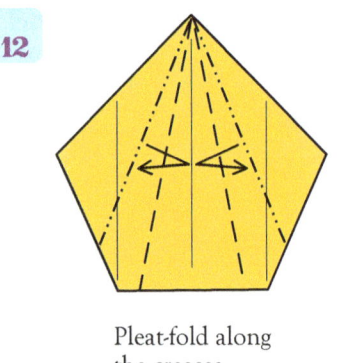

Repeat steps 8–10 on the left.

12

Pleat-fold along the creases.

13

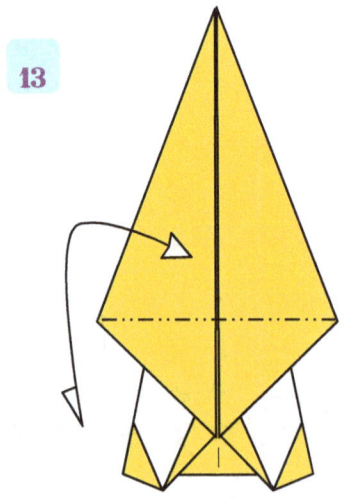

Fold and unfold.

14

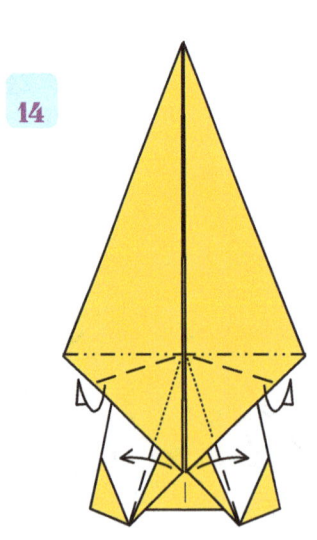

15

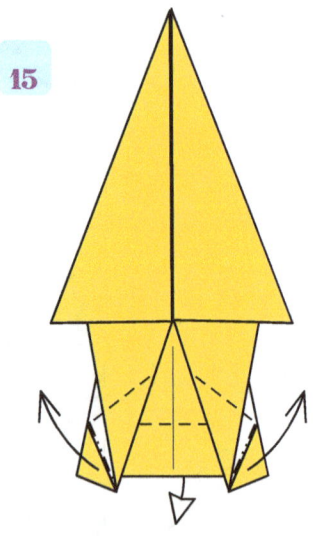

Petal-fold and swing out from behind.

116 *Origami Symphony No. 8*

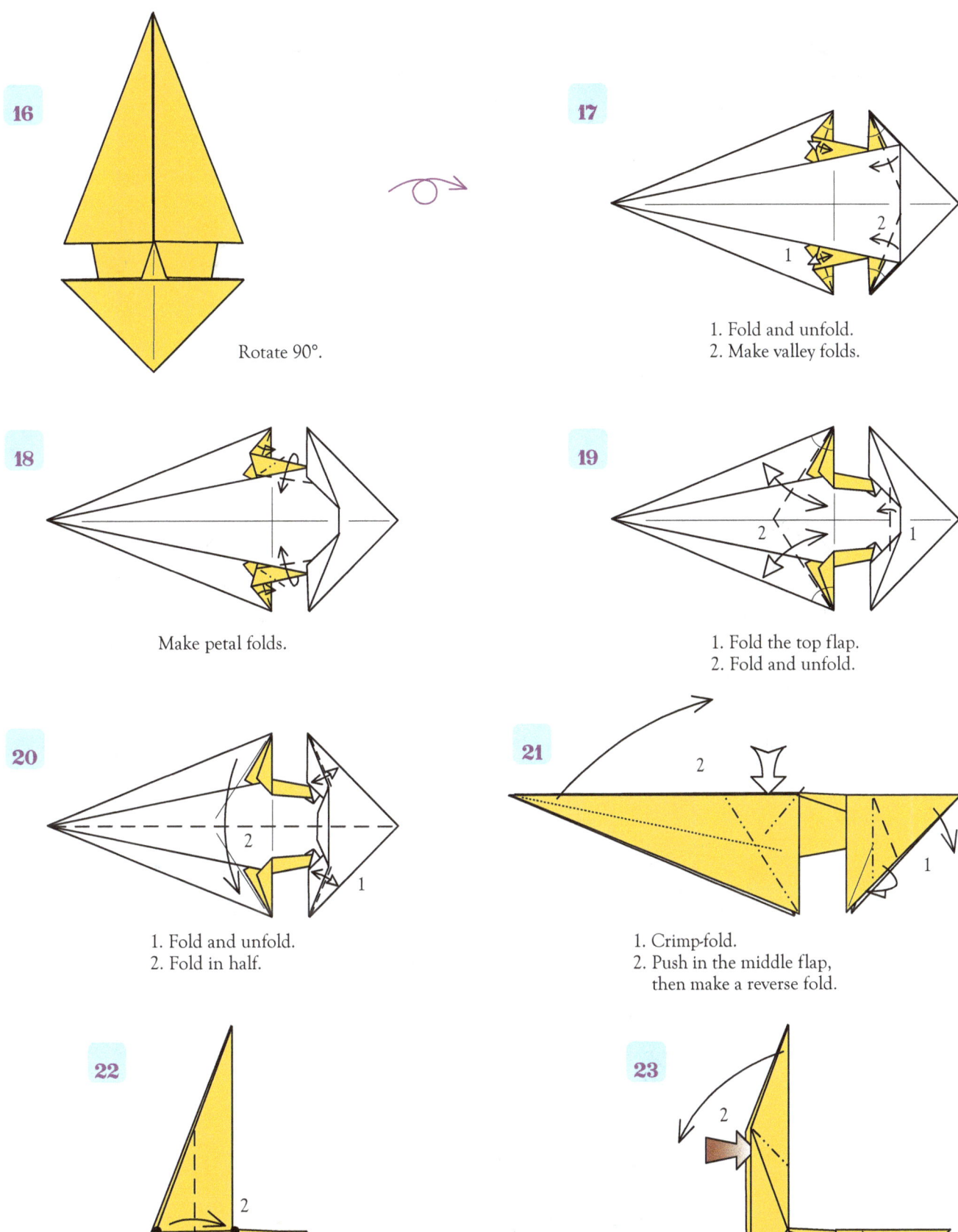

24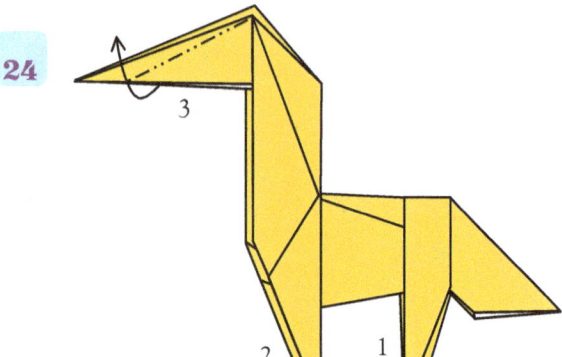

1. Squash-fold.
2. Spread to form the hoof.
3. Spread the top layer.
Repeat behind.

25

Outside-reverse-fold.

26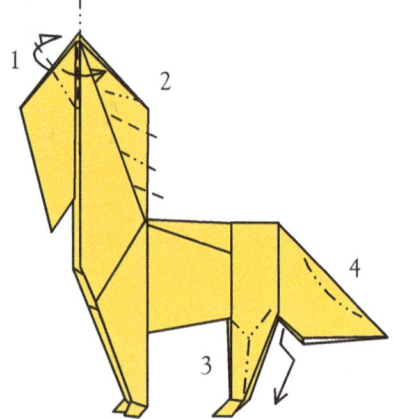

1. Crimp-fold.
2. Pleat-fold the mane.
3. Thin and shape the leg, repeat behind.
4. Shape the tail.

27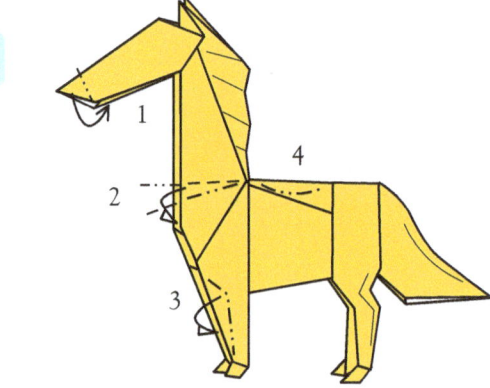

1. Reverse-fold.
2. Crimp-fold.
3. Thin and shape the leg, repeat behind.
4. Shape the back.

28

Horse

Giraffe

Giraffes are the tallest mammals on Earth. During a 24-hour day, they sleep for no more than half an hour. The horns on their heads are called ossicones. It is difficult for them to drink water from the ground but the plants they eat supply most of their water. They can run as fast as 35 miles per hour. These social animals live in groups called towers.

1. 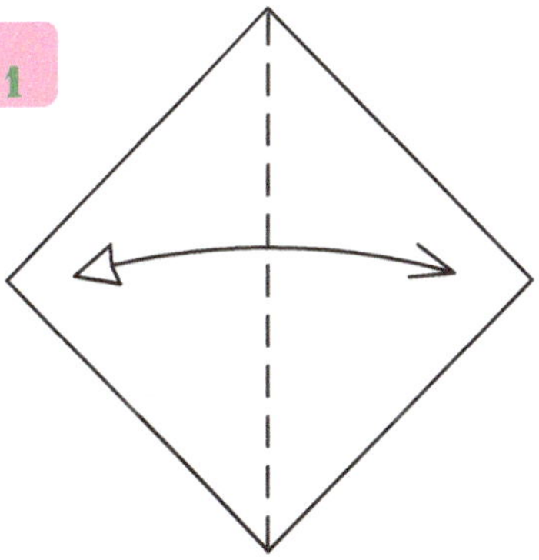 Fold and unfold.

2. Fold to the center and unfold.

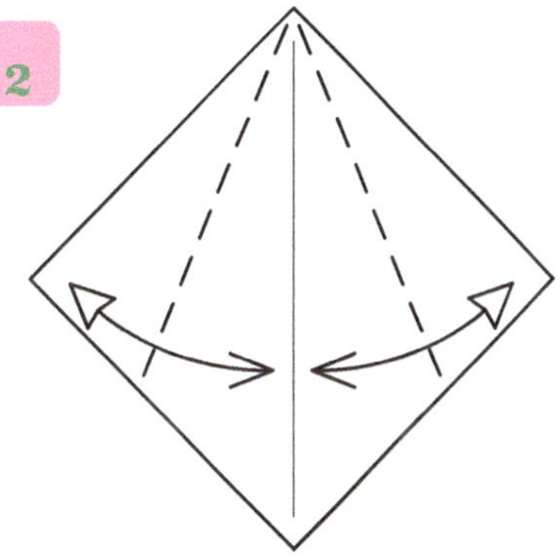

3. Fold and unfold on the edge.

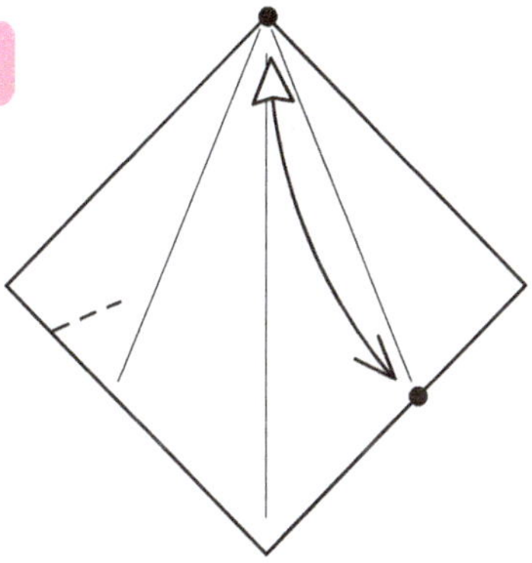

4. Fold and unfold along the diagonal.

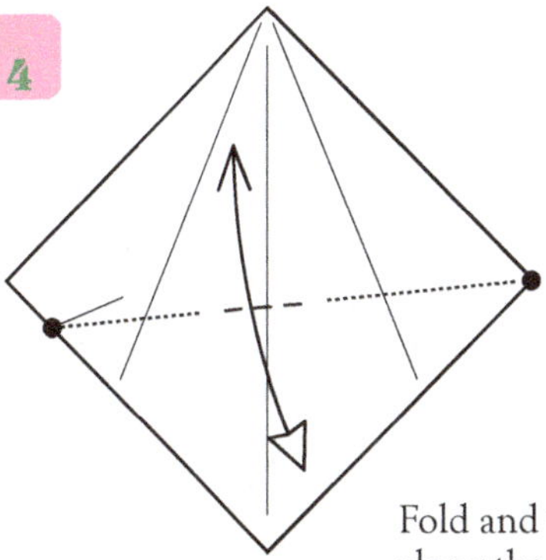

5.

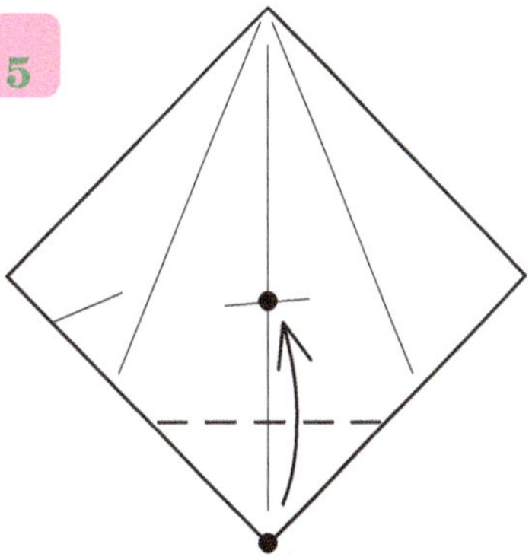

6. 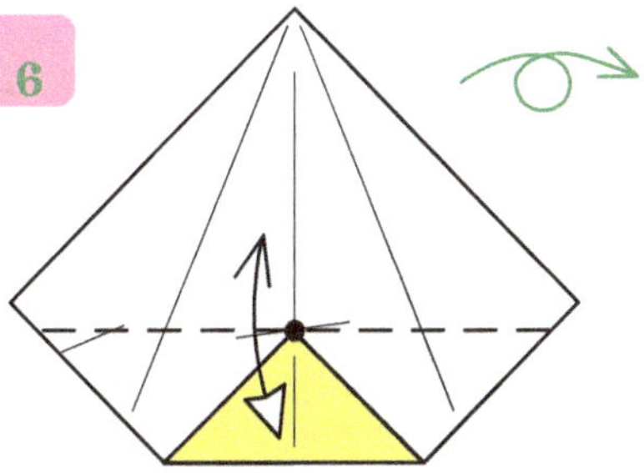 Fold and unfold.

Giraffe 119

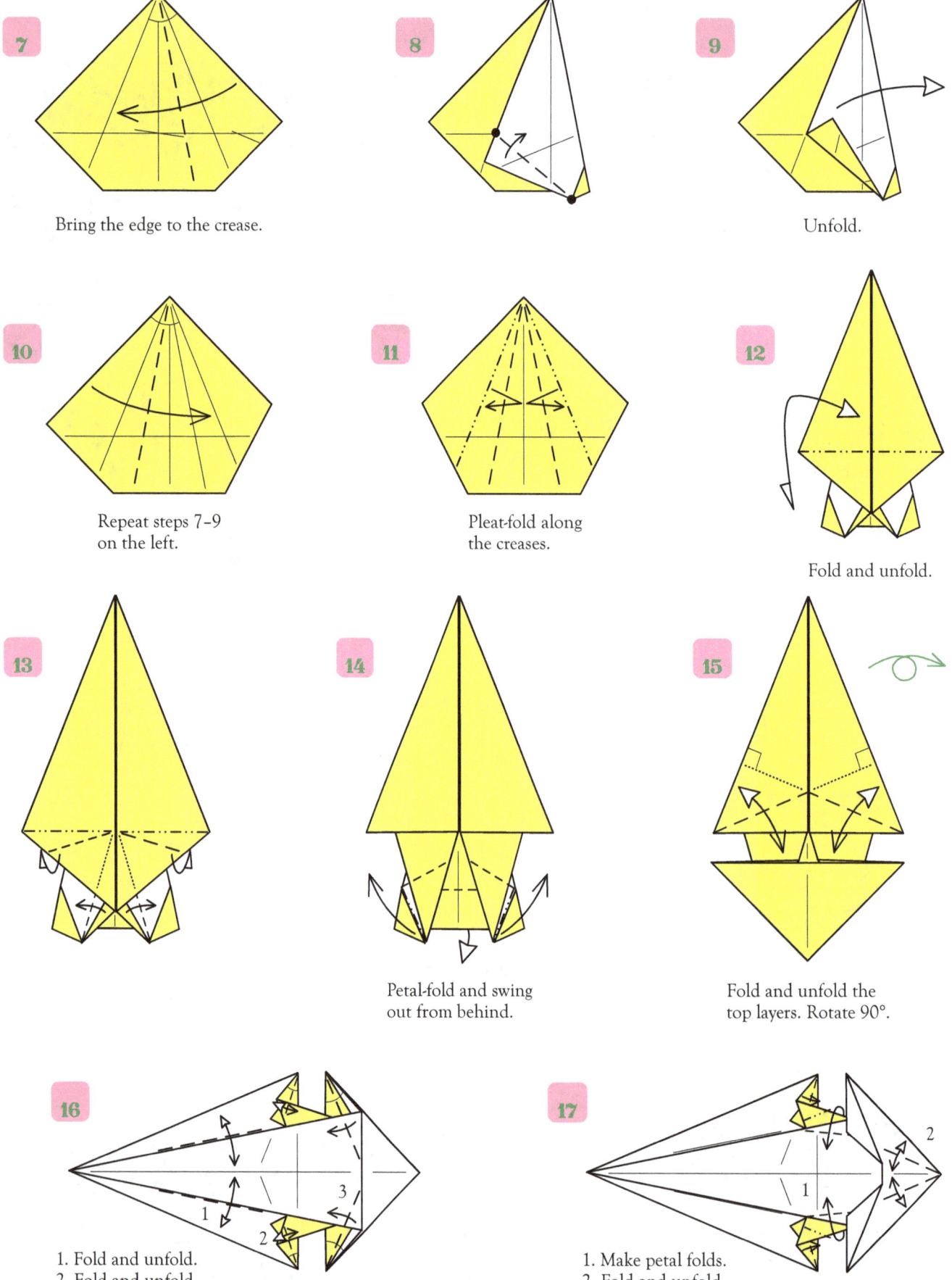

120 Origami Symphony No. 8

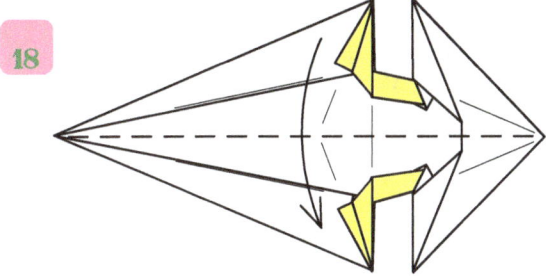

Fold in half.

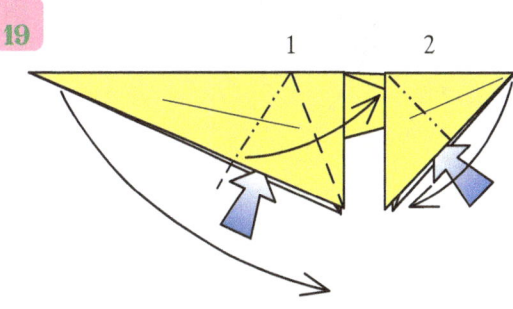

1. Squash-fold.
2. Reverse-fold.

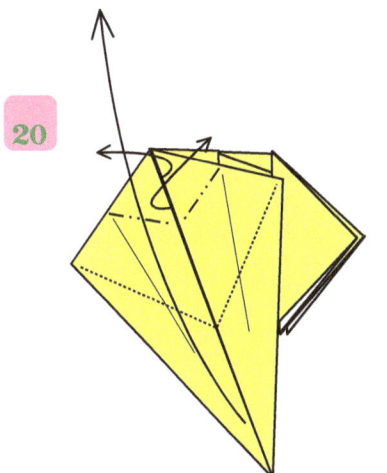

Wrap around and petal-fold.

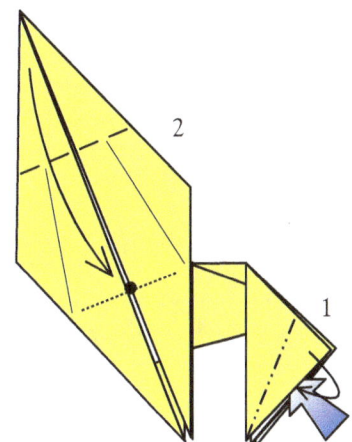

1. Fold to the dot.
2. Reverse-fold, repeat behind.

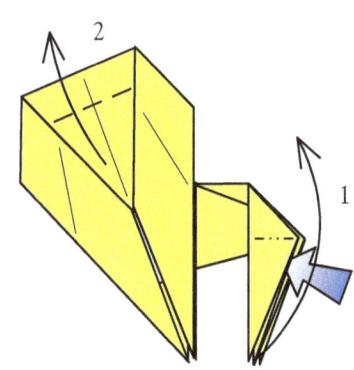

1. Unlock some of the paper for this reverse fold.
2. Fold up.

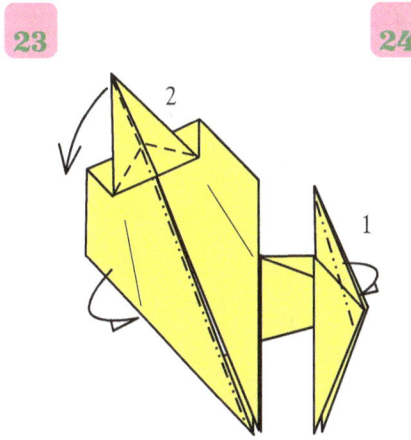

1. Fold inside, repeat behind.
2. Rabbit-ear and fold behind.

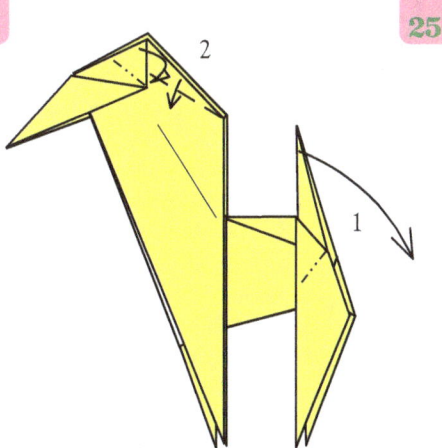

1. Reverse-fold.
2. This is similar to a reverse fold. Repeat behind.

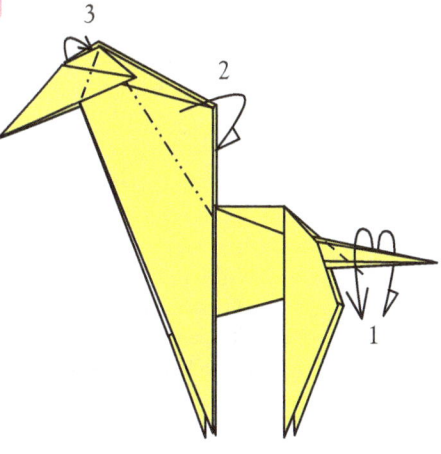

1. Outside-reverse-fold.
2. Fold along the crease, repeat behind.
3. Reverse-fold.

Giraffe **121**

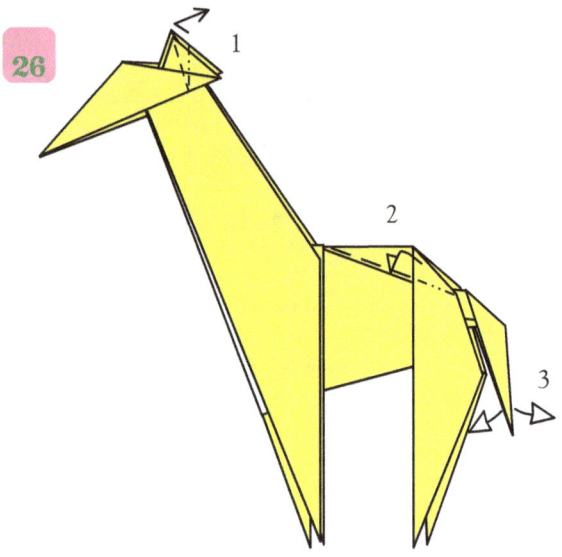

1. Pleat-fold, repeat behind.
2. Reverse-fold and tuck inside.
3. Spread the tip of the tail.

1. Make a small crimp fold.
2. Thin and shape the leg, repeat behind.

1. Reverse-fold.
2. Thin and shape the leg, repeat behind.
3. Shape the neck.
The neck and legs are 3D.

Giraffe

Elephant

Elephants are the largest living land mammals on Earth. These social animals live in groups called herds. Elephants can hear and communicate with sounds that are too low for us to hear. Their trunks have over 40,000 muscles and it takes time and practice to use them. They are excellent swimmers and use their trunks as snorkels.

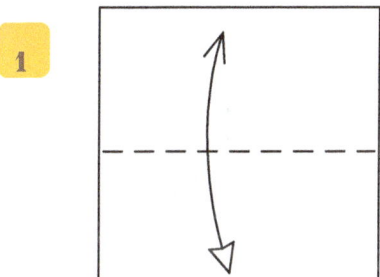

1. Fold and unfold.

2. Fold to the center.

3. Fold to the center.

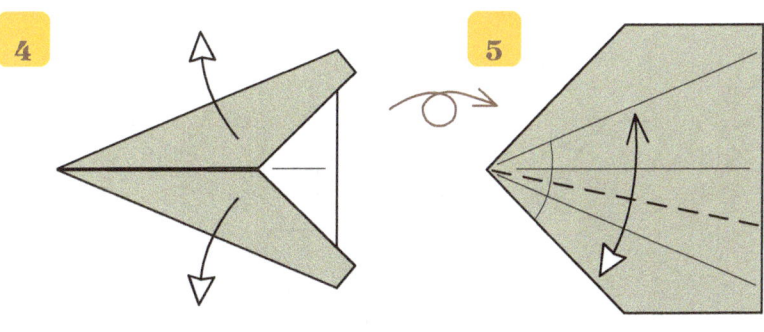

4. Unfold.

5. Fold and unfold.

6. Fold and unfold.

Elephant **123**

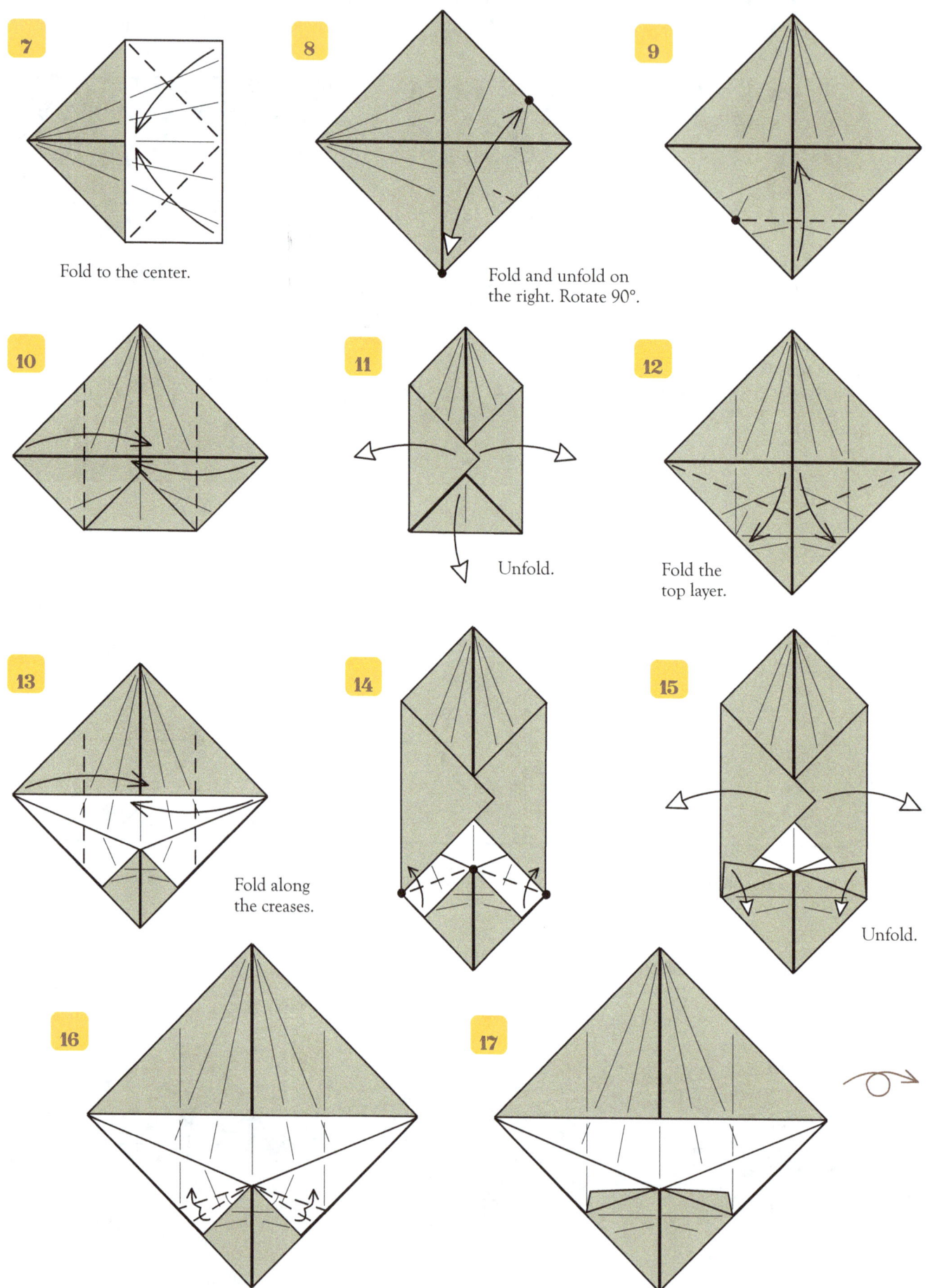

7. Fold to the center.
8. Fold and unfold on the right. Rotate 90°.
11. Unfold.
12. Fold the top layer.
13. Fold along the creases.
15. Unfold.

124 Origami Symphony No. 8

Elephant

Elephants are the largest living land mammals on Earth. These social animals live in groups called herds. Elephants can hear and communicate with sounds that are too low for us to hear. Their trunks have over 40,000 muscles and it takes time and practice to use them. They are excellent swimmers and use their trunks as snorkels.

1. Fold and unfold.

2. Fold to the center.

3. Fold to the center.

4. Unfold.

5. Fold and unfold.

6. Fold and unfold.

Elephant 123

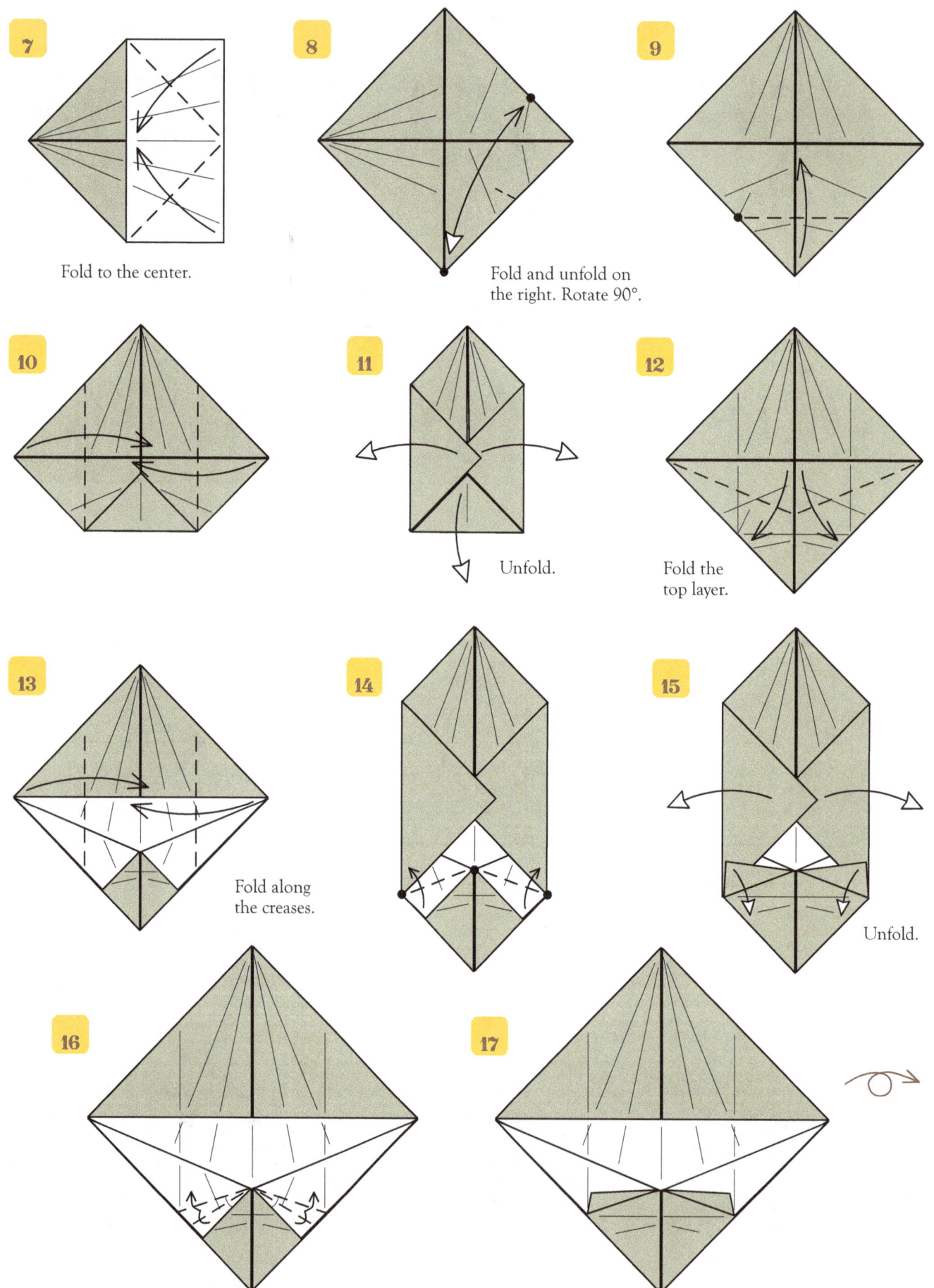

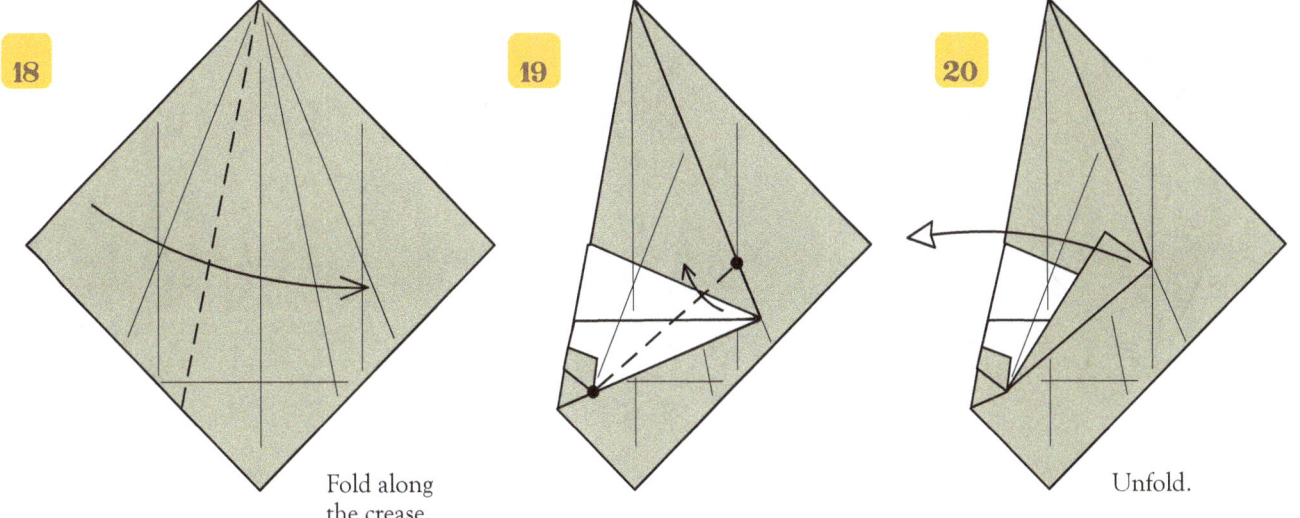

18

19

20 Unfold.

Fold along the crease.

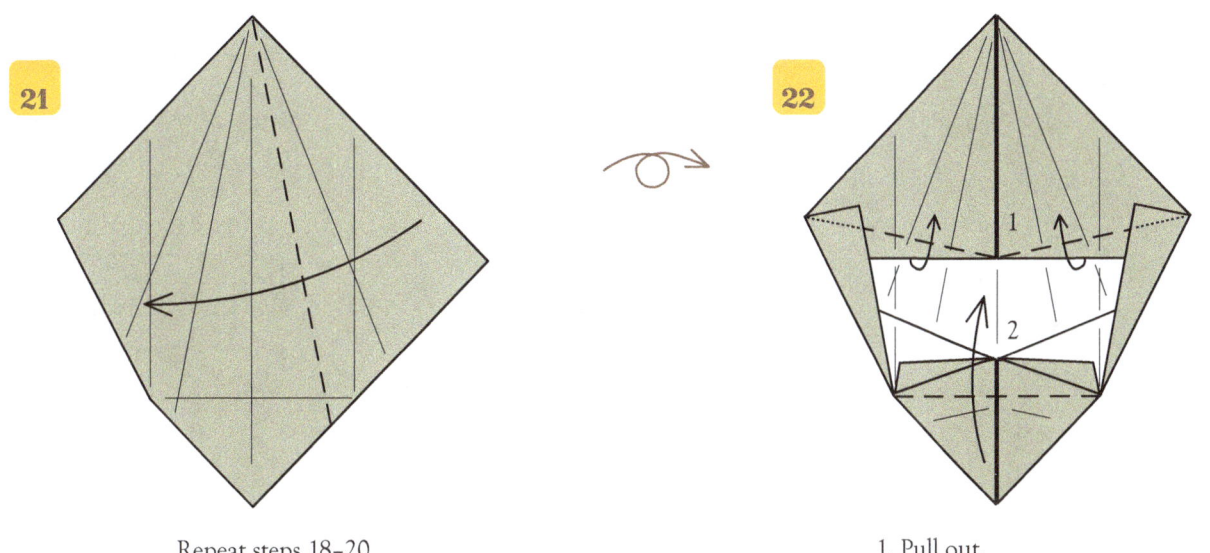

21

22

Repeat steps 18–20 on the right.

1. Pull out.
2. Fold along the crease.

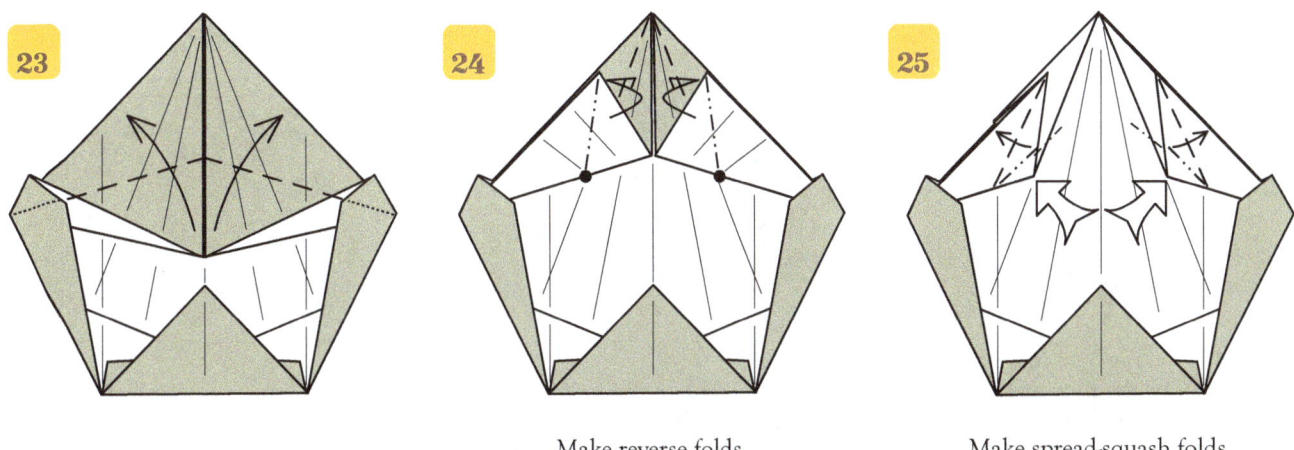

23

24

25

Make reverse folds.

Make spread-squash folds.

Elephant **125**

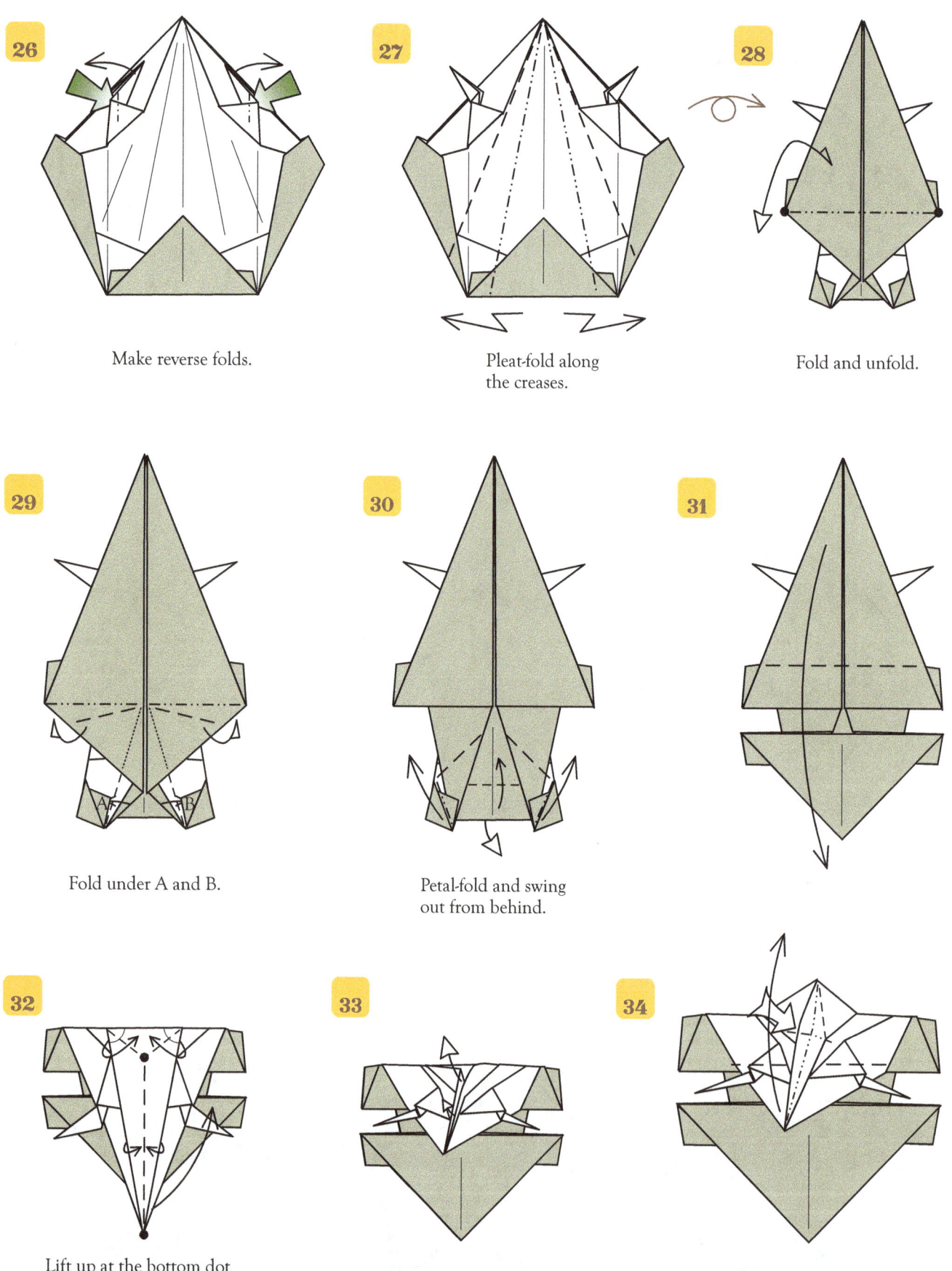

26. Make reverse folds.

27. Pleat-fold along the creases.

28. Fold and unfold.

29. Fold under A and B.

30. Petal-fold and swing out from behind.

31.

32. Lift up at the bottom dot and bring the thin center flaps together. Follow the upper dot into the next step.

33. This is 3D. Pull out from the central strip. This includes the upper dot from the previous step.

34. Push in the center flap that bulges out, and flatten.

126 Origami Symphony No. 8

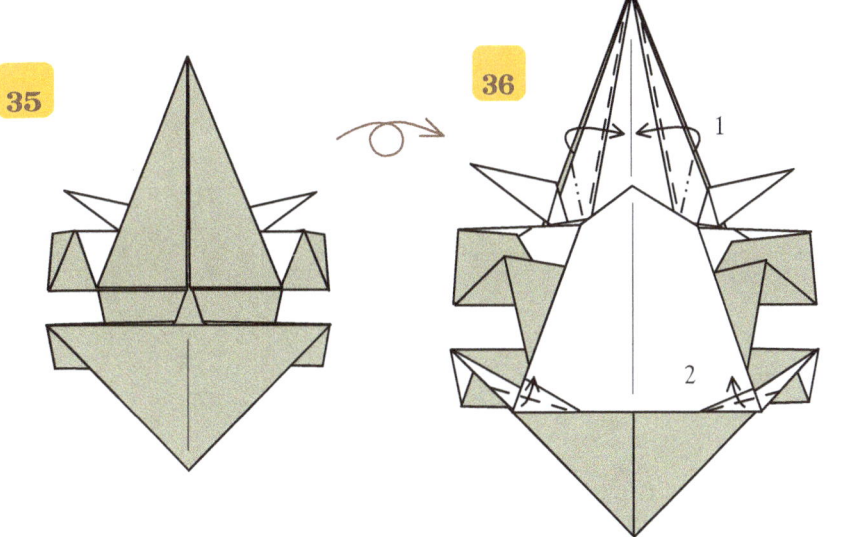

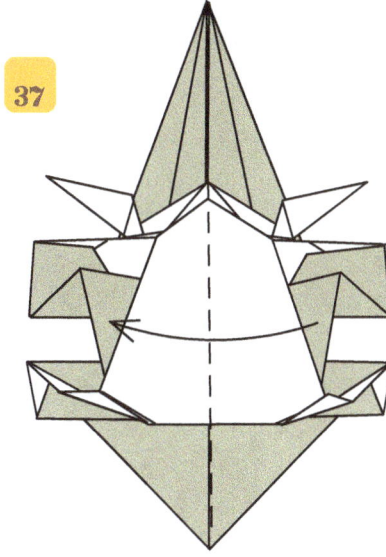

1. Cover the white flap.
2. These are thick, make small valley folds.

Fold in half and rotate 90°.

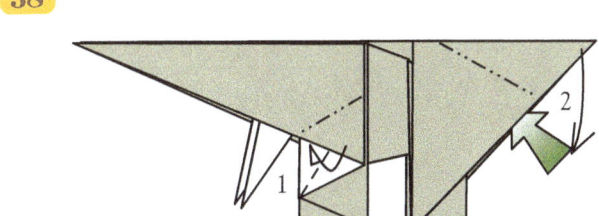
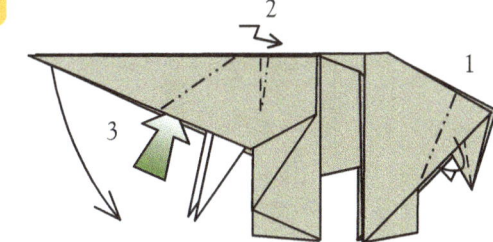

1. Reverse-fold, repeat behind.
2. Reverse-fold.

1. Reverse-fold.
2. Pleat-fold, repeat behind.
3. Reverse-fold.

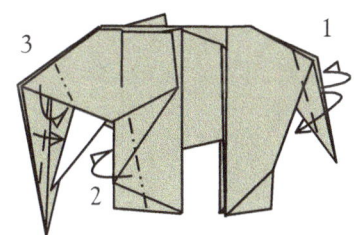

1. Outside-reverse-fold.
2. Mountain-fold, repeat behind.
3. Thin the trunk with a reverse fold, repeat behind

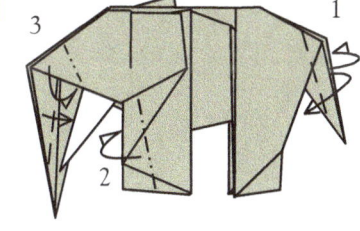

1. Shape the trunk with reverse folds.
2. Shape the tusk, repeat behind.
3. Shape the legs, repeat behind.
4. Shape the back.

Elephant

Elephant 127

www.ingramcontent.com/pod-product-compliance
Lightning Source LLC
Chambersburg PA
CBHW081620100526
44590CB00021B/3524